DATE DUE

The Other Side
of Silence

THE OTHER SIDE
OF SILENCE

Sign Language and the
Deaf Community
in America

by Arden Neisser

ALFRED A. KNOPF   NEW YORK   1983

Copyright © 1983 by Arden Neisser

All rights reserved under International and Pan-American Copyright
Conventions. Published in the United States by Alfred A. Knopf, Inc.,
New York, and simultaneously in Canada by Random House of Can-
ada Limited, Toronto. Distributed by Random House, Inc., New York.

Grateful acknowledgment is made to the following for permission to
reprint from previously published material:
Delacorte Press: Excerpt from *Helen and Teacher: The Story of Helen
Keller and Anne Sullivan Macy* by Joseph P. Lash. Copyright © 1980
by Joseph P. Lash. Reprinted by permission of DELACORTE
PRESS/SEYMOUR LAWRENCE.
Dell Publishing Co., Inc.: Excerpt from Eleanor Roosevelt's introduction to *The Story of My Life* by Helen Keller. Reprinted by permission
of the Dell Publishing Co., Inc.
Random House, Inc.: Excerpts from *Hands* by John Napier. Copy-
right © 1980 by John Russell Napier. Reprinted by permission of Pantheon Books, a division of Random House, Inc.
John Wiley & Sons, Inc.: Excerpts from *Biological Foundations of
Language* by E. Lenneberg. Copyright © 1967 by E. Lenneberg. Reprinted by permission of John Wiley & Sons, Inc.

Library of Congress Cataloging in Publication Data

Neisser, Arden.   The other side of silence.

Bibliography: p.
Includes index.
1. Deaf—United States—Social conditions.   2. Deaf—
Education—United States.   3. Sign language.   4. Deaf—
Means of communication.   I. Title.
HV2545.N44   1983   305'.908162'0973   83-48012
ISBN 0-394-53148-5

Manufactured in the United States of America

FIRST EDITION

833915

For Dick

Contents

Acknowledgments

William Stokoe, who proved the linguistic worth of ASL to contemporary scholars, has also been of central importance to this book. I thank him deeply for his help, support, friendship, patience, and redaction through all aspects of this enterprise.

I give enthusiastic thanks to Ted Supalla and his wife, Elissa Newport, who were my anchors in the deaf community, especially on the West Coast. I would also like to acknowledge Clarence Supalla, editor and publisher of *Deaf Spectrum*, an independent publication that was an invaluable source of information.

From the first day I met her in 1979, I depended on the generosity, energy, and brilliance of Laura Petitto, who spent hours, and days, and perhaps years pursuing this subject with me, who fulfilled and exceeded all my expectations. I am also grateful to Nancy Frishberg, linguist and interpreter in the widest sense; she interpreted not only the language but also many of the issues surrounding deaf life with clarity and sensitivity.

My thanks go as well to Carol Padden and Tom Humphries, who gave me a global picture of deafness as well as their own very personal perspective. The Californians who talked to me about ASL and the community of signers were numerous, but I want especially to thank Ursula Bellugi, Ray Jones, Howie and Lori Seago, Lou Fant, and Virginia Hughes.

I am grateful to Gallaudet College for providing such an open environment for inquiry, and I thank President Merrill and the

staff of the Linguistics Research Laboratory; also Dennis Coke-
ley, Charlotte Baker, and Shirley Stein. Many thanks to the National Association of the Deaf, especially Edward Carney. My
congressman, Matthew McHugh, and his staff were instrumen-
tal in facilitating this research.

I particularly want to express my appreciation to Frank Keil
at Cornell for reading and commenting on the manuscript, and
for his long and loyal interest in the linguistic and political issues
surrounding this project. I thank Kristi Lockhart Keil for her
reading of the manuscript, and for accompanying me on a trip to
a school for the deaf, as did Susan Kemper during the earliest
phase of the work in 1977. Thanks also to Barbara Lust and
James Gair.

Mark Seidenberg, Rochel Gelman, and Susan Goldin-
Meadow were extremely helpful in the areas of linguistics and
child development. David Premack gave me an opportunity to
visit his chimpanzee laboratory, which was a singular and infor-
mative experience.

Considering the question of sign language and its ecology,
my good friend, the late James J. Gibson, influenced me more
than I realized at the outset, and the discussions of the visual
world in the chapter "Signs and Science" are strongly Gibson-
ian. I thank Eleanor J. Gibson for her many contributions to this
persuasive and enlightening point of view, and feel fortunate indeed to have spent so much time with the two Gibsons, profiting
from their wisdom and enjoying their friendship.

I wish to thank Marvin Carlson for his reading of the theatrical sections of the book, and for many insights into the acting
profession. My thanks to Paul Rozin, to John Marcham, and to
Eric Seidler, my constant reader; and to Robert Farnsworth for
casting his poet's eye on some tangled portions of this text, thus
making them lovelier. I thank Lawrence Erlbaum for worldly
advice; and Chester Hartman, Sharon Shepela, Judith Spink,
and Judith Quinn, old friends who happened to live near schools
for the deaf and were burdened with the responsibility of

driving me to and from airports, as well as providing food and shelter.

I simply could not have done without the help of Sheldon White and Mary Falcon, and I thank them sincerely for expediting the entire endeavor. That courteous and determined voice on the telephone, my editor, Katherine Hourigan, has my gratitude and respect.

Present during the entire sojourn was my husband, Dick Neisser, who played the roles of saint and demon. He taught me. Perhaps more important, he let me teach him. Throughout it all he was civil, supportive, open to new ideas, argumentative, and amusing. The book would not have been nearly so much fun for me without him.

This book was written with the help of a grant from the Commonwealth Fund of New York. I gratefully acknowledge this crucial and generous assistance. I also thank the Women's Studies Program at Cornell University, where I held the position of Visiting Fellow from 1979 to 1983—with special thanks to Susan Kearl.

ARDEN NEISSER

Ithaca, N.Y.
May 1983

The Other Side
of Silence

Prologue

My first glimpse of deaf life came while listening to a research paper about American Sign Language (ASL) at a university conference on language and linguistics in the mid-1970s. This remarkable language had only recently been discovered by academic linguists; the auditorium was filled, and interest was very high. Before making the presentation, the speaker gave a brief and startling history of ASL in America: Among educators of the deaf, ASL is not considered a language. It is never taught, is forbidden in the classroom, and strongly discouraged outside of school. The aim of deaf education for close to a century has been teaching the deaf to speak and to lipread. Despite the fact that few deaf students have ever achieved these goals, it still is.

Although ASL was discouraged and even suppressed, deaf people throughout the country have continued to use it. It is the fourth most commonly used language in the United States—after English, Spanish, and Italian—with a signing population of nearly 500,000.

Deaf people have always used sign language. Even uninstructed and isolated deaf people use signs. In 1972, a Danish anthropologist came across a single deaf man on a Polynesian island—the only one ever recorded in the island's twenty-four generations of oral history—and *he* was using a sign language to communicate with his family and friends. In schools for the deaf where a strictly oral method is pursued, and the prohibition against sign language is zealously enforced, children are still known to sign among themselves at every opportunity. Observers have commented on this phenomenon for centuries, and modern psychologists have begun studying it. There is now experimental data showing that young deaf children who have had no exposure to any kind of sign language will indeed invent their own system of signs.

My own experience with ASL and the deaf community began with reading articles and attending lectures; I had never known a deaf person, never met a deaf child. I enrolled in a sign language course, and subsequently spent an entire, frustrating season signing nursery rhymes. What I was learning was not American Sign Language, but I did acquire a small vocabulary of standard signs borrowed from ASL and used in all sign systems. It was like learning a list of French words before taking a trip to Paris. Of course, it's better to go to Paris with a small list of French words than with none, and my signs, though pathetic by linguistic standards, were better than no signs at all. Later, when I began interviewing deaf people, I always used an interpreter.

ASL was a topic of considerable interest to scholars, but I wanted to know what it meant to the deaf; to understand the deaf point of view. I wondered if the recognition of ASL had improved their lives. I started with the children, and with the conviction that the new information, when filtered down to the level of the schools, could only lead to constructive action.

Most schools for the deaf are currently using some variety of sign language in the classroom as part of a new method called "total communication." When the decision was made, during the 1970s, to lift the ban on signing, no change in philosophy took place; to all other methods, techniques, training, and curricula, signs were merely added. Amoeba-like, these institutions are always eager to extend themselves, to increase their bulk and their budgets. The teachers have their own interests and traditions; their opinions were formed at teachers training colleges and special education departments. In some states, a single sequence of courses certifies a teacher to work with *any* handicapped child:

crippled, retarded, disturbed, autistic, deaf, or blind. (There are almost no deaf teachers in schools for the deaf.) Though a sort of sign language is used in the schools, it isn't ASL. A peculiar kind of trade-off has taken place: the kids don't learn to speak very well, and the teachers don't learn to sign.

For five years, I made regular visits to schools and agencies, institutions dedicated to the education and welfare of the deaf. They were all public institutions, and ranged from well-staffed federal committees in Washington to a rural school with one deaf child and a part-time hearing specialist. Few professionals in the world of the deaf have ever thought seriously about deafness. They think only about hearing: hearing loss, partial hearing, residual hearing, and the conduction of sound. They spend a great deal of time describing to their deaf clients and pupils all the things that they are missing, like music, and poetry, and birdsong. I never heard so much talk about string quartets, sonnets, and the uplifting murmurings of nature as I did at the schools for the deaf! Everybody seems obsessed with sound. They know nothing at all about silence, and have never stopped to wonder how competent and intelligent people might go about coping with it.

Although the deaf live in a world without sound, it is the same world we all inhabit. To the problems of living in the environment they bring the full range of human resourcefulness, intelligence, and ingenuity. They have created for themselves a language that is not only comparable to all the world's great languages, but is perfectly adapted to their lives and needs. They have created for themselves as well a strong sense of identity, an authentic social community, and many cultural traditions. They do not speculate long about the nature of sound, or the mechanics of normal hearing. No living creature organizes its behavior around something it doesn't have. The deaf perceive the world through skilled and practiced eyes; language is at their fingertips.

When I wanted to learn about silence and sign language, I went to talk to the deaf.

In Search of Sign Language

"We'll pick you up at the airport," Elissa Newport said on the phone. She was a professor of psychology at La Jolla in 1979, when I made the trip, and was doing research on American Sign Language. "Ted's coming with me."

Ted Supalla, a graduate student at La Jolla, is deaf. Supalla and Newport were collaborators on several studies. My pleasure at being in California again evaporated at the San Diego airport, and panic set in as I tried to face the idea of meeting and signing to Ted. Newport was nowhere in sight. A young man approached, smiled, looked me in the eye, and signed. As if paralyzed, I just stared at him, nodding my head.

The deaf, I learned, are extremely patient with this kind of behavior. They expect hearing people to be awkward and incompetent in their attempts to communicate. Their own communicative skills are extraordinary; they have spent most of their lives trying to get across to hearing people, and trying to figure out what it is that hearing people want to get across. Responsibility for any exchange is traditionally assigned to the deaf.

Getting no response from me, Ted signed again, more slowly and deliberately. He pointed to my luggage, flexed his arm (the sign for "strong"), picked up my suitcase, turned and walked towards the exit. I followed.

Ted Supalla is tall and blond with very blue eyes; a neat,

sandy beard covers the lower part of his face. He was twenty-eight years old when I met him. Both of Ted's parents are deaf, and ASL is his native language. He has an older brother who has normal hearing, and two younger brothers, deaf. Like many deaf people I've met, he has a good feeling for narrative, and when I asked him to tell me about himself he began with his forebears. Elissa Newport interpreted virtually all the conversations I had with Ted Supalla.

"My grandparents weren't deaf, but there were many deaf people in my family. My father was working in Seattle in a rubber factory, molding tires, when he met my mother. She was still in deaf school. They were married the next year in Seattle by a justice of the peace and didn't understand any of it. My mother is usually a good lipreader, she's really hard of hearing, not completely deaf. But almost. I was born in Minnesota, where my father and grandfather were working a farm together. I remember my brother going back and forth on the school bus. I really wanted to go to school. I waited for him to come home every afternoon.

"In 1956, just before my sixth birthday, my mother told me I was going to school. I was very happy. Got new clothes. Drove fifty miles. Minnesota School for the Deaf. I was shocked. I cried in the dorm. Parents made sleep sign, then counted—seven days. They would come to visit me in seven days. They came every week.

"I was the second smallest kid in class. Nobody signed in class, and only a few in the dormitories."

The following year the family moved to Washington State where Supalla's father had bought a farm, and Ted transferred to the Washington School for the Deaf. The family made the trip west by train. The school was on the way, so they got off the train, left Ted and his brother David, one year younger, at the school; then the rest of the family got back on the train and continued to the new farm 250 miles away.

Like all schools for the deaf in America at that time, the

Washington School used an oral method. The story of Ted Supalla's education is the story of American Sign Language in this
country for close to a century. The language was matter-of-
factly ignored, despised and outlawed, neither taught nor tolerated in classrooms for the deaf. Teachers in the schools were
completely unfamiliar with it, did not use it, and could not understand it. They were trained in oral methods, to teach artificial
speech production and lipreading, and to use speech in teaching
everything else. It was a difficult task and they were not often
successful. Barely 10 percent of oral students actually mastered
intelligible speech. Lipreading has an even lower rate of success—around 4 percent. As a system of education, oralism
did not foster learning. The average deaf person in the United
States during that period was found to have a third-grade reading level.

Deafness, by definition, is the inability to hear spoken language, to discriminate and reproduce speech. Oral programs
begin by teaching the children to make sounds, then words, one
at a time. Deaf children who have been in oral kindergarten programs have learned, by age five, perhaps fifty words. At the same
age, a child with normal hearing has a vocabulary of several
thousand words; and a deaf child of deaf parents who has learned
ASL as a first language has a vocabulary of several thousand
signs. But most deaf children (around 90 percent) have hearing
parents and enter school with no ASL and such a restricted
knowledge of English that they are virtually without any functioning language at all.

Yet, while few attained speech in the oral programs, all managed to learn ASL. It is estimated that 90 percent of deaf adults
who were deaf as children use ASL, and most of them learned it
at schools for the deaf—from each other. They simply signed
behind their teachers' backs.

"My brother, David, stayed with me at the Washington
School," said Ted, "in the same room; but a month later he was
moved out.

"We had speech training every day. Sat in front of a mirror and worked and worked. We watched ourselves in the mirror. *Flag is red. Flag is blue.* Over and over. We wore headphones. Watched the blackboard. Whatever teacher wrote, kids copied. The following year we did it all again. The janitor was deaf. David and I used to find him and talk to him."

The farm didn't work out for the Supallas and the family moved again. The youngest child, Sammy, was two. They rented a house one block from Ted and David's school and tried to arrange for the boys to become day students. Their requests were repeatedly denied. Everyone was disappointed. "David's classroom had a window that faced our house. I could go there and look out and see my little brother playing in the yard. We were only allowed to go home on Saturday and then had to come back for Sunday school next morning. That was all oral, too. I didn't really know what was happening for a long time."

There were so few signers in his life that Ted, at nine, was keenly aware of each one. A deaf woman arrived at the school to become a dormitory parent, and brought her son, a student Ted's age. "They were both very special to me," he said. "Even though that woman spent a lot of time telling us we had to be extra polite because we were deaf. We had to practice being very quiet, not make a lot of noise moving around, and not attract a lot of attention."

By that time there was more signing among the boys and Ted said he learned bad signs. *"Baloney!"* He showed me the sign and laughed. "That was a very bad sign, *baloney!* I used it all the time. When we got preached to about being polite, I'd sign, *baloney!* Got bawled out a lot. My fingerspelling was getting good. I practiced every day, all the time. Sometimes I'd fingerspell *b-a-l-o-n-e-y!*"

The Supallas moved again the following spring, this time across the river and into the next state, Oregon, to a farm where they still live. The children would have to go to the state school in Oregon. It was reputed to be better than the one in Washington, but they delayed getting in touch with the school or even finding out where it was.

"We were still very poor. The farm was lovely. Lots of apple trees. When the apples were ripe, David and I sold apples from our wagon. My father wrote a sign on a small card: 'DELICIOUS FOR PIE—*50¢ a bushel.*' At one house a girl came to the door. She knew sign and invited us in. We all sat around signing, having a good time, and she gave us the address of the school. We got to be good friends."

The Oregon school was more modern, but it was also a lot more oral. "The superintendent had a weird mouth. It was a bad experience trying to lipread him."

It was the beginning of the school year, September. "In the manual-vocational classes there were some big, big boys. Twenty years old. Everybody was real depressed that day because the superintendent had announced that instead of going up to eighth grade, the school would now go up to twelfth. Four more years in the manual class!

"The tradition at the school was for everybody to pop up every time the super came into the room, and when he looked at you, you said your name and the name of the town you came from. I knew I said my name really awful. It seemed ridiculous to talk to a room full of deaf kids—they couldn't hear. I wrote my name on the blackboard: *Ted Supalla, Beaverton, Oregon.*

"From then on, I was lost. Never knew what was going on. They couldn't decide about me. People who signed were usually put into the manual class, where everybody signed. They put me there because I was a signer, then took me out because I could read and write pretty well. They didn't know what to do with me. I was always in trouble. I used to forget my glasses."

Lissa stopped interpreting to ask if there was anything the matter with his eyes. "No," he answered. "Then why did you have glasses?"

"I complained of headaches, once, so they sent me for eyeglasses." He laughed. "A nurse gave me the eye test. I finger-spelled the letters on the chart. I don't think she could finger-spell. I don't know, maybe *she* needed glasses. Anyway, I got stuck with them. Fights all the time over those glasses. What I really wanted was a hearing aid. At the other school only one boy had a hearing aid, but Oregon was different. Lots of kids had them.

"They gave me a great big hearing aid. Old. It was heavy. I was excited and very happy. Later I got sick of it. It hurt. I could feel it rattling against my head but I couldn't hear anything. I got to hate it. They would lower your grade if you didn't wear it.

"A few years later, the school got new equipment. You went into a soundproof room and looked at the audiologist through a window. I was supposed to raise my hand when I heard a sound. My head started ringing. E-e-e-e. Pain. The guy got mad at me: *Stop playing around!*

"The rule was that everybody had to wear a hearing aid every day or be punished. I tried to give mine back. There were big rows over it. They kept saying I could hear real well if I wore my hearing aid, but I knew I couldn't. They were always telling you all the things you could do that you knew you couldn't. Fi-nally I think there was a meeting with the audiologist and they didn't bother me any more.

"I remember when my little brother, Sammy, came to school. He was only three or four. The deaf school put a lot of pressure on my mother and father to send Sammy to preschool. The kids down there were wild. They'd pounce on anyone who came in. Sammy was the only signer. I was allowed to visit him on Saturday afternoon. Talk to him for one hour. Preschool lasted two years. Lipreading and oral training. We were worried about him and had some of our friends look out for him. They'd contact David or me if he needed us. He did all right, though.

"When he went into the primary school there were a few signers, people he could talk to. Sammy spent fifteen years in that school, went all the way through, and graduated. When he

went to college he was a big shot. President of his class, editor of
the yearbook. Did very well. Deaf of deaf tended to go to college.
I think most of the kids from the three or four deaf families we
knew went to college."

In the school's oral program, Ted was told that he had fallen
far behind the other children. He had the impression that there
were good lipreaders in the school, but later was not so sure. In
the fifth, sixth, and seventh grades, he was at the top of his class.
He skipped the eighth grade and went into the upper, high
school section.

"I was put in the smallest track: academic. The second track
was manual-vocational. And then there was a third track. I don't
know what those poor kids were going to do. The school never
said. Some of the classes were just art work all day long, and
games.

"There were a lot of sports at all levels. My father kept writing to the school saying I didn't have to play sports if I didn't
want to. He always said the school put too much emphasis on
sports, not enough on studying. I played a little basketball, but it
really did take a lot of time. I quit after a while. Sure enough,
they said I studied too much, it was interfering with my lipreading. My father sent a lot of letters to the school telling them not
to bother me about speech training but just teach the subjects.
He was terrific."

When Ted was sixteen, in the tenth grade, the school suggested that he take the entrance examination for Gallaudet College, the liberal arts college for the deaf in Washington, D.C.

Gallaudet is known as the Harvard of the deaf, and is the
most respected institution in the deaf community. Until very recently, it was the only place in the world where a deaf student
could get a college education. Every prominent deaf person in
America (and maybe the world) has been associated with Gallaudet. Most hearing teachers and administrators who run the
state schools and organizations for the deaf have been trained
there as well, in the graduate and extramural divisions. To have
attended is a mark of distinction.

"I wanted something different," said Ted Supalla. "Everyone said Gallaudet was great fun. Social life wonderful. I didn't want to break all my ties in the West, leave my family. I wanted to go to a hearing college. Later. In a few years.

"I took the test, though, and was accepted. They were delighted at school." He began to laugh. "Because I had passed, they told me I couldn't stay at the school any more, I was finished. I talked it over with my father. He wrote to a local public high school and we visited in secret. It was arranged that I could enroll as a junior.

"They planned a big party for me at school. When I told them I wasn't going to Gallaudet, all the teachers were shocked. Canceled party. They started telling me how smart I was: 'You're smarter than most hearing people.' Some change! I told them it didn't matter. They were really pissed.

"The next year, they were still mad, and when my brother David wanted to take the test for Gallaudet, they said, 'Oh, why don't you go to a public school?'

"The public school was hard," Ted said. "I was there for two years, and embarrassed most of the time. I couldn't answer roll call. Had to explain to every teacher that I was deaf. Teachers asked for volunteer notetakers for me—in front of the whole class. I cringed in my seat. Sometimes nobody volunteered.

"The first winter, I remember having a bad cold. Sniffled a lot and blew my nose. I wondered if I was making a lot of noise. Afterwards people told me it was really loud." He tried to sit next to the good notetakers. A few of the students, he noticed, couldn't read.

"I took Contemporary Literature. Wow! Dirty Books! *Catch 22, Brave New World.* I was thrilled. Nothing like that at deaf school. The teacher was nice. She wrote me a note one day saying she wanted a conference with my parents. I wrote her a note: 'Parents are deaf.' She didn't ask again. Same teacher taught creative writing. Said I wrote well. That can't be, I thought. One girl in the class introduced herself. Next day she had learned fingerspelling.

"At lunch, I avoided the jocks. Sat with the farm boys and was real quiet. That girl kept bothering me. I went to library. Girl found me. That ended up—after a long time, almost a year—being my first girlfriend. We went to college together. Portland State.

"College was a lot harder than high school, and bigger. I met some people there I had gone to high school with. We hadn't been friends in high school, but we knew each other, and they became friendly. It was nice, and helped. I had requested an interpreter from Vocational Rehabilitation. Maybe, they said. If I told the teacher I was deaf, I didn't have to go to class. Just do the reading and write term papers. I didn't care for that. In some classes, my girlfriend took notes, especially in the second year."

At the end of the second year, Ted went home to Beaverton. His father had become active in deaf politics and was publishing a very lively grass roots quarterly, *Deaf Spectrum*. Editorial offices were in the house, production in the garage. Ted worked the farm with his father and helped put out the magazine, some issues of which ran to one hundred pages. "I was tired of being dependent," Ted said, a recurring theme of his life.

Later that year he learned about a new Center on Deafness at California State University, Northridge (CSUN). It provided interpreters for deaf students in regular classes at the college. "I could do everything myself," he said. He enrolled the following fall, 1972, as a junior. There were twenty deaf and twenty thousand hearing students at the vast commuter college outside Van Nuys in the San Fernando Valley.

The Center on Deafness was an excellent place for Ted to be. He made many deaf friends; got to know the interpreters, hearing people (some of them skilled ASL signers); and he became interested in his native language. In characteristic style, he didn't have an adviser; and though he was a psychology major, had never been to the psychology department office. "I read wonderful books by McCay Vernon, *They Grow in Silence*, about deaf children being deprived of sign language. A tragedy. Also, I read his work about deaf children of deaf parents. He said they were better students, better readers and writers, because they had learned ASL early. I had always been told just the opposite: that my writing would always be terrible. I found out that *I* was using ASL and that everybody was interested in it. Vernon was a psychologist. I wanted to be a psychologist."

Supalla learned, with some discomfort, that there were other sign languages besides ASL, and outside his immediate circle he observed signs he had never seen before. "Hearing people were teaching courses in ASL and using the wrong signs. I wanted to teach a course, but they wouldn't let me because I couldn't speak. Lou Fant and I talked about the problem a lot, but didn't know what to do about it. Lou's probably the best interpreter in the country."

Lou Fant taught at Northridge, and trained interpreters during the early days of the Center. A native signer, the only hearing child of two deaf parents, he has also spent most of his adult life trying to explain ASL to hearing people. He's been a teacher of the deaf, been on the Gallaudet faculty, has written several books and prepared courses on ASL. He is also an actor, was one of the original members of the National Theatre of the Deaf. He works a good deal in television in Los Angeles and is Hollywood's local expert on sign language, frequently called upon to give instruction to hearing actors. Fant and Supalla spent a lot of time in the college television studio making tapes of signers and filming dramatic efforts. As graduation approached, Ted, always keen on cameras, was toying with the idea of applying to the American Film Institute. Fant urged him to go, and even offered to go with him as his interpreter. It was a handsome, a princely offer; but Ted was worrying about gainful employment. He was considering it, however, when he met the Gardners.

Allen and Beatrice Gardner are the psychologists from the University of Nevada who raised the famous chimpanzee Washoe. They believed that an ape could learn language if provided with a human environment, and had spent five years trying to teach ASL to Washoe. They considered their efforts successful and claimed that the ape could use 132 signs linguistically. When the Gardners visited the Center on Deafness, they were planning a new project with a group of younger animals, and were looking for signers to work in their laboratory. They invited Ted to apply to graduate school in Reno, where he would also be a research assistant and teacher of signs to one of the infant chimps. He went and remained a year. "I think it was the longest any deaf person stayed."

The entire issue of chimpanzee sign language is a painful one for the deaf. There is simply nothing in it for them—nothing from which they might be able to take comfort or find dignity, but only the opposite. The image of an ape signing echoes the ancient and familiar charge that their language is only suited for the beasts.

Ted Supalla was determined to be above all that. He was a scientist, a psychologist, an excellent signer. "Why shouldn't I show the chimps my signs?"

At Reno, he realized that none of the large number of people who worked there knew anything about ASL, and none were using it. "I felt real uneasy about what they called signs. They made it sound as if the chimps were using signs like a language. I thought it wasn't at all.

"I tried to teach the Gardners ASL. Made slow progress. I had been reading more linguistics. I read William Stokoe on ASL, and Ursula Bellugi had started doing research on sign-language acquisition in deaf children. I suggested we borrow Ursie's tapes of the deaf kids and really compare them with the chimps. Gardners said no-no. They seemed very irritated."

Dr. Ursula Bellugi is a psycholinguist at the Salk Institute for Biological Studies in La Jolla. She and Edward Klima, a linguist, have been engaged in an investigation of the linguistic properties of ASL that is the most extensive work done in the field. She has many deaf research assistants working on the project, and many hearing graduate students from the University of California doing research. The La Jolla campus is across the highway from the Salk Institute.

Ted went to La Jolla to talk with Ursula Bellugi. Then he walked across the highway to negotiate with the department of psychology. He was the only deaf person ever to present himself to this highly prestigious department as a graduate student. The distinguished faculty responded with a display of massive, collective confusion.

"They couldn't seem to concentrate on me," said Ted, amused. "I guess I fell through the cracks. Nobody acted worried. They took the attitude that I was Ursie's problem and they kept themselves from noticing me for quite a while. When they did, I was already finished with a couple of courses, and that was that."

It is all behind him. The seminars, the statistics courses. Fingerspelling terms like *homogeneity of variance*, and worrying about interpreters, one of whom was a chain smoker. ("I hated him. He always had a cigarette in his hand or in his mouth.") Ted Supalla completed his requirements, finished his dissertation, and was awarded a doctoral degree in 1982. He now holds a position as research psychologist at the University of Illinois.

II

The use of sign language is reported throughout recorded time. There are references to it in the Talmud and in the writings of ancient Greece. During the Middle Ages there were isolated reports of deaf people being taught to read, write, and count. Around the sixteenth century, in Spain, a one-handed manual alphabet was developed to aid in the education of certain deaf children, usually those born to noble families.

Public education for the deaf began in Paris in the middle of the eighteenth century, when the Abbé Charles Michel de l'Épée, an ordinary, bookish, neighborhood priest, simply took an interest in a small group of deaf children and began to instruct them. He found them alert, intelligent, and eager to learn. Using pictures at first, then the manual alphabet from Spain, he set out to teach them how to read and write French, and how to save their souls. A small school developed, grew, received a modest amount of royal support, and after the Revolution became the world-famous National Institution for Deaf-Mutes.

Some histories credit L'Épée with inventing sign language and teaching it to his deaf pupils. He did not invent sign language. Deaf people invented it; invented, in fact, hundreds of sign languages as hearing people invented hundreds of spoken languages. L'Épée learned signs from his deaf pupils. He may have been the first educator to use a bilingual approach, because as he learned the natural sign language of the deaf, he used it to instruct them. He was convinced it was a true language, and came to believe that signs and gestures were the "mother tongue" not only of the deaf, but of all mankind. What he did invent, and add to the natural signs, were a number of conventional signs to represent French words and articles that had no signs, and to represent grammatical features of the language. (Some of these signs were borrowed from a medieval system used in Cistercian monasteries where pious monks had taken lifelong vows of silence.) This augmented system he called the *signes méthodiques*. Using it, his students acquired a mastery of accurate and stylish written French.

Students came to the school from all over France, and L'Épée began to train teachers in his method. Other schools opened in the provinces, and as more and more of the country's deaf were educated, a standard French Sign Language emerged.

The school became famous throughout Europe. L'Épée at first accepted foreign students, but later preferred to train teachers who would return to their own countries, adapt the method to their own languages, and open schools for the deaf. Most of the permanent schools in Europe can be traced to the National

Institution in Paris, and most of the sign languages of Europe are related to the French method.

Manual languages were never received hospitably in northern Europe, however, nor among Anglo-Saxons. Schools for the deaf in England, Germany, and Scandinavia traditionally used an oral method developed in Germany in the eighteenth century by Samuel Heinicke, an army officer from, as it happens, Saxony. These oral schools were organized quite differently from the manual schools founded on L'Épée's principles. They were all private schools, all run by individuals or families, and all were highly secretive about revealing lucrative methods. When challenged by L'Épée to an evaluation, Heinicke told a distinguished jury of the Zurich Academy that he would only divulge his methods for a fee. He lost the challenge, largely by default. When he died, his school died with him.

L'Épée taught speech for a short time in Paris, but abandoned it as artificial, physically unpleasant for the children, and generally not worth the considerable time and effort. He felt that the manual language was a superior means of expressing ideas and meanings to persons without hearing. Throughout his life he continued to compile dictionaries of signs, to clarify and publish his methods, train teachers, keep the school open to visitors and available for scrutiny. When he died in 1789, there were four candidates for his job, all trained by him. His successor was the Abbé Sicard, who continued the tradition of teaching and publishing. One of Sicard's books was purchased by Mason Cogswell, the father of a deaf child in Hartford, Connecticut. It contained, among other things, that useful Spanish hand alphabet, and specific instructions for making signs.

The child was Alice Cogswell. Such is the fascination of the deaf that her next-door neighbor, a young minister named Thomas Hopkins Gallaudet, was spending a good part of his time trying to educate her. Alice's father gave Sicard's book to Gallaudet, and the two men began talking about the possibility of a school. The following year, Cogswell took an informal census of deaf children in New England, convinced a number of philanthropic citizens that it was sufficient to warrant a school, and raised enough money to send young Gallaudet to Europe in search of the best possible method with which to begin the project.

Thomas Hopkins Gallaudet was born in Philadelphia in 1787. He graduated from Yale in 1805, and taught there for several years before going to the Andover Theological Seminary. He had just become a Congregational minister when he met Alice Cogswell, and was twenty-seven years old when he made the trip to Europe. Accounts of the trip give the impression that he went somewhat reluctantly and did not plan to stay long. He still had hopes of spending the rest of his life as a minister. He was gone for more than a year.

In England, his first stop, he encountered the Thomas Braidwood family, proprietors of several schools teaching an oral method. He spent almost two-thirds of the year negotiating with various members of the family about enrolling at one of their schools as a student teacher. Control of the schools amounted to a profitable monopoly that the Braidwoods aimed to keep. One member of the family, John, was in America at the time of Gallaudet's arrival trying to set up an oral school in Virginia. John's trip was only partly business; the other part was exile and rehabilitation—he drank—and the family did not have high expectations. When John failed, the Braidwoods attempted to come to terms with Gallaudet. They offered to open a school in Connecticut and run it exactly as they ran the other schools, as a franchise. They tried to extract an oath of secrecy from Gallaudet before offering him training, and refused to release any of their teachers from similar oaths of secrecy.

Exasperated, Gallaudet got in touch with Sicard and was invited to Paris to learn the *signes méthodiques*. Three months later, he returned to America accompanied by Laurent Clerc, a former deaf pupil of Sicard and a teacher at the Paris school. Clerc accompanied Gallaudet on speaking tours and demonstrations; he lobbied state legislatures as well as Congress in his already excellent written English (he is described as carrying a small slate and chalk), and was received at the White House by President Monroe. He helped Gallaudet establish the first school in this hemisphere, the American Asylum in Hartford, and became the first deaf teacher of the deaf in America. Together, Gallaudet and Clerc adapted the French method to English.

Pedagogy being what it is, the two teachers tinkered with the language, trying to make it more efficient, inventing and adding new signs. The methodological signs, originally intended to make written grammar easier, made signed grammar more difficult as more signs represented English words rather than meanings. (These signs required a double translation: from sign to word to meaning. Natural signs go directly from sign to meaning.) The situation was further complicated by the fact that since there were deaf individuals on the American continent, there was also an indigenous natural sign language. Historians call it Old American Sign Language.

Within a rather short time the methodological signs proved too unwieldy, and except for the signs already absorbed into the language, it was abandoned for a more natural system: a merger of the Old American signs and the French signs of Clerc that evolved into American Sign Language.

Clerc not only instructed children, he trained teachers— many of whom were also deaf. Teachers skilled in ASL spread the language throughout an expanding network of schools and taught it for more than sixty years before oralism forced it underground (there are deaf people living today who were educated by students of Clerc). Despite its suppression, ASL is the language used by the deaf throughout the United States and Canada. It is probably the most widely known and used sign language in the world. Deaf Europeans are tremendously impressed at the nationwide use of ASL and express envy that deaf persons from all over North America can understand each other, whereas in Europe, people from neighboring cities often cannot.

People with normal hearing learn spoken language by hearing it, and by hearing the sound of their own voices. The deaf, who can't hear and get no auditory feedback, cannot learn spoken language naturally. The inability to hear and to acquire speech is the only serious consequence of deafness; in comparison, all other sounds in the environment are trivial. For centuries the link between hearing and speaking was poorly understood. No functional relationship was considered. There was thought to be some deficiency in the brain, or a single obstruction that stopped both ears and vocal cords. Language itself had mystical qualities, a gift of God, bestowed.

Deaf individuals being taught to speak have been noted only rarely in the past. There were one or two in the sixteenth century, around the time that the manual alphabet was developed, and a few in the seventeenth. Most of the stories emphasized the miraculous powers of the teacher while giving few details regarding the pupil. Some teachers made distinctions about degree of hearing loss in their students, and some did not. Many used manual alphabets and signs, and reports of speech ability varied widely.

Beginning in the eighteenth century, and erupting in the nineteenth, a real battle began for nothing less than the identity of deaf human beings. It is called the oral/manual controversy, as inaccurate a term as the mind/body split which it also reflects. It added an unbearable dilemma to a crushing handicap.

Oralism became not only a teaching method but a philosophy of life, a model for deaf behavior, and a strong religious belief. As speech was God-given, that which separated man from beast, it was a sin to permit the deaf to remain silent. Gestures were like tools of the devil. The oralists maintained and still maintain that because signing is easier for deaf children to learn, it inhibits the acquisition of speech, that children who learn sign language lose the will to speak. Critics of oralism have called it a denial of deafness. The method is built around artificial speech production and substitute hearing: lipreading.

A great deal of mystery surrounds lipreading. It seems uncorrelated with intelligence, unaffected by motivation. "It's a talent," more than one teacher has told me. "Some kids just have it. Like perfect pitch." Most speech sounds are not made at the lips at all; only 40 percent of English phonemes are visible. Four words out of an average eleven-word sentence is considered good. The rest is gathering meaning from context, from facial expression, and from guessing. A few are remarkably good at it.

Occasionally, deaf persons will become skilled at reading the speech of certain family members and no one else; or they may be successful only under ideal conditions: face to face, and one on one. Oral interpreters are now being trained for those deaf persons who do not use sign language, though the entire rationale for oral education should make this sort of service unnecessary.

Hearing people with one practice session do just as well on lipreading tests as deaf people who have had years of training. Lipreading is not a good way to learn English, but a thorough knowledge of English appears to be necessary in learning to lipread. Adults who already know English and who are losing their hearing benefit considerably from lipreading instruction. It is also a valuable skill for persons with moderate hearing loss. Modern hearing aids often pick up enough additional information to make lipreading possible and efficient.

Speech is a different problem. There have always been two populations of deaf: those born without hearing, the congenitally deaf, and those who lose their hearing later in life, sometimes called the adventitious deaf. Modern physicians and language experts prefer to call them pre-lingually and post-lingually deaf: those who lost their hearing before or after the acquisition of language.

Estimates of the incidence of deafness in the United States range from 2 million deaf, to 14 million with some kind of hearing impairment. The most recent census, published in 1974, *The Deaf Population of the United States,* reported a total of 1.8 million deaf persons. Almost a million of those had lost their hearing after the age of fifty. The target population sought by the census was called the pre-vocational deaf: "those who had lost, or never had the ability to hear and understand speech before the age of nineteen." There were about 420,000 people in this group. Most of them had become deaf before they were three: they had grown up deaf.

The demographers identified the pre-vocationally deaf as the population receiving the maximum number of services—educational, medical, vocational—and by implication, recognized them as a cultural and political entity. The age range (birth through adolescence) is exactly the period when human beings learn and develop language skills. The size of the population corresponds closely to the estimated number of ASL signers in the country: nearly 500,000. During the years when language learning is natural and easy, deaf youngsters, whether they master English or not, learn ASL.

How children acquire language, all language, all over the world, and under every possible condition of life, is not precisely understood. All children seem to be born with the ability. It's not quite imitation and it's not exactly learning. "There are none so depraved," said Descartes, "that they cannot arrange different words together, forming of them a statement by which they make known their thoughts."

Children acquiring spoken language not only hear the words, they also notice the arrangement, the syntax. By the time children are five years old, most of them have learned the syntax of their native language. They know how to order words, and they know that words in different arrangements mean different things. This aspect of spoken language is particularly inaccessible to deaf children, especially those born deaf. They cannot hear the rhythms of spoken utterances, and develop little feeling for English syntax. Deaf children have no difficulty understanding the syntax of ASL, and pick up the rhythms of sign as spontaneously as hearing children pick up English.

Today, most children who are deaf were born deaf or became deaf shortly after birth. At the turn of the century, when oralism was gathering momentum, most deaf children had become deaf late in childhood, often through illness, after they had acquired oral language. The likelihood of retaining and improving their speech was fairly high, though not certain. The more speech and language a person had before becoming deaf, the better were the possibilities of maintaining speech through life. Indeed, for some, speech became a lifetime pursuit.

Teaching the deaf to speak is full of paradox. As they can never know or evaluate the quality of their voices, they are entirely dependent on hearing people, usually teachers, for validation. It is always the teacher who decides whether or not acceptable speech has occurred. It takes courage to utter sounds one cannot hear, and it takes trust between teacher and student. As the teachers' motive is to reward any kind of sound, no matter how imperfect, their praise often lacks sincerity. The children get conflicting cues from the hearing adults around them. Sounds that draw cheers of ecstasy from speech teachers are met with cold distaste from parents and strangers—sometimes incomprehension, sometimes derision. In a NOVA television program about deafness, Dr. Daniel Ling demonstrates his oral method with a child of perhaps eight: "Ut, ut, ut," says Dr. Ling purposefully. "Us, us, us," says the child. "No," says Dr. Ling, and begins again: "Ut, with a *t*. Ta, ta, ta." The child continues to say "Us," then switches to "Up." She never does say "ut." Dr. Ling asserts that deaf children can produce only one word in five that is understandable, and attributes this to faulty oral training.

III

Alexander Graham Bell was the hero of the oral method. With the success of his famous invention, he became its leader and principal spokesman. Early biographies say he was working on an amplification device for the deaf, and invented the telephone by accident. Later biographies emphasize the pure scientific nature of his invention and strongly deny it had anything to do with deafness, but they also say the telephone was an accident.

Bell was born and raised in Edinburgh, the second son of a family struggling to find a place in the middle class. Speech, gadgetry, and social mobility are the dominant themes of his life. As a boy he and his brother made a talking machine, and there is a story, also from his childhood, that he once taught a Skye terrier to talk. He came from a long line of elocutionists, actors, and speech experts. His father, Alexander Melville Bell, became well known as a phonetician and is sometimes identified as the model for Professor Henry Higgins in Shaw's play *Pygmalion*.

Three generations of Bells made their living coaching people who had speech problems or bad accents in Edinburgh and London. Both cities, apparently, were full of people who wished to articulate themselves into the significant classes. Young Alec Bell was teaching by the age of sixteen, and applied the family profession to the education of the deaf at the age of twenty-one. His father had developed a system of phonetic notation called Visible Speech, a rather complicated forerunner of the International Phonetic Alphabet. Bell tried to use it in teaching speech, but although it always showed promise, it never became a useful system.

In 1870, the Bell family emigrated to Canada. Alexander Melville had already demonstrated Visible Speech in the United States, and when a small oral school for the deaf in Boston invited him to lecture, he sent his son instead.

Alexander Graham Bell made New England his home and

continued the family profession. He was associated with the Clarke School in Northampton, taught briefly at the American School in Hartford, and opened a school of his own in Boston, The School of Vocal Physiology and Elocution, with a handful of private students. He was also a lecturer at the Boston University School of Oratory, and spent his free time at MIT learning about electricity and sound.

Accounts of his life portray him as a dynamic teacher and a kind man; articulate and energetic. Rectitudinous. He spent most of his young adulthood scratching out a living with considerable good humor for long hours, in low-paying jobs. He made many friends and valuable contacts. Two early backers of his electrical experiments were parents of his private deaf students. One was Thomas Sanders. Bell lived in the Sanders household in Salem and gave speech training to their son, George, while commuting daily to Boston to pursue his other ventures. The second, and more important, was Gardiner Greene Hubbard of Cambridge, a rich, well-connected lawyer whom Bell made richer. Bell began tutoring Hubbard's daughter Mabel in 1873. She was sixteen and had been deaf since the age of five. Bell was twenty-six.

Gardiner Hubbard had good instincts about making money, especially in the public sector. He got in on transportation first with the Cambridge Horse Railroad, and was first in utilities with the Cambridge Gas Light Company. As chairman of the Massachusetts Board of State Charities, he successfully lobbied the legislature in favor of oral schools, an effort that resulted in the chartering of the Clarke School in Northampton. It was there that Hubbard met Bell.

Hubbard was a patent attorney, interested in telegraphy and in the transmission of sound. Electrical gadgets were in vogue and everybody was feverishly working on inventions. Models of telephones were ubiquitous. It seems to have been a question of getting in first, a question to which Hubbard happily resonated.

"The story of the telephone will never be told," said Elisha Gray, whose own telephone missed being first at the patent office by four hours. At the time that Bell attempted to secure a patent, Gray and others were in the process of submitting designs, and over the next few years, Bell and Hubbard were tied up with legal challenges in the courts. Hubbard almost dumped the project. Facing ruin because of various financial adventurings, he was quietly trying to sell his shares in the telephone to Western Union when the litigation was fortuitously concluded in 1876, and Bell was awarded the patent. Shortly afterward, Bell and Mabel Hubbard were married.

Nothing Bell worked on afterward was in a class with the telephone, though he spent a large part of his fortune on independent "scientific" enterprises. He experimented with photophones, spectrophones, and phonographs. He invented the audiometer for the measurement of hearing loss, and the decibel (dB) is named for him. Later in his life Bell was interested in air flight; he designed and built huge, beautiful, tetrahedral kites of massive dimensions that he flew off Cape Breton in Nova Scotia, where he had a summer home. He also worked on hydrofoil boats.

Bell never seemed at ease in Washington, or with the American scene. He had taken out citizenship on the advice of his father-in-law, principally to enhance his position with the patent office (apparently good advice), but never exercised his franchise. He built a grand house on Connecticut Avenue, but seemed comfortable only in the Scottish ambience he created for himself in Nova Scotia. Throughout his life, he continued to be a powerful and prestigious spokesman on behalf of oral education. He once published a paper on the formation of a "deaf variety of the human race" that his admirers consider his major contribution to pure science.

In 1880, the French government awarded Bell the Volta Prize for the invention of the telephone. The prize amounted to $10,000. He used the money to open his own laboratory on the grounds of a house where his mother and father were living in Washington, D.C. Later it became the Volta Bureau, an organization "for the increase and diffusion of knowledge relating to the deaf." In 1893, Bell put up a permanent building for the Bureau, to function as headquarters and library. It is now the home of the Alexander Graham Bell Association for the Deaf and of the *Volta Review,* the monthly magazine of the oral establishment in America.

Oralism inspired hope; it promised to make deafness irrelevant. The oralists waited eagerly, patiently, for the exceptional deaf child who would learn perfect speech and validate their theories—and occasionally such a child appeared. But the ideal was so rarely achieved and so long in coming that they were forced to make allowances, give high marks for effort, and scale down the definition of success. The hope inspired by oralism was not borne out even in Alexander Graham Bell's own family: his wife had received articulation lessons throughout childhood, had been sent to Germany to work with special tutors, and was Bell's private pupil for years. Yet her articulation was never considered good. Bell had no patience with complaints about his wife's speech; he thought it "intelligible enough" so long as the family and old friends understood it. George Sanders, whom Bell considered an adopted son, was sent to a manual school at fifteen and was financially dependent on Bell for many years. Bell gave him a job as a printer at the Volta Bureau.

Oralism was a nineteenth-century idea, with its enthusiasm for apparatus, its confidence in the future of technology. It was reinforced by the Protestant ethic of hard work, unremitting practice, and strength of character to overcome all of life's afflictions. It flourished in the framework of Victorian manners (and Victorian science), and reflected a deep Anglo-Saxon antagonism toward all languages other than English. (Bilingualism was considered bad for the brain.) Oralism was consolidated during that period in history when the Welsh language was banned from schools in Wales; when Victoria as Empress of India made English the administrative language of the subcontinent; and when the great immigrations began, bringing foreign languages and cultures to America. Ties among English speakers were strong and there was a movement to standardize the tongue. The model for Victorian gentility was an immobile one, and a large part of "teaching the English how to speak" was directed at the elimination of gestures. Gesturing was something that Italians did, and Jews, and Frenchmen; it reflected the poverty of their cultures and the immaturity of their personalities. Sign language became a code word with strong racial overtones. It was seen as a foreign system, the invention, moreover, of a medievalist French priest.

The deaf themselves were never averse to learning speech. They fully understood its advantages, but they balked at the cost. By the beginning of the new century, it was clear to them that the price they would have to pay for speech was their own manual language. All schools for the deaf in America switched to oral methods exclusively. ASL was prohibited, even outside classrooms. Children's hands were tied, to prevent signing. Even when alone with each other, deaf children were expected to use oral language and to read each other's lips. Or pretend to. The oral schools may not have produced a large number of conversationalists, but they did produce several generations of deaf children who were quiet, stationary, inconspicuous, and quite acceptable to the hearing.

Sign language became legitimized in the late 1960s. It quickly aroused interest in the scholarly world, and was incorporated into a new philosophy of deaf education called "total communication." Within a few years, signs were being used in an increasing number of schools in the country. I wondered how the oralists were reacting, so I telephoned the Alexander Graham Bell Association to ask for an appointment. "Nobody here knows anything about sign language," was the automatic response, but they said I was welcome to come over if I liked.

The Volta Bureau is on a quiet old street corner in Georgetown, in a high, neo-classical building with columns and great heavy doors. It looks like a bank. The interior is worn, somewhat seedy; more antiquated than I had expected. I talked with a pleasant young man who seemed rushed. "I'm leaving this job," he told me confidentially, "at the end of the month." He walked me past a large portrait of Alexander Graham Bell, with a massive white beard and mustaches, and demonstrated how Bell raised his mustache to expose his mouth when talking to deaf people (his wife?) so they might lipread his remarks.

The chairman of the board of American Telephone and Telegraph traditionally sits on the board of the Bell Association. J. Edgar Hoover of the FBI was a member for years. The mission of the Association is to assure that deaf children become true Americans, patriotic and English-speaking. They regard the new interest in ASL as an academic conceit, and the introduction of total communication as a shrewd public relations campaign. After spending a few hours in the library—"We've been planning to reorganize"—I gave up. Aside from an interesting historical collection, the library was filled with inspirational volumes, poorly catalogued. There were few recent works on linguistics or language learning, and surprisingly little about deafness.

I talked at length with a very sincere woman in public relations who told me she has been with the Association for fifteen years. "Sign language," she explained, "it's not a language. It's a sort of shorthand. You can only express concrete things in sign language, not abstract ideas. There's a big difference between children who use sign language and the children who are oral." I asked her what the difference was. "Oral children think in English," she said.

I asked if the Association believed that all children could learn speech. "Well," she said, "some just aren't smart enough. Some aren't . . . aren't aggressive enough. They don't have the drive. It takes a lot of drive and perseverance. If they don't have it, well, I don't know.

"It's much easier for deaf children to learn sign language.

Because, you see, it's not really a language, it's easier. It's the easy way. If they don't know anything else, they'll use it, I guess. People who use sign language, that's fine. If they want to. We don't hate them or anything. They're just not . . . the same.

"Deaf children *can* learn to speak," she went on. "We really like to work with parents when the babies are still tiny. We train the mothers; instruct them to use language with their babies all the time. Like when they're bathing the baby. The mothers have got to talk to the baby while they're giving it a bath." She moved her hands slowly, as if pouring water over a child. "Speak, so the baby is bathed in language. Immersed in the mother tongue." She looked at me earnestly. "They can't hear, but they catch on. Some say there's no such thing as a deaf child. Not if it's done right. Education makes the difference. And amplification, of course. You've got to get them hearing aids as soon as possible. Deaf children can adjust to society.

"We are opposed to any kind of sign language. We are opposed to total communication. If only speech is used with the children," she said, "the children will learn speech and become assimilated into the hearing world."

Few deaf persons are assimilated into the world of the Volta Bureau, or the Alexander Graham Bell Association. When I inquired, I was directed to the office of Kenneth Lane, the only deaf person on the staff. He was described as an "oral adult."

Kenneth Lane is listed as Director of Publications for the *Volta Review*. He described his job as "outreach, publishing materials, proceedings of conferences, and so forth." After talking with Lane for a few minutes, I complimented him on his lipreading, and remarked that I had met very few deaf people who know how to lipread. His response was combative, lengthy, and cute. "How do you know?" he asked. "How do you know if you've met a deaf person who was lipreading? You would have no way of knowing, would you? If they're not making windmills with their hands, how would you know if they were deaf? Huh? It would never occur to you to ask them, would it? You probably meet deaf people every day who you have conversations with, and who lipread you, and you never, never have any idea, because there is nothing visible about them to let you know they are deaf!"

Toward the end of this harangue I was laughing. He took no offense, but smiled and continued. Lane had become deaf at seventeen and had attended Gallaudet College, class of 1952. He pronounced it Gal-ya-dette, not because he couldn't pronounce it, his diction was very good, but to express his contempt. His attitude toward the college was extremely negative. Also toward the NAD—the National Association of the Deaf. An extremely voluble person, Lane talked so fast I couldn't keep up with him in my notes, and hardly had a chance to ask a question. This turned out to be just as well, because after the opening moments, he didn't seem able to lipread anything I said. He could, however, lipread his secretary. He talked to me rapidly, then looked over my shoulder to his secretary, who was sitting just behind and to one side of me. She mouthed my few questions and brief contributions to the interview; you really couldn't call it a conversation.

"I studied in nine different colleges," he said. "Decided to beat the handicap, and that was all. It depends on what deaf people bring to the problem, and how much they concentrate on developing their listening skills. There are two-point-five million people with hearing impairments. Twenty-five talk for every one who knows signs. My wife never had a hearing loss with her hearing aid. She can hear water dripping. I never wear one myself, don't need it. Eighty-five percent could go this route. The rest have to go manual. They've got multiple handicaps. Learning disabilities. They don't do any better in manual programs than they do in oral programs.

"You've got to create a hearing environment, not a deaf environment. Have to forget being deaf. Have you been to Gal-ya-dette? Go to Gal-ya-dette. See what they're reading, the magazines they publish. Every article is about the deaf. It's brainwashing. Sign them up early for the NAD."

He said he was not against using signs and fingerspelling

under certain circumstances. To reduce frustration, and for clari-
fying. He said he was an excellent signer, and flashed his secretary a sign. She giggled. He had, he explained, taught her the
risqué signs.

At this point, a woman appeared at the door and said that
Mr. Lane had a telephone call. "Stick around," he said to me.
"You'll get an education."

Lane's secretary jumped up on a table and sat crosslegged,
facing him. She picked up a telephone and turned it around so
that the earpiece was at her ear, but the mouthpiece was in
empty space at the back of her head. Lane was at his desk on another extension, about four feet away, watching her. "Kenneth
Lane speaking," he said. The secretary repeated, silently, everything that the caller presumably said. Lane read her lips, then
replied into his own phone. The conversation lasted perhaps
three minutes, and was very clever. I enjoyed it. They both
seemed pleased and happy. The technique is called ancillary
transmission. Anybody in the family can act as an ancillary
transmitter for a deaf person. "Where was I?" he asked.

"Total communication schools are not providing oral training. Constitutionally, it's illegal. Language development is the
key thing. We have five senses. That's the way the brain grows.
Not four. The mouth is the focus. You've seen deaf people signing. They look at the mouth, they don't look at the hands. That's
because all deaf people know how to lipread. Natural input is the
key. Reading is not as important as speaking. Speaking and
reading are totally different. Total communication won't work.
If you want kids to have language, you have to join the team.
Hearing, learning to hear, and integrity are necessary. We are
defeating our purpose if we give them a choice. Mainstreaming?
We've been doing it for a hundred years. Alexander Graham Bell
said that the perfect educational setting would be to have only
one deaf child in a completely hearing environment. Then he'd
learn. Only a small percentage will go sign language if we do it
right.

"Oral interpreters are absolutely necessary. There are two-point-five million deaf. Only half a million learn sign language. We have students at the University of Maryland right now. Consumers. Asking for oral interpreters, face to face. Under Section 504, the university can be sued. If they provide sign interpreters, they've got to provide oral interpreters."

I had a lot of questions about oral interpreters, but Mr. Lane got another telephone call, this time on the TTY.

A TTY is a teletype machine. As part of its philanthropic commitment to the deaf, AT&T regularly donated its used machines to deaf schools and institutions. These teletype machines, permanently installed, were connected by telegraph lines to one or more other machines in different locations. This limited network served the deaf in place of telephones. In 1964, an acoustic coupler was invented—by a deaf man—enabling TTYs to be connected to existing telephone lines, and making possible the transmission of typed messages. In the 1970s, the old, bulky teletype machines were gradually replaced with small, inexpensive, portable electronic teletypewriters that could be attached to any telephone. The phone company prefers that these units be called "telecommunications devices for the deaf," TDDs, but most people who use them continue to call them TTYs. Kenneth Lane placed his telephone receiver on the TTY that had been brought to him, and began typing.

"Mr. Lane really prefers ancillary transmission," his secretary told me. "He often refuses to take calls on the TTY, but maybe it's a deaf person calling," she said.

I left him typing out his conversation in high spirits, talking as he typed. There is no doubt that the mode of the oral adult is talking.

Before leaving the Bureau I bought a copy of Bell's *Memoir upon the Formation of a Deaf Variety of the Human Race* (1883). It contains tabulations of the surnames of all students enrolled at the schools for the deaf in the United States in 1880. Some names recur; Bell concludes that deafness is highly heritable, and genetic.

In the *Memoir*, Bell suggests that the genetic trait of deafness might be submerged through marriages between deaf and hearing persons—submerged, and in later generations extinguished altogether. Oral schools would provide the means of integrating the deaf into hearing society, where they would meet their future mates. Unless the deaf succeeded in mingling with and marrying the hearing, he warned, a tragic new "defective" race would emerge.

Examining social features of deaf education, Bell finds that they all foster marriage within the group. We put them together in schools, he observes. These schools hold reunions, where the boys and girls meet as adults. They form societies, hire rooms in central locations, and meet together for social intercourse after business hours—and even on Sundays for public worship! They form statewide associations and conventions, he complains. "At these meetings they amuse themselves in various ways. Sometimes they hold fairs; have theatrical representations in dumb show, spectacular tableaux, dancing, &ct."

They have their own newspapers, Bell goes on, outraged, featuring "personals" that keep deaf persons informed of each other's whereabouts. "These newspapers are actually supported by educational institutions under the guise of teaching the deaf-mutes the art of printing." He deplores the use of sign language, saying that it further encourages the deaf to mingle with each other and fosters group feeling.

In proposing solutions, Bell considers the possibility of repressive measures, "that marriages of deaf-mutes might be forbidden by legislative enactment," although he thinks this might not work, "on account of the impossibility of proving that a person has been born deaf."

Bell was assuming, mistakenly, that all congenital deafness is hereditary. But being born with an anomaly doesn't mean it is inherited. Many things can damage the hearing of an unborn or newborn infant. Rubella (German measles) during pregnancy, Rh blood incompatibility at birth, meningitis, and a growing list of infection-fighting drugs used during pregnancy and childbirth are all known to cause deafness. Though most deafness is attributed to factors in the environment rather than to the genes, the cause of deafness most frequently listed on case histories is "unknown."

Genetic deafness usually follows a recessive pattern of inheritance; typically the deaf child is born to parents who do not show the trait, are hearing. Geneticists estimate that between 10 and 25 percent of the general population carries recessive genes for deafness. Dominant transmission is much rarer, accounting for only about 10 percent of all cases. Late-onset deafness and partial impairments are frequently genetic.

At the end of his *Memoir*, Bell rejects repressive laws in favor of preventive measures: the creation of oral schools, the banning of sign language, and the elimination of deaf teachers. "Nearly one-third of the teachers of the deaf . . . in America are themselves deaf, and this must be considered as another element favorable to the formation of a deaf race—to be therefore avoided."

Bell's argument generated considerable enmity in the deaf community. They resented his implication that they and their children were genetically undesirable. Education, they believed, was not necessarily dependent on speech and hearing; acquiring information and skills not necessarily dependent on relationships with hearing people. Suggestions that they stop associating with each other, stop making common cause, finding mutual interests, and marrying, were regarded as cruel infringements of their rights. Excluding them as teachers was a crushing hardship: It not only deprived deaf professionals of their livelihood, it deprived deaf children of sympathetic, educated, and literate adult role models and friends. Who could be better qualified to teach them?

In hearing circles, Bell's paper aroused keen interest. There was talk of sponsoring legislation immediately to prevent the dreaded marriages; but because of the strong negative response from the deaf, and because oralism was rapidly becoming entrenched in the schools, the issue was dropped. It remained alive in the private consciousness of oral educators, and despite advances in our understanding of genetics since 1894, is still relevant to the thinking at the Volta Bureau. In 1969, the Alexander Graham Bell Association reprinted the *Memoir* in a special edition that is prominently featured in their current book catalogue.

IV

Rescuing deaf children from ignorance by teaching them to read and write was a simple humanitarian act. Providing them with a college education at taxpayers' expense was somewhat more complicated. The early schools had proved so successful, however, that justifying higher education to Congress was not overly difficult. In 1864, thirteen years after the death of Thomas Hopkins Gallaudet, a national college for the deaf was opened in the District of Columbia.

The college's first president was Edward Miner Gallaudet, eighth and youngest son of the famous educator. His mother, the former Sophie Fowler, had been among the first deaf pupils at the Hartford school. Edward Miner Gallaudet was born there. When he moved to Washington to organize the college, he brought his mother, then sixty-four years old, who assumed housekeeping responsibilities and became the first matron of the new institution. From the beginning, American Sign Language was used for instruction. A stated aim of the college was to train deaf teachers.

ASL was a native language to Edward Miner Gallaudet. There is a silent moving picture of him in the college library, standing in front of a painted backdrop, signing *Lorna Doone*. He is a slight, neat figure on the screen, with upturned mustache, a tight mouth. He looks wiry and shrewd. Gallaudet remained at the college for more than fifty years and was throughout a formidable personality. In his frequent clashes with Alexander Graham Bell, he usually won.

Edward Miner Gallaudet was completely at ease in Washington. He had calmly lobbied Congress for the establishment of the college, and persuaded Abraham Lincoln to act on the charter in the middle of the Civil War. He was a regular at Washington philosophical and literary affairs, and a founder of the Cosmos Club. Equally at home in French, English, and ASL, he often interpreted at international meetings. When the oralists took control of the schools for deaf children, Gallaudet kept them out of his college. He announced that he would employ a Combined Method: signs would be used for instruction, and speech training offered according to its need and efficacy. He added articulation teachers to the staff, but refused to exclude deaf faculty. When Gallaudet tried to get federal funds to establish a teachers' training program, Bell lobbied against it and succeeded in defeating the appropriation. Without the money, Gallaudet trained deaf teachers anyway. In 1883, pointing out that Bell was no longer a teacher, Gallaudet had him excluded from the American Convention of Instructors of the Deaf. Bell in turn formed his own organization, the American Association for the Promotion of the Teaching of Speech to the Deaf—an excessively pretentious title that deaf students found hilarious and were fond of writing in public places.

Bell was convinced that spoken English, no matter how badly articulated or imperfectly understood, was essential for the deaf. Gallaudet, through a lifetime of experience and association with large numbers of deaf people, was convinced that ASL was the indispensable language of growth, education, and expression. He retired in 1911, and was the only good native signer the college ever had as president. Gallaudet College has never had a deaf president.

The oral/manual controversy continued for decades after Bell and Gallaudet were gone, but more at the philosophical than the practical level. There were not two kinds of schools, one using manual language and one using oral English—all the schools were oral. The only institution that used manual language for instruction was Gallaudet College. The college, therefore, was the single institution that could function as a target for oralist outrage. Gallaudet's reputation as the fortress of manualism was borne with diffidence. Administrators who came to Gallaudet came from the large oral state schools and had been trained to teach the deaf by oral methods. They were mostly hearing people; few deaf professionals held policy-making positions either at the state schools or at Gallaudet. Because oralist criticism was ultimately posed in terms of a strict choice between the nobility of the English language and an abandonment of all things English (especially speech), Gallaudet College was eager to demonstrate its own commitment to English. Many concessions were made, and the manual method used at the college gradually became quite different from the ASL of Edward Gallaudet.

A compromise kind of manualism evolved, known as the Simultaneous Method: speaking and signing at the same time. Theoretically, it gave deaf undergraduates an extra channel of English. They could read the words on the lips of the instructor if they chose (the few who could choose), while reading the signs. As it is quite impossible to produce two separate languages at once, and because Gallaudet was ambivalent about ASL anyway, signs were used as if they were English words.

Educators at Gallaudet did not believe that ASL prevented deaf students from learning to speak, but they did believe that ASL interfered with the ability to read and write English. Errors in student compositions could sometimes be traced to usages in ASL. It did not occur to twentieth-century teachers that the deaf might have developed a language and a grammar that were especially well suited for vision—a language that had to be, as one deaf professor described it, "light-years away from English." The hearing faculty tended to regard ASL not as a different language but as a degraded form of language, a schoolhouse slang that the deaf used because of their tenuous grasp of English. The thinking went something like this: Deaf students have trouble with tense endings in English because ASL uses no tense endings; correct word order escapes them because sign order is less constrained in ASL. Instead of correcting the student's English, or finding ways to teach English, they changed the ASL.

For a long time there have been two sign languages at Gallaudet. One is ASL, used by the deaf members of the community, and the other is a rather truncated manual form of English. These two languages are usually described as existing on a continuum, ASL being the low end (sometimes called low-verbal) and the manual form of English the high (or cultured) form of sign language. The ASL portion of the continuum, in use by the deaf community for 150 years, is quite stable. The English end is less so. Most hearing signers use a rough and ready kind of signing that varies from person to person and is rather limited in terms of linguistic expression. It's not really a language, and it doesn't have an official name, but it's usually called signed English, or English signing. It is used by hearing people at Gallaudet almost exclusively, and is used by deaf people when communicating with hearing signers. It has become the usual mode of signing between hearing and deaf—not only at Gallaudet, but everywhere. Not many hearing people know or use ASL.

Until the 1950s, Gallaudet College, without attracting much attention, continued to do its job of teaching the 7 or 8 percent of deaf students who made it to college. Few faculty members had advanced degrees; there was no tradition of scholarship. It remained a sleepy educational backwater that was considered just about right for a handicapped population. During the decade of expansion that followed World War II there was a move to upgrade Gallaudet: to build a library, to hire better-trained faculty, and to become an accredited institution. As part of this plan, the college hired William C. Stokoe, Jr., a Ph.D. from Cornell with ten years' teaching experience at Cornell and at a smaller women's college at the north end of Cayuga Lake, Wells College. He took the charge of upgrading Gallaudet seriously. He also took a good serious look at American Sign Language.

Within a few years of his arrival, Stokoe published a linguistic analysis of ASL. At the core of the oralists' complaints was the charge that ASL was not a language but a primitive system of hideous hieroglyphs, with no syntax and no grammar. The Stokoe analysis showed that ASL was not a cipher for English or a gestural code, but was in fact a true language with an enormous range of expression, abstract as well as concrete; that it had a complex grammar and a well-regulated syntax.

The work opened up a new field of linguistic inquiry; it made a positive difference in the lives of deaf people who used the language; and it made an international reputation for its author. Most of his colleagues at Gallaudet thought he was crazy.

Early in 1979 I went to Gallaudet to meet William Stokoe.

V

Gallaudet College has a good-looking campus, modern at one end, Victorian at the other. Exceptionally loud rock music came from the dormitory rooms. From one building the sound was so distorted that I thought the record must be set at the wrong speed. Loud rock music is common at Gallaudet. I think that for young people who are deaf, it's a lot of fun just to hear something occasionally—anything. Over the next few months, every time I passed that particular building, the same, loud, distorted record was playing.

A large part of the campus was torn up by construction. Several high-rises were just being completed. It seemed like a terribly ambitious building program, somewhat too large for the limited population. Later, I learned that the college is getting ready for the children who were born during the rubella epidemic of

1964–65, an epidemic that doubled the school-age deaf population. Gallaudet expects one thousand new students during the 1980s.

I entered a Victorian building near the front gate and was inside a large hall, looking into a model of an enormous plastic ear. It was a walk-through, multi-media display with photographs, posters, video films, and printed material depicting the history of the deaf. There were pictures of the Gallaudets, the Abbé l'Épée, Cadwallader Washburn (an artist famous for drypoint engraving), and Beethoven. I read the material as I made my way through the display. Three spelling errors. It was very quiet.

As I walked into an adjoining building, I met a woman who signed to me and spoke at the same time, asking if I was looking for someone. When I found the linguistics laboratory, the secretary did the same thing, she signed while addressing me in speech. At Gallaudet, people who work in the offices, if they don't ignore you altogether, give you their whole attention. They stop what they are doing, look into your face inquiringly, and raise their hands, ready to enter into a signed exchange if that is your mode. When I spoke, she lowered her hands to the desk and said, "Bill's waiting for you," and he stepped out of his office.

Bill Stokoe is tall and athletic-looking. He has a pale complexion, deep-set eyes, and brown hair topped with gray cut straight across his forehead. It's an unusual face, like an English farmer's in a story by Thomas Hardy. At sixty, he is youthful-looking, very soft-spoken, and perhaps shy. Several staff members at Gallaudet have said: "Of all the people for it to come from! Nobody expected it from Bill." He had originally come to Gallaudet as an English professor and chairman of the English Department.

Stokoe was raised on a dairy farm in northern New York State, outside Rochester. Good in school as well as sturdy on the farm, Stokoe went to the ultimate upstate institution, Cornell

University, where he majored in classics and criticism and remained to take a doctorate in 1946. He is an expert on Chaucer and on medieval romances. "After I got my Ph.D., I accepted a job at Yale, but also had an offer from Wells College, in Aurora, New York. My wife, Ruth, is from upstate too. We decided that maybe we weren't ready to leave, and Aurora seemed a beautiful spot to start raising a family."

In 1953 Stokoe took a sabbatical leave, and the whole family went to Scotland: Bill, his wife Ruth, and their two children, Helen and Jim. They found a castle that was for rent, in East Lothian, and moved in. Bill was finishing some research on a fifteenth-century Chaucer scholar. "What I really did was become a reader of European linguistics, and become involved in Lowland Scottish culture." His neighbors in East Lothian spoke Middle Scots at home and standard northern English when they went to Edinburgh.

He bought bagpipes, and now plays with a bagpipe band in Washington. Ruth, who is a writer, published an article about housekeeping in an old castle. Helen, a musician, got interested in folk music and has since become rather well known in American fiddle circles. Jim just got interested in castles and is now an architect. They are a family who not only make the best of their environment but enter into active engagement with it.

In 1955, this quiet Chaucerian, at the age of thirty-five, moved to Gallaudet College. He found himself in a unique linguistic environment of sign language, an ambience he found altogether engaging. Stokoe says that he has always been interested in philology, more so than in the literary aspects of language. He often characterizes himself as an anthropologist. The deaf community at Gallaudet and American Sign Language were not, for Stokoe, qualitatively different from the community in the Lothian Hills that used Middle Scots as their daily vernacular. Nor was ASL the most esoteric of the many languages he had already observed. "I always thought it was linguistic," he said.

In 1956 and 1957 he was editor of the *American Annals of*

the Deaf, a journal that began publishing in 1847. Laurent Clerc had been a contributor, and Edward Miner Gallaudet. Stokoe read back through the original volumes (he frequently cites them) and found much to admire in the philosophy of the early teachers. As he learned the history of ASL, he also began making appointments in his office with native signers—people who had learned the language as children from deaf parents. In his serious way, he tried to organize discussions of ASL on campus, and pleaded at faculty meetings for a regular gathering place where teachers from various disciplines could meet, discuss problems, and keep up with research. None of these suggestions aroused any enthusiasm. He took his ideas and the data he had been collecting to the Roundtable on Language and Linguistics at Georgetown University; and there he found a great deal of interest and support.

Linguistics used to be anthropology. Linguists accompanied anthropologists into the field, identified a particular language, analyzed its structure, and compiled a lexicon—wrote it all down—sometimes for the first time. It was in this anthropological tradition that Stokoe analyzed ASL, calling it at the time "an almost unknown language." This study, "Sign Language Structure," was published in 1960 in an obscure anthropological journal (*Studies in Linguistics,* occasional paper number 8, University of Buffalo). In addition to basic information about the signs—handshape, movement, location, and descriptions of grammatical features—it contained historical and sociological material, and an extremely useful notation system that made transcription of the signs possible.

A handful of faculty were interested in the work, but the general reaction at Gallaudet was one of irritation. "They kept asking me why in the world I'd be interested in a thing like this. And reminding me that my job was teaching English. If the deaf wanted to fool around with ASL, that was their business. Certainly not the English Department's. Bringing up the whole matter of ASL was . . . well, obfuscation. They were so annoyed with me, they kicked me out. Removed me as chairman." He smiled. "They thought I was crazy. Not just a little odd; clinically insane. I suppose it was a good thing I had tenure."

There were many implications in Stokoe's research. Most of the faculty and administrators at Gallaudet took the attitude that all of them would only make the work of the college more difficult. Suppose it was a language, so what? "That sort of reception on the home campus was kind of daunting," Stokoe said.

He applied for and received support for further research from the American Council of Learned Societies and from the National Science Foundation. (Two descendants of Alexander Graham Bell wrote letters to *The Washington Post* protesting the grant.)

"The dean of the college, George Detmold, was very interested in ASL, and he always encouraged me. There were a few others, too, but mostly it was the young people who got excited. The young deaf faculty and students. They came to me all the time with ideas, and taught me their language. We decided to do a dictionary of ASL on linguistic principles, a project that was generally regarded around campus as the compounding of an absurdity." Except for a small number of handbooks published by local groups for their own use, sign language materials had been out of print since around 1918.

ASL is rarely observed by hearing people. It is used by the deaf when they are together. By definition, true languages are those that have been used and elaborated by generations of native users. There are relatively few native signers of ASL in the country: deaf children of deaf parents (about 10 percent of deaf children have one deaf parent; around 5 percent have two deaf parents); certain hearing children of deaf parents (natural bilinguals and the traditional interpreters for the deaf); and the generation of deaf people born near the turn of the century when ASL was still taught to young children. Though most other deaf persons in America know and use ASL fluently, they typically learned it late in childhood at schools for the deaf. They learned it from those among them who had deaf parents, and from each other. ASL is said to be the only language in the world that is transmitted from child to child.

It is a natural language. Deaf people think in it, have internal monologues in it, dream in it. Almost everyone I've asked has said that they translate everything into it. They also rehearse— much as dancers and athletes report that they mentally rehearse their movements.

The signs of ASL refer directly to meaning rather than to a specific English word, and often contain information about how a thing looks or behaves in the environment—valuable information for people who cannot hear. (Signs contain no information about sounds.) The feature chosen to represent an object is often interesting, economical, stylish, and might be compared with figures of speech in oral language where a part is used for a whole, or one important characteristic symbolizes a meaning. In the sign for *cat*, for example, the signer makes a small, short, tugging movement away from the upper lip, at the place where, if she were a cat, she'd have whiskers. These kinds of signs are called iconic—picture-like—but an actual picture of a cat would have more information than merely the suggestion of a half-set of whiskers. Historians say that signs lose iconicity over time, become more abstract and less picture-like.

Since this is an action language, many of the signs represent action, and are known as mimetic, mimelike. The sign for *bread* might be described as one hand holding an imaginary loaf while the other hand slices it. But most signs are not easy to explain, and in most cases the original act or image is lost in time. Explanations are useful as memory devices for the hearing, but the fact is, most deaf people learn and use their language without being aware of its iconic or mimetic origins, as English speakers use their language without being aware of its Latin and Greek antecedents.

It is not an easy language. It has its own sign order, its own rules of grammar, and its own consistencies of inner form, all of which are particularly well suited to being perceived by the eyes rather than the ears. It lacks the linear quality of spoken languages in which one word follows another in a time sequence: in ASL, two or more concepts can be expressed simultaneously. Modulations changing the meaning of a sign often occur within the signs themselves, where in spoken language an additional word or words might be needed. Many ideas and events can be expressed more efficiently, accurately, and gracefully in ASL than in spoken language.

Before linguists began studying it, ASL was thought to be a language without nouns and verbs; that was found to be false. It was thought to have no inflections (tenses) on the verb; now it is regarded as one of the world's more highly inflected languages, and is compared with Latin and Navaho. Investigation has turned up virtually all the properties that ASL supposedly lacked. It is a well-developed, sophisticated, highly polished human language. But throughout the deaf community, and especially in the view of the educators, it remains socially inferior. It is not unusual to find deaf individuals still apologetic about their language and some who continue to characterize it as incomplete, a broken form of English. Socially, it has a status somewhat, but not precisely, comparable to Black English—a vernacular, not suitable for public display. In formal situations, and in gatherings that include hearing people, most deaf signers avoid ASL and use signed English. Ted Supalla caused a sensation at a symposium on the study of sign language in 1978 by delivering an academic paper in ASL.

Fingerspelling is an indispensable addition to ASL, and all sign systems use it. It is a letter-by-letter spelling out of English words using a one-handed manual alphabet. Every literate country in the world has a manual system to represent its alphabet (some use two hands), and it is probably as old as writing. Anything can be spelled out in the manual alphabet; it's like writing on a typewriter one letter at a time. It's not difficult to learn, but it is quite a bit easier to send fingerspelled messages than it is to receive them: the letters tend to run together, fast, and one or more might not be clear. And, of course, the users have to be able to spell. Deaf children have a reputation for being rather good spellers (and fingerspellers) because they don't make the phonetic mistakes common to English—they just learn the word and the rules for spelling. Some manual systems rely entirely on fingerspelling, the Rochester Method, for example, and methods used by the deaf/blind. Helen Keller learned how to read and write and learned the English language by having it fingerspelled into her hand.

It takes forever—fingerspelling is three or four times slower than either speech or sign. It is extremely useful for technical and scientific terms where no sign exists, or until one is invented, and in situations where accuracy is essential, and for names. Introductions are always fingerspelled. At a high school basketball game I watched at Gallaudet, two coaches stood in the center of the court, back to back, and fingerspelled the names of the players as they were called over the loudspeaker and lined up on the court.

In conversation, deaf people fingerspell very rapidly and skillfully, but politely slow down for hearing persons and for children. Stokoe's "Sign Language Structure" has a long section devoted to fingerspelling and some of the educational issues involved in its use. Recent research has noted a number of ASL signs that evolved from fingerspelled words through long usage over time.

With two collaborators, Carl Gustav Croneberg and Dorothy Casterline (both young deaf colleagues from the Gallaudet faculty), Stokoe compiled the *Dictionary of American Sign Language on Linguistic Principles,* published in 1965. Informants volunteered from the Gallaudet community, the photographs were made on campus, and the book was designed by its editors. Stokoe's symbols for writing the signs are explained in detail and the notation accompanies all 2,500 entries. The dictionary includes discussions of syntax, usage, and English equivalents; in addition, there are two articles by Professor Croneberg, one about the linguistic community and the other on regional dialects.

By 1965 the field was starting to fill up. New manuals and handbooks for teaching sign language had already appeared. Requests for sign language instruction were on the rise, and the deaf subcultures were beginning to surface. In the political climate of the sixties, deaf youth took tremendous encouragement from the work of civil rights activists and demanded rights of their own. Many observers believe that the entire handicapped movement started with the appearance of "Deaf Pride" on the Gallaudet campus in the 1960s. Sign language was the important issue.

In the sixties, the National Theatre of the Deaf came into existence, and during its second season gave a performance in sign language on American television. The National Association of the Deaf initiated a census of the deaf population; the U.S. government had not taken one since 1930.

During the sixties, linguistics itself was in a state of revolution. Noam Chomsky's *Syntactic Structures*, published in 1957, was having enormous influence on the field. On several fields. According to Chomsky, syntax is something we are born with, and language part of our unique biological makeup, coded in the genes and specific to the species. In the past, it had been the prerogative of the grammarian to say whether or not we were using language correctly. Chomsky, who proudly called himself a grammarian, declared that we are all innate grammarians.

At the close of the 1960s, two ideas gradually came together: the innate ability of the human species for language, and the failure of oral education. The language that all deaf children learned without being taught was sign language. Far from its having to be taught, it was all but impossible to stop them from using it. The 1970s began the second era of sign language in the schools.

"How long does it take to become a good signer?" I asked the admissions director at Gallaudet, who was introduced to me in the lunchroom.

"Maybe five years?" He shrugged. "Some people never get very good. I've been here twenty-five years, and I don't sign very well."

In 1979, more than nine hundred undergraduates out of just over a thousand endorsed a petition complaining of the signing ability of the faculty and asking for better instruction and evaluation procedures. (Only since 1970 has sign competence been considered in making tenure decisions.)

It is very difficult to produce signs and speech at the same time and maintain accuracy in both. Experimental evidence shows that one modality tends to deteriorate—almost invariably the signs. Stokoe, who now edits his own journal, *Sign Language Studies*, recently published a study of classroom teachers in total communication schools using a speech-and-sign method. A large number of deletions occurred in the signs over time; the longer signing and speaking went on, the greater were the number and kinds of deletions. But a controlled study is hardly necessary. Merely watching many of the hearing people at Gallaudet, you can easily see that a good deal of signing is haphazard. Often, only the principal words of a sentence are being signed at all. The best simultaneous signers are individuals who are fully competent in both ASL and English. These are far more likely to be deaf than hearing people. (There are bitter complaints about "deaf English"; the real travesty may be "hearing sign.") Deletion is characteristic of the signing part of the sign/speech simultaneous method, and it is only because deaf people have become so skillful at working around these deletions that they can understand what is going on. I marveled at the intelligent questions

Gallaudet students asked after lectures that were accompanied by quite minimum signing.

The admissions director, Bernard Greenberg, gave me a large amount of interesting data. He wanted to know if I was a teacher (I'm not), and asked about my family. He wanted news. "Nothing very interesting is apt to happen here," he said. "If there's a demonstration, it's usually about the portions in the cafeteria." He smiled. "Even during the war there were no demonstrations." I pointed out that deaf students were in no danger of being drafted.

"Well, perhaps you're right," he said. "Anyway, we don't have much political activity on this campus."

"What about ASL?" I asked.

He smiled at me benignly. "It surely is a thorn in our side," he said, then went on, seriously: "Being deaf is an enormous handicap. A monumental handicap. No matter what method is used, education of these students is very difficult. It is a miracle that the schools have achieved so much."

I asked him about the high proportion of very bright students.

"Geniuses," he said. "We have quite a few more than most colleges this size. It's a statistical artifact. In the general population, almost fifty percent go to college. Among the deaf, it's only the top eight or ten percent, and most of them come here. Since NTID opened, we have had a change. All of a sudden, we've got math anxiety at Gallaudet and we never had it before. I think that more of the good mathematicians are going to Rochester for a technical education."

NTID, the National Technical Institute for the Deaf in Rochester, New York, is an adjunct of the Rochester Institute of Technology. It was opened as a second college for the deaf in 1968, and now has an enrollment almost as large as Gallaudet's.

Greenberg gave me statistical profiles of incoming students. The scores were, as he put it, "pathetically low." Over the past five years, scores of students admitted hovered around the twentieth percentile nationally in reading and vocabulary, which means that 80 percent of high school seniors scored higher. These are mean scores, an average of all scores gotten by all applicants who were accepted. In math and science, the Gallaudet group was somewhere around the thirty-fifth percentile, but were ranked against ninth graders rather than the twelfth-grade seniors. On the nonverbal IQ tests, however, they averaged seven points higher than the national norm.

The dropout rate at Gallaudet is close to 50 percent. The median hearing loss is profound, greater than 90 decibels down in the better ear. This figure has been unchanged since 1966. The median age at onset of deafness (also since 1966), birth.

These are stark data, with very sharp edges. Not easy to deal with directly. I found attitudes toward deafness constantly shifting, not by degrees, but in wide swings from extreme to extreme. At Gallaudet they insist they're just another college, "a collection of dusty academics," educating a group of bright young people. Should anyone question whether the education is all it might be, the questioner is advised to contemplate the limitations imposed by deafness, and told that achievement will always be defined by these limitations. The institution is solidly entrenched, singularly immune to any kind of criticism. Yet most of the people I met there seemed very thin-skinned and almost defensive; quick to question motives, keen for reassurance. Requests for detailed information were interpreted as innuendo, and answered with recrimination: "Well, some people think it's a waste of time and money to try to give these deaf kids a college education. We don't happen to think that way."

With variations, it was a remark I heard often. Some information—like the budget—I had to get through the office of my congressman. For fiscal year 1981–82, Gallaudet had an operating budget, for all three units—Kendall Demonstration Elementary School, Model Secondary School, and Liberal Arts College—in round numbers, $50 million.

. . .

There seemed to be very few strong personalities at Gallaudet, and no controversial issues except ASL, which is effectively isolated at the fringes. It was interesting, therefore, to talk with Mervin Garretson, a personality both strong and politic. Whenever I come across the phrase "leader in the deaf community," I think of Merv Garretson. He's been a teacher and the principal of a state school in Montana (one of several Western states that did not exclude deaf teachers). He was a faculty member at Gallaudet for eight years, and is a past president of the National Association of the Deaf. He played a major role in the creation of the Model Secondary School for the Deaf (MSSD), the high school on the Gallaudet campus completed in 1977. Garretson was director of the school during the planning and building phases, and described himself as the receiver of federal funds for the new building (many millions). He left MSSD before the new school actually opened to take his present job as special assistant to the president of Gallaudet.

Garretson had been characterized to me as an irresponsible supporter of ASL, someone who had "gone overboard on this bilingual education thing," a charge that he smilingly denied. "I'm not overboard at all," he said, "I'm right on board and in the boat." I laughed at his turning the English idiom around, a deaf joke that happens just often enough to catch you by surprise. Garretson used his voice and signed rapidly. "Yes," he said, "I've talked with the Office of Education about getting bilingual programs started. It's something to think about. They've funded lots of programs in all sorts of languages. Choctaw, Blackfoot. As far as ASL goes," he said, "they are amenable. So far."

Garretson graduated from Gallaudet in 1947. He said he took the last course that was offered in ASL. "They didn't call it ASL even then, it was a course in public speaking. The teacher was a great signer, Harley Drake, one of the old-timers. We weren't allowed to speak or move our lips—pure ASL. Drake retired in 1949. Then nothing was really offered in ASL until Bill Stokoe came along." I asked him what his reaction had been to Stokoe's ideas.

"We were all surprised by it," he said. "Never thought it would amount to anything. Now he's a folk hero, I understand. ASL definitely has a legitimacy it never had before. It's amazing, really." I asked him, again, what his own reaction had been. "Bill had been here only a couple of years. Had been signing for a very short time." He smiled. "If it had come from a good signer, we might have paid more attention. But, Bill was not a smooth signer—especially not then, in 1958. Oh, he knows ASL, it's not that. He understood it right away," he said, thoughtfully. "Bill's more like the football coach who can't play the game himself but who can show you how to win. It's made a big difference. I audited a graduate course over there in the linguistics lab." He smiled. "The ideas were good, but the delivery was only fair.

"It's unbelievable how it's caught on. I went to a symposium in San Diego last year. People gave papers in ASL! I signed mine in English. Felt like an outcast. After the papers, there was a forum. Everything was slanted toward ASL. I lost my hearing at age five. All my education was at residential schools," he said, just a shade bitterly. "I can give a talk in ASL with the rest of them. These young people want to divorce themselves from English. Divorce themselves from their parents, divorce themselves from other people. They want to be *very* deaf signers.

"The students' complaints about the hearing faculty are certainly justified. Some of them are disgraceful signers. Two left hands. But many universities have this problem. Foreign-born faculty who have accents and no one can understand a word. Sometimes the institution has to choose—a good teacher or a good signer.

"The young people, well, I think it's kind of a catharsis. They are the way black people were in 1964, after Selma. Needed to get it off their chests. Now, we need a time for the emotions to settle down. The newspapers and books are all in English. I am a strong supporter of total communication."

VI

While I was in San Diego, I met Carol Padden and Tom Humphries, two young deaf professionals who regard ASL as the most serious political issue in the deaf community. Elissa Newport arranged the meeting in a sprawling, crowded Mexican restaurant called Fedele's. We had to wait in a small, noisy bar for them, but the table, when we got one, was in a quiet corner. Not that it would have mattered to them, of course.

Carol and Tom had been married for only a month. Carol was a graduate student at La Jolla, the second deaf student admitted (Ted Supalla had been the first). Tom Humphries had just resigned from a teaching job at Gallaudet to accompany Carol to the West Coast. I had been told that Tom learned ASL at Gallaudet when he was seventeen years old. He seemed tense and said he had a cold. "I can't use what little voice I have," he apologized.

Carol was perfectly at ease. She is small and graceful and has the kind of self-assurance I have come to associate with deaf children of deaf parents. Her voice was good. She spoke directly to me, and signed at the same time, then looked at Elissa, who interpreted my questions into sign. Tom only signed, Carol interpreting his signs into speech. It sounds complicated, but they managed it very comfortably.

Carol is twenty-three years old, third-generation deaf. Both her parents teach at Gallaudet. She has a brother five years older who is also deaf. I had already run into him, and was beginning to realize how small the community is. "Everybody knows everybody else," Carol said. "My father and Ted's father went to school together at the Minnesota School for the Deaf."

She is militant about ASL, and often discusses her own deafness in political terms. "My mother thinks I could hear as a baby and didn't become deaf until I was two . . ."

"Everybody in your family is deaf," Tom interrupted, "how could you not be deaf?"

"Maybe it meant something to her to have a hearing child. Like black families used to want light-skinned children. Anyway, I was tested around age two, and it turned out I was deaf.

"I went to Kendall, the elementary school at Gallaudet, until I was in second grade. It was horrible. They had kids there who were thirteen, fourteen, fifteen years old. I was six. Most of them didn't have deaf parents, didn't know sign. I was teased and picked on a lot.

"The audiologist at Gallaudet suggested public school. My parents were afraid I'd become withdrawn and lonely, but they found a nice small private school in Maryland and drove me every day. It was all right. I never had special training, just picked up the language. Later, I went to a neighborhood school. I don't remember not understanding. I didn't have bad experiences, like in *Deaf Like Me.* Nothing like that. My parents really doted on my brother and me.

"I can lipread pretty well with my hearing aid—I think. You can never be sure what you're not getting." She smiled at me. "I wasn't an outcast or anything. I think I was sort of admired, in a hostile way. In high school I was just dying to be popular. I had a couple of dates," she added with no enthusiasm. "Oh," she laughed. "I was a cheerleader! They almost died when I showed up to try out. But they *had* to let me in. I did a fan-tas-tic split jump." She showed me the split with her fingers. "Practiced it all summer till my muscles ached.

"The last year of high school I began to recognize that I couldn't understand. I had to admit how hard it all was. I was always listening real hard, always on the alert, trying to find out what's going on, what the hearing people are doing and how they're behaving. What are they laughing at? Is it something I couldn't quite catch, or is it me?"

Tom began signing. "I was an expert on hearing people," he

said. "I studied them. One thing I noticed was that when they talk to each other, they never maintain eye contact. They're always looking around the room or looking at your lapels. So I made a point of never looking a hearing person in the eye. I know I looked cool, but of course I knew even less of what was going on." He demonstrated his technique, his eyes moving around our heads and over our shoulders. "Even now," he said, seriously, looking away, "it's sometimes very . . . hard . . . to look a hearing person in the eye."

"There's an administrator at Gallaudet," Carol said, "who always sits in the back of the room and way over on the side, where he can't possibly see the signer. He gets up and walks around during meetings, and turns his back—like a hearing person. And he is. He's a hearing deaf man. It's like a white black man. An Uncle Tom.

"At opening ceremonies for MSSD a couple of years ago, they had the Marine Band! For deaf people? We're really supposed to love those vibrations," she said, very sarcastic. "And the principal—the brand-new deaf principal of MSSD—did not sign his own speech. He made it in spoken English and had an interpreter."

In 1974, after some hesitation, she applied and was accepted at Georgetown. She was a linguistics major and had interpreters in all her classes. She also worked on research projects in the Gallaudet linguistics laboratory with Stokoe, and with another sign language linguist, Charlotte Baker. By the time she had a bachelor's degree, she had done some interesting original work and had a nice list of publications.

A few days later, I visited Carol and Tom in their apartment in La Jolla. It was a bright winter Sunday afternoon. Tom was watching a football game with the sound off. There were many books on the shelves. *Song of Solomon, Love Among the Ruins.* A number were about language and linguistics.

Carol sat opposite me. I was uneasy because I hadn't brought an interpreter and I wanted to talk to Tom, but Carol reassured me. "I can hear you now," she said. The room was very quiet. "I couldn't hear you at Fedele's the other night, but this is all right." I asked her how serious her deafness was. "It's in the severe range in both ears," she said. "Actually, I have what is called a flat audiogram, with no peaks. The loss is uniform across the range. It's the best kind to have for hearing aids. In a quiet room I can pick up a lot. In a classroom, in a crowd, I can't hear anything. I'm very deaf, just as deaf as Tom."

I asked if she was wearing a hearing aid. "Yes," she said. "Both ears." There was no sign of them and rudely I asked where. She was embarrassed, but brushed her hair back and showed me the plastic ear molds behind each ear. I was impressed. "Ah-h-h," she laughed, "isn't technology wonderful? When I was a child, I wore a body aid. I was completely wired.

"I don't tell people what my audiogram reading is any more. Because my quote oral skills unquote are so good everybody asks what my decibel loss is. They want to know *exactly* how deaf I am. I don't tell them. What difference does it make? I'm the same person. They can deal with me if they want to. Not with my hearing loss."

When Tom joined us, he asked: "Do you want to hear about me before I got ASL, or about me as I am now? I was a totally different person."

"Tom's a convert," said Carol. "And you know how *they* are."

He grew up, he said, in a small town in South Carolina. Very poor. "Poor and Pentecostal. The county next to ours was listed as one of the twenty poorest counties in America, and it was just like ours. We weren't any better off. I became deaf when I was six. Had already started school and did O.K. There were only twenty or thirty children in the school, and I knew most of them. Went through all twelve years of school with the same children. Some were my cousins. My mother had seventeen brothers and sisters, so you can imagine how many cousins I had. One year the teacher was my aunt. I had lots of help from the other kids. I don't remember much. My older brother was very supportive, protective.

"There was never a question of special classes or anything like that. I was the only one. I thought I was the only deaf person in the world.

"When I was finishing high school, Vocational Rehabilitation got in touch with me for the first time. Told me about Gallaudet. I wanted to go someplace else. Anyplace else, but VR said there was only Gallaudet. It was that or the textile mill, so I went.

"I had a terrible time adjusting. When you're the only deaf person in the world . . . it was a shock. Those deaf people acted *nothing* like hearing people! I lost thirty pounds the first year. I was very condescending about ASL and took a lot of abuse. Non-signers were a small group of social outcasts. Maybe fifty out of nine hundred students. We banded together and that made it worse. But we were all learning signs and we were aware that signing was really improving our lives. There was a lot of conflict. It took a long time to come to a comfortable place, and especially not to have regrets. You try not to think, All the signs I could have had; all the friends I could have had.

"You find yourself in an odd position, and suddenly, you can't wait to learn this language. You can't *wait* to be able to talk—really talk—to all the beautiful girls. There were big changes in me. My values. It took a long time. I had wasted my life becoming an expert on hearing people. I had no idea how to be deaf."

After graduating from Gallaudet, Humphries went to American University in Washington for a master's degree in accounting. "They kept telling me I could probably find a job where I didn't have to use the telephone. Posters all over the place, Hire the Handicapped. It was depressing. I dropped out. Went back to Gallaudet and took an M.A. in education."

He looked at me and smiled. "All teachers of the deaf have to be qualified to teach speech," he said. "In principle. I thought that was pretty funny. How was *I* going to teach speech? Well, in order to get my degree, I was required to make a speech therapy box—with a feather, a candle, and a mirror. I was outraged. That's what Alexander Graham Bell used! I just refused. They couldn't understand why I didn't want to make a box with a candle and mirror and a feather. I asked them if I had to go out and catch a chicken. Finally, they let me do something else. Shrugged it off. Even offered me a job at Gallaudet, teaching English. I took it.

"I taught a remedial course for incoming students with language problems. Of course, they didn't have language problems—there was nothing wrong with their *language*, they all knew ASL—they had English problems. And problems of inferiority. I'd have to say that a lot of the work we did was affective. Getting over the stereotypes and the guilt."

"Hearing people," said Carol, "are very chauvinistic about English. ASL is a deficiency label. But the only thing wrong with ASL is that it isn't English. Deaf people who use ASL have incredibly rich lives," she said.

"The educators, and a lot of them are deaf, are pushing signed English and the new English manual codes because they don't understand ASL. They worry about making a distinction between rage and anger. In ASL the distinction is clear. We feel that ASL has been vindicated. Turning it into a code for English is seen as another compromise. A big compromise.

"The issue is whether we have the right to decide. In the oral/manual controversy, the hearing people decided. Now that they've decided to let us go manual, they want to control which manual language we will use. Of course it's going to be English—it's more convenient for them."

Tom said: "The debate over ASL versus an English sign system is being carried on in English. There's no equal time. ASL is not used in the classroom, or given a chance in any of these debates. It's not even an educational issue. It's an issue in human rights."

Signs and Science

I

Jonas Salk built his Institute for Biological Studies on one of the most beautiful sites in America: a high point beside the Pacific Ocean in La Jolla, California. When I visited in midwinter, the temperature was around 65 degrees; the acacia trees at the entrance were in full and fragrant blossom. A courtyard at the center of the complex of somber concrete buildings opened to a magnificent, endless view of the sea. It was impressive; windswept and austere. Nobel laureates cross paths in this courtyard.

American Sign Language research is conducted in the Laboratory for Language and Cognition on an upper floor. All the windows faced the ocean. Dr. Ursula Bellugi, the director, greeted me warmly. She is a middle-aged woman, very short—barely five feet—with bright red hair and bright brown eyes in a bright expressive face. She was dressed in a voluminous colorful floor-length gown. Three years earlier I had seen Ursula Bellugi, wearing just such a costume, deliver a scholarly paper on ASL that had received the closest thing to a standing ovation I've ever witnessed at an academic meeting. Her skill in explaining American Sign Language, the eloquence and wit of her demonstrations, have made her something of a diva.

Before moving to Salk, Bellugi had done research on children's language acquisition at Harvard. When she arrived at La Jolla in the late sixties, construction of the Institute was not quite finished. The staff was very small, mostly biologists and medical researchers. Jacob Bronowski was there, the mathematician, physicist, and litterateur whose reputation in the international intellectual community was something close to cosmic. Bellugi's first published work about sign language was an article co-authored with Bronowski that appeared in *Science* in 1970. In it, they discussed the claims made by Allen and Beatrice Gardner regarding the signing ability of their chimpanzee, Washoe, in the light of Bellugi's experience with children's language, expressing some skepticism that the two were comparable. Not long afterwards, the ASL project at Salk began. Originally, Bellugi planned to gather information about the acquisition of signs by deaf children of deaf parents, and compare it with the data she already had on hearing children. She realized very quickly that nothing was known about what the deaf children were acquiring, so the emphasis of the research shifted to an investigation of ASL itself.

The project was headed by Bellugi, and by Edward Klima, professor of linguistics at the University of California. Separate from questions of how ASL was learned were those concerning its linguistic properties and whether or not it could be considered a language. The only research they had to draw upon was the work of William Stokoe.

When Stokoe began his research, he was working from within a signing community. Gallaudet had the largest concentration of signers in the world—he was part of it himself. Although deaf people decline to make claims about ASL in public (especially in the face of scornful oralists), informed deaf opinion for the past one hundred years has insisted that ASL is a complete and highly expressive language. Stokoe's own daily observations confirmed these historic claims, and his research was undertaken to prove them. His motivations were idealistic as well as intellectual: he wanted to bring the linguistic and cultural identity of the deaf to the attention of American scholars.

Not so at Salk. They began with an attitude of scientific detachment, and were, they stated repeatedly, completely open-minded about the linguistic status of ASL. They considered it unlikely that ASL had evolved as an autonomous language. Nonetheless, they wanted to investigate it anyway. If it did prove to be less than a language, more in the nature of a simple communication system, they thought it would still be interesting to find out how such a system worked and how it was learned. They started the project with one deaf individual, and over the next few years made contact with large numbers of native signers of all ages, taking their cameras and video equipment into schools and homes all over California. There is hardly a deaf adult on the West Coast who is not aware of the research.

Klima is a linguist and Bellugi is a psychologist. Their staff consisted of research assistants, graduate students, and native signers (hearing and deaf); it also included professional linguists and psychologists interested in particular aspects of the investigation.

In the popular understanding of the term, psychologist means practitioner: one who manages some aspect of mental health or personality development. Indeed, the majority—perhaps sixty percent—of psychologists in America are so employed. They are the therapists, the test givers, the counselors, and the ubiquitous school psychologists. The remaining forty percent, like Ursula Bellugi, are academics and experimentalists. Psychology is a discipline that straddles several others and is close to both the humanities and the sciences. Some psychologists characterize themselves as humanists who take data. William James called psychology the science of mental life.

Within the spectrum of academic psychology there are at one end neuropsychologists, whose work shades off into biology, and comparative psychologists, who work primarily with other species; and at the other end the social psychologists, who study cultural, social, and political questions. In the center (more or less) experimental psychologists study thinking and perception, memory, learning, and cognition (sometimes called mental processes). There are developmental psychologists, who study babies and children; psychoacousticians, who know a great deal about the way we hear; and, of course, psycholinguists, the psychologists of language, who bring their skills of data-collecting and experiment-designing to questions about human language.

Psycholinguistics became a specialty in the 1950s. Not since Wilhelm Wundt in the nineteenth century did academic psychologists show much interest in the nature of language. Wundt, the founder of experimental psychology, opened his first laboratory in Leipzig in 1879. A legendary scholar in the German tradition, he had an encyclopedic mind and a prolific output, producing massive works on almost every aspect of psychology. Many remain untranslated; but a portion of his work on the psychology of language dealing with gestures and sign languages was published here in English for the first time in 1973. Between Wilhelm Wundt and Ursula Bellugi, psychologists displayed no interest whatever in sign language.

Historically, the profession regarded deafness as a pathology, a speech and hearing disorder that might, to some degree, be corrected. The deaf were studied as anomalies—like asphasics and severe mental retardates—human beings without language. Most research about deafness consisted in assessments of the deficit, and of the effect it had on emotional adjustment, achievement, and thinking. Unless deaf persons had speech they were considered to have no language, and questions were continuously raised about their ability to think at all (and if so, what did they think *in*)?

Linguistics is the study of language itself. It is an ancient discipline; the earliest known writings on the subject are inscribed on palm leaves, fragments of which are preserved in the vaults of the British Museum. The first linguist was probably Panini, a contemporary of Plato (circa 350 B.C.), whose grammar of Sanskrit was translated in the nineteenth century. Panini set down rules for proper written Sanskrit that were based on usage found in a small number of sacred texts. It was a literary accoutrement, designed to perpetuate a high standard of writing. For the next two thousand years, all grammars were similarly prescriptive. English grammars of the last century were based on the classical prose style found in the sublime writings of Latin and Greek.

In addition to the writing of grammars, an enormous amount of work was done in comparative and historical linguistics. By the end of the last century virtually all of the world's known languages had been classified as to original linguistic family, geographic distribution across various parts of the globe, and type of structure—the method used by speakers in putting their languages together and elaborating them.

Modern linguistics began in the twentieth century. Prescriptive grammars were replaced by discovery methods, ways of learning and describing how particular languages were structured: structural linguistics. Interest shifted away from written language to focus instead on the spoken tongue, especially on those primitive languages for which no written form existed. Cultural anthropology rather than literary criticism became the umbrella for linguistic research. European anthropologists established field stations in Oceania, while Americans began the task of studying the large number of indigenous Indian tribal societies on their own continent.

The great voyages of exploration in the nineteenth century had always carried along a naturalist, who observed and collected local plant and animal specimens. In the same spirit, the cultural expeditions of the twentieth century always included a linguist who collected the exotic flora and fauna of speech. Like the naturalist before Darwin, the linguist in the field was unencumbered by theory. Nothing was known; specimens were plentiful. Nobody asked what it all meant. Structural linguistics was regarded as a classificatory science, "a sort of verbal botany." Utterances were collected and recorded by means of phonetic notation. Sentences were segmented; their parts sorted into words, word classes, parts of speech. Words also were broken into smaller parts: morphemes, the minimum unit of meaning. The word *speak* (for example) is one morpheme. *Speaking* has two: *speak + ing*. *Unspeakable* is made up of three morphemes: *un + speak + able*. The invention of the tape recorder greatly facilitated this kind of linguistics. The tape could be slowed down and utterances segmented into structural units with greater efficiency.

Below the level of word and morpheme, all human languages are made up of a very limited number of small, interchangeable units that are combined and recombined to form meaning. These are the phonemes, the sounds of speech. With about forty phonemes, we are able to produce all the words of English. (The alphabet is an imperfect representation of the phonemic system of English.) *Cat* has three phonemes: /c/, /a/, and /t/. *Bat* and *cat* differ in one phoneme. It is characteristic of all human languages that meaningful units like words are always composed of smaller units that have no meaning in themselves. This is called duality of patterning. Animal communication systems lack this two-level structure. Other species have a small number of different cries, or calls, or songs, one for each "message," but do not combine them into different patterns or sequences. All definitions of true language include a two-level structure. When William Stokoe demonstrated that ASL has duality of patterning, and identified the discrete components that make up all signs, linguists began to believe it was a language.

All languages have rules for the ways that phonemes can and cannot be combined (*Nkat* is not a word according to the rules of English, but it might be in some other language). There are rules, also, for combining and changing morphemes, and syntactic rules governing the formation of sentences. These have been less well defined and understood than the rules for stringing phonemes together, but were considered, in principle, the same. The main trend in structural linguistics was not to dwell on words or sentences, but to make finer and finer distinctions in the speech sound and to further analyze the phoneme.

Beginning in about the 1930s, the phoneme yielded another level of analysis. The sounds themselves were made up of small (atomic) parts: bundles, or clusters of distinctive features. Roman Jakobson, eminent Russian-born linguist who has pursued his work in the United States since World War II, is best known for his detailed working out of the theory of distinctive features in several languages. This theory quickly becomes quite abstract; but what the phonologists actually study are the sounds that human beings are able to produce and hear naturally. The system of distinctive features describes how these sounds are made inside the mouth and vocal tract, and is not particularly aesthetic to contemplate. It specifies, for example, whether the glottis is open or closed; whether the tongue makes contact with the teeth; whether air passes through the nose. Distinctive features are said to exist in a relationship of binary opposition: there are only two possibilities—the glottis is either open or it is not—and it is impossible to make a sound that is a compromise between two phonemes. We produce and hear (for example), a /b/ or a /p/, but never something in between.

Jakobson's insight into the structure of the phoneme proved vastly influential. That an unlimited quantity of meaning could be produced from a handful of meaningless features seemed too good an idea to be left to the linguists alone. Scholars in other fields (mostly in Europe) were convinced that a great many human endeavors might be explained in terms that exactly corresponded with the distinctive feature analysis of the phoneme. The French anthropologist Claude Lévi-Strauss built a school of structural anthropology based entirely on Jakobson's theory of the phoneme. Features in binary opposition were found in the structure of rituals, kinship systems, myths, table manners, food preparation, ceremonial exchanges. Inevitably, a structuralist literary criticism emerged in which narrative and poetical works were treated "as if they were a language." Characters existed in relationships of binary opposition; and plots revealed a sub-phonemic level completely accessible to structural analysis.

American linguists were ambivalent about phonology. They acknowledged its importance as the most well developed branch of linguistics, but showed little inclination to draw analogies between cultural practices and aspirated consonants. The European speculations were too finicky for domestic tastes, and too literary. American structural linguists continued, steadfastly, to pursue their goal of recording every indigenous language on the North American continent. Their mission took on a degree of urgency from a certain awareness that traditional Indian life would soon disappear. They went into the field enthusiastically, armed with their discovery methods, tape recorders, and the international phonetic alphabet. Typically, the linguist did not know or attempt to learn the language under investigation; the ability to communicate directly with native informants was not considered necessary. Linguist and informant (who sometimes knew English) merely walked through the village, the linguist pointing to things, the informant supplying the appropriate term in his own language. A list of lexical items—words—was compiled in this way. From the patterns of sound sequences that emerged from this data, phonemic rules could be inferred. From the larger collection of utterances, word classes were identified, and the whole language arranged into sentence structures: the syntax.

While the linguists concentrated on language exclusively, the anthropologists in the field gathered a wide range of ethnological material: facts about the particular culture. The two enterprises were quite autonomous. Occasionally a fluent anthropologist might provide information to a linguist, and frequently the anthropologists consulted the dictionaries compiled by their linguistic colleagues. The dictionaries proved extremely useful (though no one would claim they rivaled Dr. Johnson's) and were used by generations of scholars. The purpose of linguistic research, however, was not to provide tools for the anthropologist, but to analyze and document the structure of Indian languages. In doing so, these linguists extended knowledge about the universality and complexity of human languages to all parts of the world and all peoples. Their greatest contribution was the dispelling of many popular myths about the inferiority of primitive languages. "We know of no people that is not possessed of a fully developed language," the American linguist Edward Sapir wrote in 1921. "The lowliest South African Bushman speaks in the forms of a rich symbolic system that is in essence perfectly comparable to the speech of the cultivated Frenchman." Though emphasizing the great diversity among languages, Sapir considered them all to be "essentially perfect."

It is interesting that neither anthropologist nor linguist seemed to take any notice of Indian sign language during the intensive early period of ethnography. Today, it is becoming a lively research topic, but for almost a century there was no official mention of it. Excellent works were published in the 1880s by the Smithsonian Institution, but since then, updating and reprinting material on Indian signs have been done solely through the efforts of amateur anthropologists and Boy Scouts.

In 1930, Benjamin Lee Whorf, a student of Edward Sapir, asserted that with careful analysis, important non-linguistic information could be found within the structure of all languages. Whorf, an immensely influential linguist, spent very little time doing field research. He compiled a dictionary of the Hopi language and constructed a grandiose hypothesis regarding the Hopi's view of the universe that was based entirely on information he received from a single Hopi Indian who lived in New York City. (Whorf's first visit to the Hopi reservation in Arizona came three years after the dictionary was completed.)

The Whorfian hypothesis stated that language overwhelms perception. Whorf believed that all people live in a linguistically conditioned environment. We understand the world, he said, not by experiencing it personally and directly, but by having our experience shaped by our particular language. We see only in ways our language permits us to see; we think only in ways our language directs us to think— "A change in language can transform our appreciation of the Cosmos."

Whorf based his hypothesis on linguistic devices used by the Hopi in describing the passage of time: "In our language [English]," he wrote, "[we have] real plurals and imaginary plurals. . . . We say ten men and also ten days . . . but ten days cannot be objectively experienced. We experience only one day, today . . . the other nine are something conjured up." In contrast, the Hopi language allowed its speakers to reach a particular day by an objective count. "Instead of saying *they stayed ten days*, the Hopi say, *they stayed until the eleventh day.*" Whorf considered this way of speaking vastly less subjective than our own. English speakers, he maintained, had a conditioned perception of time based on a three-tense system of past–present–future, with "the observer being carried in the stream of duration continuously away from the past and into a future."

According to Whorf, the English speaker's view was characteristically Newtonian, but the Hopi's language was more relativistic, and therefore Einsteinian (the theory is sometimes called linguistic relativity). Whorf believed that the Hopi's world view as expressed in their language was close to the world view expressed by Einstein in his theory of relativity. Because their minds had been so objectively shaped, he suggested that the Hopi would make superior physicists, and called for research to discover the world views imposed by other unknown languages.

Of course, there were no physicists among the impoverished population of Hopi; nor was Einstein's theory in any sense a personal or philosophical world view. Many societies share similar languages, yet have different cultures and systems of belief; and many societies are known to have almost identical cultural institutions but speak vastly different kinds of languages. Nevertheless, the hypothesis was taken very seriously, possibly gaining in popularity after Whorf's death in 1941, and it continues to be discussed today. At its peak, it spawned a literary movement of its own known as general semantics. (S. I. Hayakawa is just about the last of the general semanticists.) They insisted that the ills of the world were due to a widespread confusion of terms, to the inability of language to reflect reality; and to the use of imprecise speech in general.

The Whorfian hypothesis rephrased and consolidated a lot of hackneyed academic ideas and popular prejudices about the relationship between thinking and language that had already been argued, unproductively, for generations. Is French, because of its logical word order, better suited to higher levels of discourse than English? Or (a favorite of English speakers), because there is no word in the German language for fair play, do Germans not have the concept? (There is no word for fair play in English either.) When scholars noticed that there was a paucity of color terms in the classical Greek vocabulary, there were spirited arguments over the possibility that all ancient Greeks were colorblind.

Color terms seemed to provide a good way to test linguistic relativity, to find out whether language overwhelmed perception. Whorf's hypothesis suggested that persons who did not know the names of specific colors would be unable to identify them accurately or remember them. Subsequent color-naming experiments with English speakers did show that people remembered and recognized colors with names that were familiar to them. Subjects picked out red and blue color chips from an array more easily than they picked out aquamarine and heliotrope.

From several isolated parts of the world, languages had been reported that had limited color terms; some had only two, black and white (or light and dark). In the late 1960s a young psychologist, Eleanor Rosch, took a set of color chips with her on a field trip to study the Dani in New Guinea. She described the Dani as "a Stone Age agricultural people who have a basically two-term color language." When she did the color experiments, the Dani responded the same way as the Americans: they too recognized red and blue better than heliotrope. Rosch then taught her subjects a set of words to correspond to the color chips. After they had learned the color names, she tested them again. Again, the same colors were easier to remember and the same colors easier to forget.

The colors hard to keep in mind were, in fact, also difficult to categorize; they were indeterminate, of mixed hue, often falling between two major color groups. The ones everyone remembered, regardless of language or culture, were the focal colors: the true, often primary colors, highly saturated and unmixed, basic reds, bluest blues. Rosch concluded that we recognize these colors easily not because we know their names but because they are easiest to recognize. They probably have short, familiar names for the same reason.

In agricultural societies with few material objects of any kind, it may not be appropriate or necessary to distinguish things according to color. Rosch showed that gaps in vocabulary do not necessarily imply gaps in knowledge of the world, and that the importance attached to color terminology was entirely false. More generally, she destroyed the Whorfian notion that language overrides perception.

At present, the status of the Whorfian hypothesis is that it is partly false, partly unproven, and the remainder most likely untestable. It functioned in the absence of any other theory, and seemed to strike some deep feelings that people have about language. For native speakers their own language is so natural, automatic, perfect; so much a part of their national and personal identity, even their identity as human beings, that all those who do not have it must be qualitatively different. Mark Twain, who made a lot of jokes about language and national character, gave Jim and Huckleberry Finn a dialogue concerning the doubtful humanity of Frenchmen that Jim concludes with the exasperated question: "If a Frenchman is a man, why don't he talk like a man?"

Much of the traditional objection to the use of sign language has been explicitly Whorfian. If the deaf used sign language, they would think in pictures, not words. The language itself would make them deaf, imposing not merely a different mode of expression but an alien mode of thought. This opinion is expressed almost daily by educators of the deaf; but an encounter with almost any unfamiliar or exotic linguistic group brings similar opinions to the surface. Now, as Arabic-speaking nations have begun to play a larger and highly confusing role in world events, their language is being scrutinized as a possible major source of our conflicts with them. A front-page story in *The New York Times* (December 30, 1979) carried the headline: "Language a Key to the Spirit of Islamic Revival," and asked if there is something in the syntax and structure of the Arabic language that predisposes many Moslem leaders to what seems an extravagant, irrational mode of speech and behavior.

Whorf also turned up recently in the work of a Marxist scholar, the contemporary Polish linguist Adam Schaff. *Language and Cognition* was published here in translation in 1973 and is devoted in large part to a positive account of Whorf's hypothesis. In the introduction, Noam Chomsky, characteristically, has the last word. Chomsky states that, independent of Whorf's problems with Hopi, his understanding of English was incorrect. Whorf believed that English speakers, because of their three-tense system of past, present, and future, conceived of time as "a point moving constantly from past to future." But English, Chomsky pointed out, has only two tenses: present and past— *jump, jumped; run, ran.* What we have instead of a future tense is a handful of auxiliary words called modals that exist as an independent system. These can be superimposed on a sentence to specify concepts like possibility, necessity, obligation, and future: *might, must, ought,* and *will.* The future *will* is not distinguished in any special way from the others. "Approaching English from a Whorfian point of view," Chomsky wrote, "we would conclude that an English speaker has no concept of time [as] a point moving constantly from past to future, but rather he conceives time in terms of a basic dichotomy between what is past and what is not yet past. . . ."

Noam Chomsky, taking everybody by surprise, and over a number of dead bodies, revolutionized linguistics in 1957 with the publication of his first book, *Syntactic Structures*. He was not yet thirty years old. Shortly afterward, he became professor of linguistics at MIT. MIT didn't even have a linguistics department. Today, it's like Mecca.

From the beginning, Chomsky combined the presentation of his own theories of language with sweeping, detailed, and manifest criticisms of traditional linguistics. The structuralists believed that stringing words together into sentences was no different, in principle, from stringing phonemes together into words. They had devised a number of syntactic rules for this purpose: how to diagram a sentence, and how to form one correctly—subject, verb, object; where to place the nouns and verbs; how to handle the adjectives and adverbs; and how to avoid ending a sentence with a preposition. Any deviation from this syntactic scheme was attributed to a lack of intelligence on the part of the speaker, a willful or ignorant disregard for standard speech, or possibly to some fragile condition of mental imbalance that was beyond the scope of linguistics to explain. Beyond the scope of linguistics, too, was any interest in language as something that people used, or any curiosity about how they used it. Linguistics described, but made no attempt to explain.

Chomsky found that existing rules could not even adequately describe many ordinary English sentences. What worked for combining phonemes into words did not (even in principle) apply to the formation of sentences. He began asking questions that linguists had tended to avoid. He pointed out, for example, that the number of sentences in any language is essentially without limit; and that a large number of sentences produced daily by all speakers are entirely new—have never been spoken before.

Chomsky asked, How is it that we are able to speak sentences we have never spoken before, and understand sentences we have never heard? Nothing in linguistics could handle these questions. Chomsky said that all native speakers know, intuitively, how to produce and understand grammatically correct sentences in their own language. They understand grammatical relationships within sentences, and know the rules for expressing them. The purpose of linguistics, he said, was to formulate what the native speaker already knows: a set of rules that would generate all (and only) the grammatically correct sentences in the language. A grammar, therefore, was a theory of language.

Chomsky came to linguistics from philosophy and mathematics. The theory he proposed would be precise, formal, logical, and deductive. He expressed the opinion that it was nothing less than foolhardy to suppose that a grammar could be obtained merely by recording a sample of sentences in an unknown language. He told linguists to study their own languages thoroughly, and to test their hypotheses against their own intuitions.

Chomsky continued to ask difficult and interesting questions that were completely novel to practicing linguists: How do children learn language, and how do all children all over the world happen to learn it at about the same young age, when they might not be expected to learn anything? Isn't it interesting that the dullest child, but not the brightest ape, learns language? He suggested that the similarities among languages were more compelling than their differences, and postulated a universal grammar: a set of principles underlying the organization of all natural languages that corresponds to an innate ability in the human child to grasp linguistic principles. Language was not something that came from without to shape human thought and behavior, but rather something that came from within, an attribute of the human mind, a biological endowment, innate, and particular to the human species. Linguistics, then, said Chomsky, was psychology; to study language was to study mental life.

When Chomsky made these statements, both mental life and innate endowment were ideas virtually without adherents in the United States. Many American scholars, in fact, stood in a tradition devoted to eliminating them. In the years before ethology (decades before sociobiology), instincts had a very bad name. To attribute anything to an innate biological endowment was considered a sign of serious intellectual, and possibly moral, sluggishness. Americans were empiricists, concerned only with the observable. In the social sciences this inclination found expression in behaviorism, which had been the dominant trend in psychology since its introduction by John B. Watson in 1912 (best known in recent generations through the works of B. F. Skinner). Though theoretically threadbare, behaviorism set down a handful of principles that narrowed and simplified psychological possibilities. Human babies, according to Watson, were born with only three instincts: fear at noise or of being dropped; rage at having their movements hampered; and love at feeling their skin stroked. Everything else was learned, instilled, conditioned; a particular response to a specific stimulus in the environment. It only remained to discover the exact identity of the stimuli and which responses they controlled.

Behaviorists believed that language, like everything else, was learned. Mothers taught children. A mother might go about teaching her child the word "dog" by showing him a dog (or a picture of a dog), and repeating the word "dog." She would continue displaying the stimulus (the dog) and repeating the word until the child had made the association and responded, saying "dog." The child was then reinforced—rewarded—sometimes materially, sometimes merely with expressions of love and approval. Other objects were then displayed by the mother, and responses elicited from the child, one word at a time, until all the words were learned. It was a grim picture of domestic pedagogy.

Behaviorism seemed to embody some peculiarly American ideas about egalitarianism, but gave them an odd twist: all people were born equal and equally empty, the human mind a vessel to be filled. It claimed that anyone could be taught anything if the circumstances were correctly controlled and the learning accompanied by an appropriately reinforcing pay-off. There was a disturbing mechanical quality about the whole thing. It carried empiricism as far as it could go and influenced areas of scholarly thought beyond the social sciences. Some philosophers considered behaviorism liberating, a scientific outlook that freed them from all that was not observable, and found in this meager theory a strong affinity with logical positivism, a branch of philosophy important at the time.

Chomsky's assertion that human beings possessed special skills at birth was, in the minds of American empiricists, a dangerous return to mentalism. The outcry against him was loud, personal, and often vicious. He was accused of being a confidence man, a thief, a viper. Nobody said he was stupid, and few claimed that he was merely wrong; the general opinion was that Chomsky, for reasons of his own, was spreading outrageous and deliberate falsehood. Considering the intensity of the reaction, one would have concluded that only Noam Chomsky, and no one else, had ever noticed that other species don't talk. Before long, a number of behaviorists had placed orders for chimpanzees and began making plans for the ultimate refutation of this mentalist.

Meanwhile, a new generation of linguists had been trained. Rancor remained high (and still remains high), but there is not much doubt that Chomsky has been a constructive influence. Constructive and permanent. His linguistic theories are now compared in importance with the emergence of modern chemistry that followed the long period of medieval alchemy. Two decades ago, there were few linguists who subscribed to any of Chomsky's theories. Today, there are few who do not accept a large number of his principles.

Before Chomsky, linguistics had been languishing. Linguists of the older, well-known and written languages of Europe and Asia continued to teach and interpret them. Linguists in the field continued recording unwritten languages, but opportunities for field work declined steadily. Predictions made at the beginning of the century have been sadly realized. The urgency about perusing those "human documents" (as Sir James Frazer called them) was well founded; few now remain to be perused. Linguists who go into the field today are likely to be adjuncts of missionary organizations. The dictionaries they compile are used for translating the Bible into hitherto unwritten tribal languages and serve as a basis for bringing Christianity and schooling to primitive people—an enterprise that might be considered somewhat Victorian.

Chomsky brought life into a discipline that was stuffy and pedantic in one corner, Victorian in another. He made language interesting again, human and intellectually rigorous. His work attempts to state explanatory principles, and to formalize them. It is highly technical, mathematical, abstract, and difficult. The movement he started is called, all over the world, the Chomskyan Revolution. Outside linguistics he is equally revolutionary, and has become a public figure because of his unpopular political activities. He associates with Marxists, socialists, pacifists, Third World organizations, Arabs. He has criticized the university, the role that intellectuals play in society, and was arrested for protesting the Vietnam War. He has been accused of seducing young intellectuals with his politics rather than his scholarship. One linguist wrote: "I should like to enter an informed doubt that the more than a thousand who attended his lectures on language and mind at Oxford in the spring of 1969, or who filled the streets in London waiting for a lecture there, were moved by visions of a better base structure." This statement reveals how seriously the writer has underestimated the fascination that language has, especially for the young, and how short-sighted linguists have been in the past about the nature of their own discipline. Language and mind is a subject of nearly overwhelming interest: it is not so much about base structure as it is about human nature.

A multitude of young scholars were galvanized by Chomsky. It is perhaps for this that the linguistics establishment cannot forgive him. While they caricatured his theories, a growing number within the academy were studying them; not only linguists, but psychologists, philosophers, neurobiologists, logicians. Throughout the sixties new works were published on the biological basis of language, and on child language acquisition. There was a proliferation of conferences and symposia on the general subject of innateness. At one of these meetings, called "Brain Mechanisms Underlying Speech and Language" in 1964, Chomsky gave a frequently quoted definition of language competence. Command of a language, he said, involved knowing a "specific sound-meaning correspondence." When asked how he would account for sign languages of the deaf, he rephrased his statement, saying instead, "signal-meaning correspondence," and added: "It is an open question whether the sound part is crucial. It could be, but certainly there is little evidence to suggest it."

This remark irritated traditional linguists immensely. If they didn't have the phoneme, they didn't have anything. But the sign-language linguists have come to cherish it.

II

By 1979, ASL research had become a large, visible project within the Salk Institute's biological laboratories. The research group seemed confident and happy. The first book to come out of the project was finished: *The Signs of Language*, by Klima, Bellugi, and ten other authors, two of them deaf. Ursula Bellugi showed me around the lab.

We walked through a darkened studio where a signer was waiting to be recorded on videotape. The lights went on and he began signing. It was—it always is—riveting. I stopped, and Dr. Bellugi had to come back for me so we could continue the tour.

The corridors were lined with shelves of videotape cassettes. In the offices the research staff worked at large desks, many with video monitors playing tapes of signers, some at slow speeds. On several screens, the signing subject was a very young child. Large charts of Stokoe's notation system for ASL were tacked to the walls. Conversations in ASL, interspersed with laughter and a certain amount of desk-thumping, were going on all over the room. I stepped into someone's sightline and she rolled her chair into the aisle and ducked her head to look around me. She was signing to a young man behind a glass partition in the next office. He smiled at me, signed for me to move a little more, and resumed. Only Bellugi and I were speaking, the only voices audible. I never observed any simultaneous signing and speaking at Salk, just straight ASL.

Ursula Bellugi stopped at an empty desk, shoved a video cassette into a vacant monitor, and showed me a signer with lights attached to his fingertips, wrists, and elbows—a new technique. She is trying to find out whether the signs can be understood using only the minimum information provided in the light trajectories.

Back in her office, Bellugi and I talked about her work. I realized that she was not entirely comfortable with me, especially after I told her that my interest in ASL was not purely psycholinguistic. I wanted to know as much of the story as possible, I told her, the social and personal aspects, the important educational issues, the politics. Her reaction was one of horror, and she recoiled from saying anything that might feed into the controversies within the deaf community. She insisted that she knew only about the formal properties of ASL. Her findings applied to deaf children of deaf parents, and to those who had learned ASL as a first language. She was not aware, she said, of any information at all about any other sign system used in the schools. Perhaps signed English would be successful for deaf children of hearing parents, but she had no opinion about that. She gave me some background information, but steadfastly refused to be quoted. I was welcome, of course, to quote from her published material—of which she gave me a mountain.

I was irritated but not surprised, and all things considered, I thought she was probably justified in wanting to avoid getting involved in deaf politics. (After I had spent more time at the various institutions and schools for the deaf, I felt even more inclined to appreciate her point of view.) We confined our interview to ongoing research and the new book.

Until ASL was studied, the search for the biological foundations of human language focused entirely on the vocal tract, ear, and brain as an intimately linked system. Because the human voice could only produce speech sounds one after the other in sequence, it was reasonable to assume that the ear was especially adapted to perceive this kind of information, and that cognitive processes in the brain were also specialized for speech. The structure of spoken language—from segmental phoneme to the ordered syntax of phrases and sentences—had very likely been determined by these anatomical limitations as well. This theory, like earlier ones, continued to define language as something that happened from the neck up. In the absence of anything except spoken language, it was an excellent account. With the new evidence about ASL, it now seems too narrow.

William Stokoe's insight about ASL was based on his observation that signs are *also* made up of segmental units—small interchangeable parts. Unlike phonemes (sound sequences in time), the structural elements in signs are presented simultaneously in space. All signs have three parts (or parameters), meaningless in themselves, that can be combined and recombined to form meaning: the shape of the hand; the location of the sign in relation to the signer's body; and the movement of the hand (or hands) while executing the sign. Within these parameters, Stokoe identified nineteen different handshapes; twelve possible locations; and twenty-four basic kinds of movements. Fifty-five features in all. These formed the sublexical level of

ASL, analogous to the phonemic level of spoken language. There were rules for the ways in which these features could and could not be combined.

By showing that ASL was based on structural principles similar to those of spoken language, Stokoe's work suggested that language was not determined by the biological limitations of speech and hearing. Language appeared to be a more general kind of cognitive ability, rather strongly ingrained in the human organism. The Salk Institute confirmed Stokoe's findings and undertook new studies to identify other features ASL might or might not share with spoken language. There were already standard experiments in the psycholinguistic literature about the ways hearing speakers use and process speech. These experiments had shown that phonemic structure was not merely a useful descriptive invention of linguists, but also played a role in language use—it had "psychological reality." Klima and Bellugi adapted these experiments for use with deaf signers, and designed new ones. The results with both speakers and signers were remarkably alike.

In short-term memory studies, hearing speakers confuse words that are structurally similar and sound alike: *chair* and *stare*. Errors in recall are not made because of meaning; subjects do not confuse *chair* and *couch*. In ASL experiments, signers also made structural errors, and tended to confuse signs that looked alike: *home* and *flower*, which are identical except that *home* is made near the cheek and *flower* near the nose (the two signs differ along one parameter). Like speakers, signers did not confuse signs that had similar meanings, *home* with *house*. This suggested that both languages are similarly encoded by their users: speakers organize their memories according to the sound segments of the words, and signers according to the visual, structural components in the signs. This experiment, and others as well, tended to confirm the existence of the interchangeable sublexical level, and duality of patterning in ASL.

In an early study, the Salk group compared the speed of

speaking with the speed of signing, and found them nearly identical. Although it takes longer to make a sign than it does to say a word, it takes fewer signs to make a statement. In fact, it takes the same amount of time to state a proposition in ASL as it does in English. (In a version of the experiment using a signed English system called *Signing Exact English*, the same proposition took more than twice as long to sign.) The authors concluded that cognitive processes underlying all natural languages might well be the same and might also create an optimal rate for stating propositions. ASL can be produced at the same rate as spoken language because there are grammatical devices in ASL that allow signers ways of packing information into individual signs instead of adding more signs.

The psychological aspects of ASL were less difficult to find than the linguistic: it is easier to know that a linguistic transaction is taking place than to know exactly how it is being conducted. To live closely or work together with a group of deaf ASL signers is to have no reservations about their linguistic competence. They express themselves. They chat, gossip, discourse, argue, convey to each other all the nuances of information and meaning that hearing people do. It is quite difficult, however, to see (perceive by the eye) exactly how they do it. Klima and Bellugi watched ASL signers for a very long time before becoming aware of all the things that can go on in a sign.

A particularly instructive chapter in *The Signs of Language* with the intimidating title "Aspectual Modulations on Adjectival Predicates" represents a breakthrough in understanding ASL. It was written with Carlene Canady Pedersen, a young deaf linguist, a native signer, who demonstrates how signs are modulated to change their meaning.

In English, words can change meaning according to their use in a sentence, or can be modified by the addition of other words. *Sick*, for example, can be used to convey a range of meanings: *she is sick; she has a tendency to be sick; I haven't been sick for twenty years*. Independently of its use in a sentence, the form of the word *sick* can also be changed by adding affixes: *sickly; sickness; sicker.* ASL can also express these variations, not by adding other signs or by affixation but by changing movements. Changes and complexities of movement are executed within the framework of the basic sign; they are simultaneous and spatial, and are superimposed directly on the sign. The difference between *being sick* and *getting sick* is a very small difference in movement. For example, the sign *sick* in its simplest form (called the citation form or the frozen sign) is a two-handed sign made with an open handshape, the middle finger bent. One hand makes simple contact at the chest, the other makes similar contact at the forehead and maintains a brief hold. *To get sick* is made in the same way, but with a straight movement to the forehead and a hold at the offset. The sign that means *to have a tendency to be sick* (predispositional aspect) is made with no change of movement at the chest, but the hand approaching the forehead does not make contact. It moves without pausing to form circles in a smooth continuous movement in three cycles.

There are aspectual markings in ASL that can specify meanings like: *sick for a long time, sick intermittently, frequently sick*, and many others.

Signing (like playing tennis, dancing, or even peeling an apple) involves complex, many-dimensional physical movements quite beyond verbal description. The dynamic events that are signs become lifeless, diminished, they lose their own prosody. Linguistic terminology, unfortunately, is more difficult to follow and less interesting than ordinary English. The only way of talking about signs that makes them easy to remember and fun for hearing people is to relate them to some familiar concrete activity: "as if cradling a baby in your arms . . . like grasping the peak of a cap . . . weighing things, one in each hand." In a sign language handbook, *Talk with Your Hands* by David Watson, the sign *sick* is illustrated with a single cartoon drawing of a wretched-looking man holding one hand at his head and one at his mid-section. The text reads: "Ailing in mind and body." The instruction for making the sign is: "Bend slightly over, as if in some distress." This description is pantomimic (and iconic) rather than linguistic. It emphasizes that *sick* is a subjective condition and directs the signer to act out the distress. Deaf signers rarely add this sort of pantomime; the likelihood of a deaf signer in an ASL conversation acting distressed when signing *sick* is about the same as any hearing person's when speaking the word *sick*. In most of the sample sentences given for *sick*, distress is not even appropriate—as in *I haven't been sick for twenty years*, or *He is prone to being sick*. The role played by pantomime in signing is largely extra-linguistic and not part of the language system.

Most sign language classes for hearing people stress gesture, facial expression, and all the picture-like, iconic aspects of signing. Students are encouraged to get the idea across and not worry about using the correct sign. Though it is possible to communicate with a deaf person in this way, it's not ASL. (It's possible to communicate with a Frenchman in this way, but it's not French, either.) Deaf people use expressive gestures in approximately the same way that hearing people do, as an accompaniment to language. Good ASL signers use far fewer gestures with each other than they do with people who are unfamiliar with ASL. Conversations in ASL can be as sedate and gesture-free as any polite discourse between English speakers. ASL does not *need* gestural embellishment any more than English does.

Scholars and laymen alike have shown great reluctance to believe that ASL signs are linguistic symbols. Traditional definitions of language insist that symbols must be completely arbitrary and bear no physical resemblance to the things, objects, or events they signify. (The word *dog* is arbitrary; barking to signify *dog* is not arbitrary but iconic. The word *sick* is arbitrary; acting sick is iconic.) Many signs in ASL are arbitrary, but many others bear visual clues to their meanings and can certainly be classed as iconic. Another group of signs appears to be arbitrary yet are known to have originated in a more iconic, gestural form. Nancy Frishberg's historical research (in *The Signs of Language* and elsewhere) has shown that signs tend to lose iconicity over time and to become more arbitrary. They have moved away from gestural origins and toward more abstract forms.

Iconicity seems to play no role whatever in deaf people's use of ASL, but hearing people—both critics and enthusiasts—continue to put their intellectual money on it. Quite literally, it is all that they can see. Critics disparage ASL because it's not arbitrary enough, because the signs look like pictures and pantomimes. Enthusiasts adore ASL because they think they can look at a sign and know what it means. It's a powerful feeling, but false. Hearing people are almost never able to understand a sign by looking at it. Ursula Bellugi got very low rates of accuracy when she tested hearing subjects. Even on multiple-choice tests, where the correct meaning was listed along with three others, hearing subjects scored little better than chance. When told the meaning of a sign, most hearing people eagerly constructed gestural explanations to match—and even those were not always correct.

A deaf linguist who sometimes teaches ASL told me, "Hearing people can't seem to remember signs without a lot of explanation. They can't learn the sign for *milk* without imagining a real cow being milked. They must have an image of a man with his elbows sticking out of his jacket or else they won't remember the sign for *poor*. An old, brown Harris tweed jacket with a hole in the elbow!" She shook her head and laughed. "We never, never think of those things."

Deaf signers give every indication that signs are to them as words are to the hearing: arbitrary symbols. ASL is a highly evolved language. From concrete representations (if representations can ever be concrete), abstract forms have developed. Hearing people, who lack the visual sophistication of the deaf, overlook the arbitrary forms of the language and insist on moving ASL away from the abstract, back toward more concrete and iconic forms of gesture and meaning.

III

Those of us who can hear, hear just about everything. Physicists have told me that if human hearing were any better we could listen to the molecules bouncing around outside our ears. We hear, and can identify, a large variety of sounds: footsteps on dry leaves, keys jangling, wind in the trees, animal noises, footsteps on wet leaves. Many things in the environment, however, make no sound at all, and some only when in motion. The amount of information conveyed to the ears is always limited, the quality fragmentary and ephemeral. The most salient sounds in the environment—for all species—are the sounds made by members of the same species. We are all tuned to the music of our conspecifics.

In contrast, the visual world is infinitely rich. When we open our eyes, we see a world full of things, objects, shapes, color, movement: information. We get immediate information about size, dimension, texture, velocity, distance, density. Light travels faster than sound: we can see over great distances, can tell if an object is moving away from us, or, if toward us, can sometimes estimate how long it will take to arrive. We can see through things: water, glass, foliage, dust, rain. There is so much information that we can identify things when we can see them only in part, or indistinctly: a branch of a tree, a portion of a structure; the outline of an animal, the shadow of a man. A sound signal is lost soon after it occurs, almost instantly. But we can look at an object in the environment for as long as we like: as long as it doesn't move away, as long as there is light. The information we receive about most objects and events in the world is so complete, rich, and multifaceted that any of a number of features might provide the basis for a representation. They can be depicted, mimicked, characterized, symbolized (rather easily) by the human body, and especially by that part of the body most frequently in our line of vision, our hands. Ancient Chinese characters contain representations of hands "reaching, grasping, holding, and otherwise indicating manual activity."

Gestural representations are associated with cave drawings, pictographs, and the earliest writing systems. All graphic and pictorial art probably originated in gestural communication. Primitive woman drew pictures in the air, then began scratching her tracings on solid surfaces. Visual images tend to be fairly specific. Everything looks like something: a line, a root, a lump of earth, a cloud, a scar on a rock, an inkblot. Non-representational artists are highly constrained by the nature of the visual world, and their struggle to escape the forms and shapes of nature, to be truly non-objective, has only rarely been successful. Few abstract works are inaccessible to interpretation; the images of nature have often been replaced by the images of industrial society, less familiar, but no less referential.

All theatrical and ritual displays, dance and drama, are in the visual and gestural tradition. Classical Hindu dance drama is so precisely structured, the meanings assigned to each posture and gesture so exact, that it is sometimes described as a closed grammatical system, unchanged for millennia. In ancient Persian poetry, a gesture was frequently used in place of a word at the end of a line to convey the essential meaning of the line as well as to complete the meter. European theatrical art, in that long period between the ancient Greeks and the Elizabethans, was almost entirely mime and dance, often accompanied by music and sometimes by song. Spoken plays were used as fillers during intermissions between the more popular masques and commedias. Since performances were usually outdoors—in amphitheaters, enclosed roofless areas, or village squares—most with negative acoustic properties, the actor moved little, faced the audience,

and in his loudest voice declaimed his lines. The blank and me-
tered verse of early playwrights was used to overcome acoustic
difficulties and to provide audiences with clues for following the
thread of the unfolding dramatic "action." Modern spoken
drama derives from poetry, where the manipulation of words
alone produces special meanings—images. The making of pictures with words is not an inaccurate description for a great deal
of the world's poetry. In many cultures, the shape of a poem on a
page and the relationship between the meaning of the words and
the visual configuration of the script are parts of an integrated,
artistic whole. Today, poets occasionally draw pictures with
their typewriters.

Questions about the origin of language can never truly be answered, yet scholars theorize and even debate these questions
with verve and conviction, "like eyewitnesses," as one linguist
complained. At present, a widely held theory is that gestural
language preceded speech or accompanied speech until about the
time that tool-using occupied the hands exclusively. (The British author Anthony Burgess, who is also a keen philologist, believes that gestures were used by day and speech after dark.)
Gestural communication continued as a human activity long
after the invention of tools, and is documented even into modern
times.

Vision is surely our most important perceptual contact with
the environment. Without it, our understanding of the world is
vastly restricted and our movements within it limited or impossible. If language shifted from the visual to the auditory, perhaps
it was not the case that primitive hands were too full of tools, but
that the eyes were too full of meaningful images; the visual world
already saturated with information. It seems likely that early
language was in an interchangeable modality, human representations varying between manual/visual and vocal/auditory. (It is
not unreasonable to assume that early writing systems, and number systems, represented signs as well as words.) Gradually, to
the cries, calls, and other compelling and emotive human sounds

were added vocal symbols taken from the visual and gestural: words used in place of signs.

Gestural languages have been reported all over the world. They were in extensive use throughout the Mediterranean region and Asia Minor until a few hundred years ago. There is no indication that they were ever the primary language mode; they were probably used alternatively with speech. The decline of gesture is generally tied to the spread of literacy—the replacement of one kind of visual symbol (gesture) with another (writing).

Gestural languages can be used only in communities where face to face contact is still the most important form of social interaction. Perhaps they were overlooked by history because they were highly esoteric and preserved as private languages, not readily displayed to strangers, armies of occupation, or itinerant ethnographers. (The Sicilian Vespers of 1282 was an insurrection that resulted in the massacre and total expulsion from the island of thousands of occupying Norman troops. Legend has it that the conspiracy was planned and discussed on the streets of Palermo entirely through the use of signs.)

There seems to be a tendency for people to have more than one kind of language. The sign language of the Plains Indians was used as a lingua franca for communication among tribes with different spoken languages; but it was also an alternative language, sometimes a ritual language, sometimes a poetic language. Becoming fluent in sign was a cultural accomplishment. In its more formal mode it was used by the men, and some accounts of its use are reminiscent of Church Latin, the language of priests, used not only for prayers but for conducting all important church business. On the Plains, there were centers for instruction in sign language, and certain tribes became famous for their skill in using and teaching them. It was the best signers in each tribe who were chosen to be representatives at intertribal councils, and who conducted ritual and narrative performances. It was those fluent signers, also, who went to Washington at the turn of the century to compare their signs with college students at Gallaudet. The Indians were said to have been dazzled by the deaf signers, and considered their own signs inferior to ASL, though there was a great deal of mutual understanding.

Although traditional Indian life and language were treated with a certain scholarly respect, the more general cultural attitude in this country toward Native Americans was one of hostility. Indian sign language was considered a joke, and Indians were said to use it because they lacked the intelligence necessary to learn English. LaMont West, who conducted the only substantial study of Plains Sign Language in this century, found that the majority of Indians on the reservations were completely fluent in English, fluent in their tribal languages, fluent in signs, and a few of the best signers he met were fluent in a European language as well. For some individuals, interest in sign language was clearly part of an intellectual and linguistic pursuit of some sophistication.

Sign language has the reputation for being unrestrained and emotionally primitive, but after observing deaf signers using ASL for several years, I have come to consider it highly controlled and cerebral. It is, in fact, a very cool medium. Far less anxiety is generated by signing than by speaking. The all-encompassing energy released by a stream of speech can be brutal, and an aggressive shout finds all within earshot. Without giving consent or provocation, we are constantly being addressed, commanded, lectured, harangued—barraged with words. The arousal level caused by a voice at high volume is considerable; several voices, a room full of voices, strain endurance. Sign language is far less arousing, more purely linguistic and expressive, less emotive. Because signing is a face-to-face exchange, it is less possible for an outsider to intrude in a conversation, to bully his way in. No one gets shouted down. Signs are given and received by mutual agreement. All exchanges seem more focused. In gatherings of deaf people, hearing people instinctively lower their voices.

If language began with gesture, it must have become obvious fairly soon that the emotion-arousing qualities of the voice provided a most effective method of transmission. Our linguistically minded species filled the auditory channel with its most interesting sound, the human voice. Meanwhile, members of the species who were deprived of hearing continued to make representations. When given the opportunity for contact with older generations of signers, they proceeded to refine and elaborate their representations in the sole modality available to them. In American Sign Language, a lucky accident of history, they created a most civilized language.

Even without the accidents of history, and without the cultural transmission from one generation to another, deaf individuals continue to make symbolic representations and to express them linguistically.

Nature: The Innate Language Endowment

The plain conclusion to which all examples point with irresistible force is, that the origin of linguistic stocks is to be found in what may be termed the language-making instinct of very young children.—Horatio Hale, Presidential Address, American Association for the Advancement of Science (1887)

I

The idea that children know about language goes back to antiquity. The Greek historian Herodotus wrote during the fifth century B.C. of an important language experiment. The Egyptians and the Phrygians had both claimed to be the most ancient people on earth, and both considered their own language original to mankind. Wishing to settle the matter, the king of Egypt ordered that two children "of the common sort" be isolated at birth from human society and language, but fed and cared for. "His object herein was to know, after the first indistinct babblings of infancy were over, what word they would first articulate." The shepherd who tended the children obeyed these orders strictly, and two years later reported that both children had run up to him with arms outstretched, calling "*Becos, becos,*" the Phrygian word for bread. "In consideration of this circumstance, the Egyptian king admitted the greater antiquity of the Phrygians," and the children were presumably returned to their families.

King James IV of Scotland (1473–1513) was interested in repeating the experiment with Scottish children—he hoped they might speak Hebrew—but there are no clear records of the experiment or its outcome.

Sensitive observers have noted, for hundreds of years, that deaf children who aren't taught sign language use a spontaneous and idiosyncratic system of signs and gestures among themselves. Oral schools usually ignore it, or deny it. In the deaf community it's called home sign. In 1974 two graduate students at the University of Pennsylvania, Susan Goldin-Meadow and Heidi Feldman, working with Professor Rochel Gelman, a developmental psychologist, began a study of home sign. They wanted to find out what sort of language it was, where it came from, and whether the children learned it from each other or knew it even before they got to school.

The group decided to study children who had never been taught sign language or exposed to it—children of hearing parents who might already be receiving oral training. The students received a list of children from private speech therapists, contacted the families, and obtained permission from the first six on the list.

The children ranged in age from seventeen months to four years. All had hearing losses that prevented them from acquiring speech normally, even with a hearing aid. All were receiving special speech training, but none had learned to speak more than a few words, and several had no speech whatever. All lived at home while attending oral day schools. The six children attended five different schools and did not know each other; the two who went to the same school were in different grades and were not regular playmates. Each of the schools had requested the parents not to gesture or sign to the children and to discourage all signing by the children at home, offering the traditional explanation that signing has negative effects on oral training. All the parents were committed to oral education, and all had agreed.

Taping of the subjects was done every six to eight weeks, in their homes, for three years. From the earliest sessions, all the children were observed using signs and gestures spontaneously in making their thoughts and wishes known. They began using signs at about the same time and in the same way that hearing children begin using speech. They signed about the same things that hearing children talk about. Not only did they invent signs, they joined signs into phrases and sentences the way hearing children combine words during the early stages of language. Most interesting to the linguists, all the children used a structured way of ordering the signs grammatically. They had syntax.

At the University of Pennsylvania, I watched an early tape of the subject called David. By now it is rather well known, shown at linguistics conferences and included in syntax courses. David is on the floor surrounded by toys and books. He is almost four, a lovely child, blond and chubby. It is a summer day. David has just been shown a picture of a snow shovel. He proceeds to make six different statements, in sign, about his experiences with a snow shovel during the preceding winter. He signs:

1. *The shovel is to dig with.*
2. *I put on my boots and take the shovel from the basement and go outside and dig.*
3. *Me. David!*
4. *I dig when it snows outside and I shovel the snow.*
5. *Yes, I dig.*
6. *The shovel is kept in the basement, what I dig with is kept down in the basement.*

The tape is old, and was copied from an earlier one, but David's remarks are quite clear, his signs stylized, economical, and expressive. After each statement, he returns his hands to a neutral position on his lap.

For three years the two graduate students spent a great deal of time in dark rooms peering at the data—the videotapes—separating out signs from what they called the stream of motor behavior. They cross-checked their observations with each other, and with other professionals and faculty at Penn. Then they designed a system for segmenting and coding the signs. They did linguistic and developmental analyses comparing the skills of the deaf children to skills found in the larger population of hearing children the same age.

When it was all over, and the results of the study clear, the conclusion was that the deaf children had not learned their language from anyone, they had each, independently, invented it. They were like the children in the ancient story of Herodotus, linguistically isolated from the spoken language of their culture by their deafness, and linguistically isolated from the sign language of the deaf community by the educational philosophy of their time. Without a model, they still showed a strong desire to communicate and an impressive talent for representing their thoughts symbolically. This urge toward language was so strong, and the human organism so adaptable, that children without hearing extracted from the visual environment a structured and compelling language of their own—as deaf individuals have always done.

Articles about the study were published in scientific journals and in collections of linguistic writings. Perhaps the best known, and the one I like most, is *Beyond Herodotus*, by Feldman, Goldin-Meadow, and L. R. Gleitman (1979). It has a narrative quality rarely found in scientific writing, and a portrait of the deaf children creating their own language that is hard to forget. The authors present the work as further evidence for linguistic innateness, and acknowledge their intellectual debt to Noam Chomsky. Throughout the work, the authors describe the home signs as "language-like." Though similar to other child languages, it was an open question how much like a full, adult language it would become. With continued isolation—and none of the children had anyone to talk to, or anyone who would answer—they might abandon their signs altogether. Given greater contact with other deaf children who signed, the languages would surely expand. By 1979 the project was over; but Susan Goldin-Meadow, who had received her doctorate for the work, decided to continue collecting data on three of the original children.

It is not unusual in this kind of study to have a "best" subject. In this case it was the subject known as David. Looking at the table headed "Total Occurrences of Two Signed Elements," the numbers read like this:

Kathy	33
Dennis	27
David	248
Donald	84
Tracy	24

A table showing sentence-length in the older children reads as follows:

Donald	4
Tracy	5
David	9+

From the first, David was consistently more inventive and accomplished than the other children. No one knows why. Perhaps he is more intelligent than the others, the experimenters suggested; perhaps his parents are more good-natured about his signing. Aside from these general speculations, there is no explanation. David is just a very fluent little boy, they said, the Shakespeare of home sign. Some of Susan Goldin-Meadow's recent work is concerned exclusively with David, and his sentences show increasing complexity. I was interested in meeting this talented child, and wrote to Goldin-Meadow asking permission to accompany her on her next videotaping trip to Philadelphia, and a meeting was arranged.

II

Susan Goldin-Meadow picked me up at the grimy Thirtieth Street Station in Philadelphia on a hot, muggy morning at the end of June, driving a rented compact car with her cameraman in the front seat and the back filled with video equipment. Professor Goldin-Meadow was twenty-eight years old when I met her, and was teaching at the University of Chicago. She comes to Philadelphia every three months to make tapes of her deaf subjects.

Larry King, the cameraman, an undergraduate at Penn, gave me the front seat and managed to crawl in among the TV equipment in the back.

Susan said she was particularly looking forward to this visit with David. The family had a new baby girl, and this would be the first time Susan had seen her. Susan was hoping that David would have a lot to tell us about the event. We planned to spend the whole morning at home, perhaps four or five hours. "They're a terribly nice family," she said. (I will call them Baker. The names of all subjects and their families have been changed.)

It was just past nine o'clock, and 93 degrees. We turned into a quiet street and stopped in front of a neat brick row house. The door burst open immediately, and there was David standing on the top step. He smiled, and signed: folded his arms in front of him, close to his body, as if cradling a baby. He pointed to the front window of his house, and there was his mother cradling the real baby in her arms. Mrs. Baker waved, Susan waved, everyone smiled.

David ran down the stairs and helped us carry the gear into the house. In addition to the video equipment, there were several boxes of toys that Susan always brought with her. She had a small gift for the new baby, too.

Inside, Larry made for the farthest corner of the room where he began moving furniture and setting up his camera; then he wedged himself inexorably behind it. Introductions were made matter-of-factly, and they found me a seat out of the sun, where it was cooler and where I wouldn't be in the way. Most members of the Baker family were dressed in shorts. David's father was home; a civil servant who works odd hours, today was his day off. He went to walk the dog. That left David, who was eight and a half, a baby, and David's sister, Molly, a tall dignified little girl of ten.

Mrs. Baker seemed an extremely cheerful, outgoing woman, very pleased with her family. The new baby, one month old, sat in an infant seat until time for a morning nap. The cause of David's deafness had never been discovered, and I understood that the decision to have another child had been a big one.

Susan, David, and Molly spread themselves out on the floor. Molly stayed with us all morning. The things Susan had brought included games, books, and many action toys: trains that moved, cars that ran on tracks, an antique bank with a soldier who shot a penny into a slot.

I had expected David to be a nice little boy, smart and attractive. I had expected the family to be nice. But I wasn't quite prepared for the completely friendly and cheerful atmosphere I found that morning; I think I had expected them to be at least a little depressed. I looked closely for signs of anxiety. But they weren't depressed, and they really weren't anxious. There was not a trace of hostility in their attitude toward each other, the experimenters, me, or the deaf educational establishment when we got around to talking about it. They chatted openly about themselves, what they had been doing, of summer plans at the seashore. But most of the conversation was about David. Susan often asked about his signs. Is that the sign he always uses for the ocean? How long has he been doing that? They all seemed to understand David's signs.

Molly, David, and Susan played a game of Chutes and Ladders, and David was losing. He sulked and frowned. "David doesn't like to lose," his mother said. Molly left the group and went to talk to Larry. David then set up some toy cars and constructed a ramp for them. Someone came to the door; children's voices were calling for David. His mother tapped him and pointed to the stairs. David stood at the head of the stairs and signed down to his friends: *After lunch, you knock on the door, and I will come.* The message was clear, the signs very readable. At that moment David looked almost like an ASL signer. Not so fluent nor so quick, but very stylish and smooth.

David had been playing with the cars on the floor, and the pattern of the tracks edged close to my chair. As he set up a complicated jump, he turned and looked at me, directly into my eyes, very steadily. His expression was not unfamiliar. Many deaf children have given me that direct, measured, addressing look. Who are you, it asks? Do I have your attention; are you in this with me? No one, of course, had tried to tell David who I was, or why I was there. It was too complicated. At schools for the deaf where signs are used, many children ask about me, and are given an answer—usually an inadequate one, but something. More than David got. He was curious. He had noted my presence, and several times during the morning I had noticed him checking to see what I was doing and where my interest was.

Now he set up the ramps, and, Evel Knievel style, lined up three cars, side by side, in the space between the two ramps. He wound up the car that was going to make the jump, then turned again to see if I was ready. I gave him a signal, and he let the car go. It made the jump and a perfect landing, but failed to manage the turn at the end of the track and flew across the room. It was going too fast, he explained. He'd try it at a slower speed next jump, he said as he retrieved the car and set it up again. He signed all this to me, though afterwards I couldn't remember any of the specifics of his signing. Looking through my notes the following day, I wasn't sure how he had expressed himself and had to consult the tape again. It was all in sign.

David spoke only a few words, and those were not terribly clear. He also made some rather random sounds that may or may not have been intended as words. His home signs were numerous, complex, and fluent by comparison to his oral language, though certainly not so impressive as the signing of deaf children who know ASL. David did not appear to read lips, but he could read people and situations. When the children came to the door with bathing suits, he knew they were going swimming. He knew that when Susan and Larry came, they stayed for lunch; therefore, he told his friends to come back after lunch. When he was addressed by one of his parents, like all children, he often knew what they wanted before they told him. Sometimes he just guessed. He would try something, and if it was not what his mother had in mind, he'd try something else. The situation did not offer too many alternatives.

No one interfered with David's signing, or suggested that he stop. They paid attention to everything he signed and seemed perfectly aware that communication in the family would be greatly constrained if David were not permitted to use his hands. The only person I observed actually signing back to David was his sister, Molly. Susan thinks that it may be Molly who understands David's language best.

It was rather late in the morning, after eleven o'clock, when Mrs. Baker asked me what my interest was in David. I answered that I was writing a book, had heard about David's signs, and wanted to meet him. She was pleased and wished me luck. She told me that David went to an oral school, had never been taught sign language, but had made up all the signs he used. The Bakers had read some of Susan's published work and had found it interesting. They said they were thinking of sending David to a total communication school in Cincinnati, St. Rita's. Had I heard of it, they asked?

The school had an excellent reputation but I had never been there. St. Rita's students were usually near the top of all the achievement scores I had ever seen.

David's father had joined us shortly after we began talking about David's education. I was surprised at how much of their time and resources the family had devoted to being well informed, and how thoughtful they were, but was more surprised when they asked if I knew about cued speech. The previous summer, the family had all gone to Gallaudet for a week of cued speech training. "How did you hear of it?" I asked.

"I saw a notice in a civil service employees magazine, and sent for information," was Mr. Baker's answer.

Cued speech is a lipreading system. Because many of the phonemes cannot be discriminated visually (*pit, bit,* and *mit,* for example, look identical on the lips), the speaker uses handshapes to aid the deaf lipreader in knowing which sound has actually been made. It is very similar to a Scandinavian hand/mouth system developed in the last century, used on and off without much success over the next seventy years. The present cued speech method was invented by Dr. Orrin Cornett, an administrator at Gallaudet with a Ph.D. in engineering physics. Several Scandinavian visitors to Gallaudet told me that they wished Cornett had talked to them before undertaking the present cued speech program. It has never been adequately tested in this country, and the reasons I decided not to investigate it in any depth were that nobody seems to use it and deaf people hate it.

Cued speech uses twelve handshapes (cues) to help the lipreader: four for vowels, eight for particular consonants, and a glide to indicate the dipthong. Cornett contends that after learning to lipread with the cues, they will no longer be necessary and can be discarded. Cueing, he claims, forces the deaf child to focus attention on the lips, more so than standard lipreading techniques. Cornett reasons that the "brain" uses only the cues it needs, and not all lipreaders need all the cues. As lipreading gets easier, he says, no one will bother to read the cues. But the evidence is to the contrary: Scandinavians discarded the system because they found that people who use cues become increasingly dependent on them and can only communicate with speakers who have been trained in the method. Still, if it works, and a family, school, or group is willing to learn and use cues with a deaf person, communication might improve. Lipreading is so difficult that any additional information seems likely to improve performance. The real question is, Can hearing people really use cues comfortably while speaking and can deaf people read them during ordinary conversational exchanges?

"It's a nice place, Gallaudet," said Mrs. Baker. "It was an interesting experience going there. I had no idea, and it's been there so long. We stayed in one of the dorms and went to cued speech classes every day. The kids came too, all of us. Everything was set up really well. Lots of things for the kids to do, and they had a special program for the deaf kids where David went. It wasn't expensive, either."

"Is there a book?" I asked.

"Well, they said you didn't *have* to buy the book; but," Mrs. Baker indicated her husband, "he bought it and," she laughed, "he really learned the whole thing from the book. He can learn things like that, all by himself. I was too agitated or something, I had to go to the classes."

"By Wednesday," said Mr. Baker, "I just had enough of sitting in classrooms, so I went over to the bookstore and brought the book back to the air-conditioned dorm."

"Did David learn the cues?" I asked.

"He doesn't have to do anything. Just us," she said. "He'll pick it up naturally. That's the nice part of it. I had a meeting here. Tried to get some other parents interested. As you say, it's no good if nobody uses it. I don't know how it's going to turn out, but I think we'll go ahead. Dr. Cornett called yesterday and I told him I guessed we would. He's called a lot and seems very, very keen to get David into the program."

David's father laughed. "What an intense man," he said. "I think he really turned a lot of parents off with his speeches about how you've got to make a strong commitment or else forget the whole thing, it won't work, get off the pot."

"He has a reputation for being excitable."

"But," said Mrs. Baker, shaking his head, "if he ever does get that computer working, wouldn't that be something?"

Cornett is attempting to computerize his method with a three-part hardware system: microphone, speech analyzer, and a pair of heavy eyeglasses. The microphone is to be worn somewhere on the clothing (necktie is recommended). It picks up incoming sound and relays it to the analyzer (worn in the breast pocket). The analyzer searches for the kinds of phonemes that can be represented by cues, and relays that information to the eyeglasses, where more complicated relays involving mirrors present the cues (colored lights) to the eyes of the deaf person.

Aside from the formidable task of trying to decode speech on the lips while simultaneously decoding flashing lights dancing before the eyes, there are many other difficulties. It is yet another one-way communication system—from hearing to deaf. There is no way in the system for a deaf person without good speech to answer the hearing person talking into the microphone; and no way for deaf people to talk to each other except by using speech good enough to be processed through the many machines.

The entire argument may be moot because no analyzer has ever been built that can accommodate ordinary speech. Bell Laboratories has a multi-million-dollar machine called the Visible Speech Translator that can print out, or display, a spectogram of the human voice that a few skilled individuals can read. The problem seems to be the quality of the input; it doesn't do well with just any voice. The best account of it I ever read states that "slow, carefully spoken sentences [can] be successfully communicated with much practice. . . ." The analyzer that Cornett plans for his system is quite a bit more complicated, specialized, and more difficult to design than the Bell Lab's translator, but engineers are optimistic, and the entire system is being developed at Gallaudet along with a drive to recruit more users of cued speech.

Cued speech alone, without the computer, is now seen as an intermediary step. If a growing population uses cued speech, they can also be said to "need" the computer system. By the time

the plan gets to the computer stage, many of the original as-
sumptions about cueing seem to be lost in contradiction. If cues
are easy and automatic for hearing people, why should a computer take over the task of making them; and if the cues are
merely a temporary device for teaching lipreading, there is no
need to design permanent electronic equipment. At any rate,
money for computer research appears plentiful. When I met
Cornett in 1981 he was anticipating a $5 million grant. (I often
suspect that ASL is unpopular as a teaching method because it
doesn't cost anything; it can't be copyrighted, it doesn't require
sophisticated equipment; and no educational specialists are
needed except for skilled and/or native signers.)

"Cued speech is used a lot in other countries," Mrs. Baker
said. "Australia."

"You know Daniel Ling, of the Ling Method?" asked Mr.
Baker. "He's come out for cued speech in oral schools. Just recently, I think. Cornett told me."

A great deal of anxiety had begun to show itself in the Bakers' conversation. They were trying hard to be reasonable and
open-minded and do the right thing. In cued speech they saw
something they could give David that was more than he was
getting.

"I don't care if he talks," said Mrs. Baker. "As long as he gets
an education. He can just barely read. And he's got so much . . .
potential. He's really bright."

"There's no question about that."

"What do you think about cued speech?" Mrs. Baker asked
me directly.

"I've read a couple of articles," I answered. "That's all. I
never thought it was used enough for me to find out about it, and
the chief drawback is that so few people in this country use it. If
it helps David with lipreading here in the family, and you're
willing to try, it might work fine. I really don't know. I don't
think," I added, "that you should count on the computer being
ready soon."

"Oh, that'll never be ready," said Mr. Baker. "I know that!"

At the next conversational opportunity, Mrs. Baker began cueing David. He watched her attentively. She made a mistake and tried to erase it from the air. David turned and began to walk away, but she stopped him and began again. He watched until she was finished, then turned and left. "He didn't understand," she said. "It's not him, it's me. I forget the cues. I don't know how to use them yet."

"We need more practice," her husband said; "we'll get it."

"I know, I know," she said, and went into the kitchen to make lunch, calling over her shoulder to me, "You'll have some hot dogs with us, won't you?"

We all trooped into the kitchen. Lunch was very pleasant, and David was very animated, signing about a lot of things. He was eager to get on with the summer afternoon, though, and expressed a desire for us to leave. He told Susan he would pick up the toys and then he was going swimming. Molly sat beside Larry and passed him a large number of hot dogs. The baby woke up. David went into the living room and began putting toys back in boxes. The morning was over. We left directly afterwards.

On the return drive to town, Susan told me about some of the problems connected with the research and the criticism she had encountered "from both sides," as she put it. The oralists were somewhat suspicious and considered that her work might undermine their attempts to teach speech. The manualists thought she was irresponsible in not advising David's family to seek ASL instruction for him. I had heard some of these criticisms, too. She was sensitive to them, but felt strongly that she had no advice to offer.

The project could easily get out of hand, she said. Her analysis of the tapes lagged by several years and she was still sifting and writing up results of data that had been collected in 1977. In addition to traveling to Philadelphia, she was currently taping two children in Chicago. She had to continue seeking funding for these projects, write reports, publish articles, carry a full teaching load and work with students. Meanwhile new developments were constantly turning up in the home sign languages. "How long do you plan to keep on gathering this information?" I asked.

She raised her eyebrows. "Maybe forever. Who knows," she said. "As long as I can. Sometimes I think I'll never catch up, but even if I don't, I'm sure it's a valuable record. Nothing like the language of these children has ever been documented."

We drove back to the university to return the video equipment and dropped Larry off in the center of campus. He would be graduating soon and had been with the project since his freshman year. "I'm really going to miss those people," he said.

In 1833, Harvey Peet, principal of the New York Institution for the Instruction of the Deaf, commented on home sign in his fifteenth annual report to the state legislature. The deaf children were ten or older when they came to the Institution, and had received no previous schooling:

> It is a remarkable fact, that, in a state of ignorance, this unprivileged portion of the human family, create, themselves, the means of communicating with the world around them. Each individual presents the phenomenon of an immortal and thinking spirit, pent up within what is, without metaphor to him, a prison house of clay. The imprisoned spirit seeks to effect its escape. . . .
>
> In endeavoring to communicate with his fellow, the deaf [person] is compelled, in the absence of words, to resort to the indication of present objects, and to the delineation, by motion and gesture, of those which are absent. Ideas belonging to the world of intellect solely, he must call up strictly by metaphoric representation, since he presents a material emblem of that which is truly ideal. As the facility, however, with which he finds it possible to

make himself understood, increases, his language extends itself until it becomes as copious as the circumstances of his situation will allow. This language he brings to the institution, in which he is to receive his education. He meets with many, who, in like manner, have constituted their individual languages; but who, by common consent, abandon them for the more copious dialect. . . . This dialect constitutes, in every institution, the medium of familiar intercourse.

The charm of my visit with David gave way in a few days to extreme uneasiness. I wondered how far he could take his home sign language—or rather, how far it could take him. Interesting as David's language was, it was not the rich, cultural thing, shared with family and community, that hearing children and deaf children of deaf parents all have. I felt considerable awe and respect for the generations of deaf children who invented language for themselves—and a sense of tragedy that they have to.

I went to the library to find out why Daniel Ling was interested in cued speech.

III

Before the appearance of Daniel Ling the oralists hadn't produced a theoretician, or a new textbook, for thirty years. Ling is professor of aural rehabilitation at the School of Human Communication Disorders, McGill University, in Montreal. Speech is what Daniel Ling believes in. His very name means tongue. Lipreading plays an incidental part in his method. What he wants the deaf to do is hear, and his contribution to oralism is the concept of residual hearing.

The Ling Method is built entirely on the utilization of residual hearing through maximal use of the new technology in amplification: hearing aids turned to high volume. His declaration that every bit of hearing, no matter how small, can be used in perceiving speech is now the received view, and is often quoted and passed on from one teacher to another. The key to understanding speech is also residual hearing, not lipreading, which Ling considers a secondary and inferior visual skill. "They don't want the deaf kids to use their eyes," one parent summed it up.

I watched a demonstration of the method at the Lexington School in New York City, where all children have individual speech therapy every day. The therapist announced to her pupil, a girl of about six: "Now we're going to practice listening." The therapist then covered the entire lower part of her face with a large piece of cardboard, so the child couldn't lipread or pick up her facial expression, and shouted: *"Ba-a-a."* After several trials, the child said: *"Ba-a-a."*

"Good!" cried the speech therapist, and bestowed a hug. "Wonderful! *Good* listening!"

Ling has been very aggressive in criticizing oral education in the United States and Canada. He repeatedly points out the failure of oralism, the bad speech of oral students, the laxity of the teaching, the low level of teacher training, and the absence of psychological input. The whole thing lacks method. In a position paper he prepared for the Bell Association in 1977, he conceded that certain proponents of sign language were justified in their criticisms: ". . . [their] indignation has, of course, been shared by oral teachers." The trend toward manual communication he considered "explicable," but "anomalous." He also felt that it was "retrograde and should be halted, if not reversed." His response to failed oral education is more of the same: more speech training, begun earlier, and pursued more aggressively.

The term "deafness" occurs infrequently in Ling's writings. The children are hearing-impaired, a condition that calls for treatment and habilitation, sometimes "(re)habilitation." As if it could be cured, the impairment restored by finding and using the child's residual hearing. Ling does admit, reluctantly, that there are some children who have no useful residual audition. For these, he is willing to consider manual communication.

Ling was strongly influenced by the British psychologist Donald Broadbent, whose theory of attention essentially separates the two channels of vision and hearing. According to Ling's reading of this theory, individuals switch back and forth, using primarily one channel or the other, but not both. While one channel—hearing, say—is in use, the other—vision—is put on hold, and monitored in case of need. If needed (suppose the lights go out), the reserve channel is switched on, and the original goes on hold. One modality seems always on hold. Ling wonders "whether or not deaf children can switch or can be trained to switch auditory and visual channels in time to perceive enough of both sensory inputs to make linguistic sense of them."

Even though deaf children, by definition, do not have an auditory channel, Ling worries that they might not switch to it. (Most psychologists no longer believe in Broadbent's isolated channels, or in the problem of switching time.) What deaf education is all about, according to Ling, is giving children practice making sense of whatever comes roaring out of their hearing aids. They must be trained to listen more industriously and more efficiently. He assumes that deaf children do not try to hear useful sounds in the environment. He's afraid they have become, or might become, "visual processors," and will rely on visual information when interacting with the world. He'd just as soon have them not use their vision at all. (By this argument, people who are blind and deaf have an advantage over people who are merely deaf.)

These concerns were spelled out in the only two evaluation studies I was able to find about cued speech. Ling and a colleague, Bryan R. Clarke, tested a group of eight children in Vancouver in 1975 who had received one year of training with cued speech. The children's scores were rather poor: 9 percent of the responses were correct. A year later, 1976, a follow-up study was done. The same eight subjects, the same kinds of tasks, not markedly more difficult. The children were a year older, and had an additional year of cued speech experience. None of the tests was very demanding, and the children were well acquainted with and practiced in the material. The second year, lipreading scores were much higher when lipreading was accompanied by hand cues. However, Ling found that the cued speech scores were the same *whether or not the children were wearing hearing aids.* Residual hearing "appeared to be ignored when hand cues were used." He concluded that the children had been using all their resources in the visual channel; watching the lips and the hand cues had prevented them from switching to the auditory channel. Because of this obvious reliance on the visual, Ling's endorsement of cued speech was not enthusiastic, and his preferred method continues to rely primarily on the use of residual hearing.

Deaf adults manage, somehow, to keep a sense of humor about all these theoretical issues. In the grass roots magazine *Deaf Spectrum*, I found a satire entitled "Residual Vision" written by George Johnston. The scene opens in a doctor's office where a doctor is trying to soothe the mother of a child who has become blind. "Relax," says the doctor, "your child can be normal." He prescribes a vision therapist who will teach the child to see and walk straight. "See, see, see," recites the doctor, "that is their motto."

In the next scene, the vision therapist declares that the child is not blind but only seeing-impaired, with lots of residual vision. Normalization, he assures the mother, will take place provided that the child is not given canes, dogs, radios, tape recorders, or Braille. (In the education of the blind, Braille is almost as unfashionable as ASL is for the deaf. Braille isn't English, either.) The therapist advises the mother to buy 500-watt light bulbs, and to have a TV set going in every room with the sound disconnected. She must discourage the child from relying on his hearing: "Don't talk to him," and make him use his eyes. "Write!" The therapist stresses that these activities must be made visually enjoyable. "Please. Let's make him like seeing people."

Dr. Ling himself is completely indifferent to the opinion of deaf adults and denies that their experiences are relevant in any way to the experiences of deaf children. He writes: "Members of the deaf adult community are not, by virtue of their deafness, experts on the education of hearing-impaired children and to argue otherwise is comparable to claiming expertise in pulmonary medicine simply because one breathes."

Nurture:
Schools for the Deaf

I

In Hartford there is only a marker on the site where the first school stood, for one hundred years, on Asylum Avenue. During the 1920s it moved to its present buildings on fifty green acres in a quiet, lovely neighborhood in West Hartford. The American School for the Deaf claims to be the first school in the western hemisphere for handicapped children. Set well back from the road, the main entrance is in a huge red-brick, Georgian-style building with three-story white columns. Like all schools, it is operating with somewhat fewer students than it can accommodate; there were around 370 the day I visited. The staff numbers two hundred. My immediate impression, reinforced during the day, was that it is too big. It was also very noisy.

I was put in the charge of a volunteer who led a tour of about forty people through the school, mostly nursing students and their teachers from a nearby community college. We began some distance from the main building at the Lower School, with quarters and classrooms of its own. The youngest children the school accepts are two-and-a-half. Physically, it was very pleasant—all the schools are. Sweet and sad, the small beds piled with stuffed toys and dolls, neatly made and arranged in rows in sunny cheerful rooms.

The youngest children are the most interesting to observe. They all seem bright, happy, interested. They all wear "trainers," classroom hearing aids that are more powerful than hearing aids used outside school, and are, in fact, radio receivers designed for use in rooms especially wired (looped) for transmission. A trainer is about the size of a transistor radio, worn on the child's chest, attached by a harness of nylon webbing. Wires run from the receivers to standard earpieces in both ears. It looks awkward and uncomfortable, but the kids don't seem to mind.

The teacher speaks into a microphone/transmitter worn around her neck. If the children can hear anything, they can hear the teacher's voice as she speaks into the microphone. If they cannot actually hear the teacher, they might hear something, and great importance is placed on "the rhythms and cadences of the English language" getting through. "Say *ba-a-a*," says the teacher, smiling. "*Ba-a-a*," says the child. During class, the teachers sign and speak simultaneously. The American School is a total communication school. Every few minutes, the lesson is interrupted and the children are asked, one at a time, to make a sound related to the work or the story in progress. "*Ba-a-a.*" Or sometimes, "*Ba-a-a-l-l-l.*"

Classrooms in schools for the deaf are gardens of electronic delight, filled with television sets, overhead projectors, filmstrip machines, slide projectors, electric typewriters, Polaroid cameras, tape recorders, and a variety of other audiovisual equipment that I was unable to identify.

In the Middle School, the children seem to be doing the same sort of work as those in the lowest grades. The teacher's signing is very rudimentary, truncated, while her English seems rather formal: "Jonathan, do you want to use your pencil or your crayon to draw a picture?" she asks a child, then repeats verbatim. And again. The third time she asks, she also signs: "*You pencil or pencil?*" (sic). Finally, the child responds by picking up a felt-tipped marker. The teacher turns to the next child: "Amy, do you want to use your pencil or your crayon to draw a picture?" Later, I ask her if she finds it difficult to sign and speak at the same time. She appears not to understand the question, and seems in a very bad mood, which is unusual. Most teachers at schools for the deaf are sweet-tempered and kind; they usually all have the look of contented, well-paid professionals.

In the corridor on our way to another classroom, the tour guide warns us about the apparent lack of activity, which must not be misunderstood. "It looks as if nothing is going on," she says, and laughs pleasantly. "It looks like the children are not working, or learning anything that we think of as school subjects. In schools for the deaf, a big part of the education is incidental learning. It's very important. Things that do not have to be taught to hearing children—things they just pick up—must actually be taught to the deaf. The teachers have to explain everything. Simple things like what a bank is. What a check is. About paying rent, mortgages, interest. Everything." As we entered the classroom, the teacher was explaining the evils of cigarette smoking, exhorting the children (they seemed about eleven) not to smoke.

In the High School, the atmosphere was relaxed, happy, and busy, especially in the vocational classrooms. Many rooms are equipped for instruction in various visual trades, printing, photo offset, drafting, and so on, traditional occupations open to young deaf persons. The insurance companies of Hartford have always employed deaf typesetters in the vast printshops that turn out the policies, forms, and brochures of the industry. In a large studio a high school student worked, silent and engrossed, over an illuminated drafting board. The guide gave her entire talk, and we left without his ever having looked up or been aware that we had passed through.

We stopped at the school's video studio where closed-circuit TV programs originate. The teacher declared that the equipment in the room had cost $46,000, and showed us a tape of four deaf students moving in pantomime to a rock record. It ran about three minutes. "It took those kids six months to learn to pantomime that song," he said proudly.

The guide concluded the tour with a few facts. The American School has had more than five thousand graduates, 60 percent of the present graduates go on to post-secondary education. Most students leave the school with achievement levels that are five to seven years below the national average; that is, with around a fourth- or fifth-grade education.

Afterwards we went to the auditorium to watch a film. Nanette Fabray, who is hard of hearing and a celebrity among deaf educators, explained sign language. "Sign language," she said and signed, "helps deaf people understand our conversation." Then she stopped signing. There were various scenes of the school, the playing fields, the classrooms. A teacher was vigorously trying to explain, orally, the rhythms of English. "Fresh and sweet and clean," he sang and tapped out the beat: "Ba-baba ba ba. Repeat . . . Comedy. Com-a-dee."

Major criticisms leveled against deaf education all through the sixties resulted in the adoption of total communication in a large number of schools. The American School brochure defines total communication as ". . . the realistic use of the full language modes: child-devised gestures, the language of signs, speech, speechreading, fingerspelling, reading, writing, and auditory training." ASL was still considered unsuitable for classroom use and incompatible with English, so new sign systems were invented, copyrighted, and sold to the schools. They were especially designed to be manual codes for English and were intended to be used simultaneously with speech. There was a proliferation of new and unknown signs, and a tendency to make the systems conform to the phonetics of English: *right* (correct), *right* (the opposite of left), and *write*, all used the same sign.

There were controversies about the new manual English codes, but the arguments became moot immediately because most teachers worked out a very personal signing style to accompany their spoken remarks. Total communication in practice meant the addition of English signs to all existing techniques in the classroom. Oral training continued at about the same level. The children, who had been able to understand only a fraction of what was going on, began to understand a much larger fraction. There was a move to hire more deaf teachers, but deaf teachers remain a small minority; the only ones I encountered at the American School were in the printshop. Most deaf teachers are instructors in the manual and vocational tracks, in home economics and shop classes that both sexes traditionally take in all schools for the deaf.

After the tour and the film, I find myself on my own. I read the bulletin boards, watch the students, pass the cafeteria, and decide to go in and sit with the teachers.

As soon as it had been established that I was neither a Connecticut State official nor a parent, the teachers began to seem friendly—in a dispirited sort of way. "Oh, a writer. Writers come here all the time." Very openly they gave me their opinions about deaf education. All seemed convinced that teaching deaf children was a difficult, maybe an impossible task; that a fifth-grade reading level was an acceptable goal. One teacher asserted that his deaf students could not grasp abstract ideas. "It's not particularly their fault," he said. "It's deafness. They can only get hold of concrete notions, nothing abstract." No one disagreed with him. Several teachers wandered off, some to other tables. I asked him if by abstract things he meant things like love, hate, greed, envy . . .

"No, no," he said. "They understand those things. But democracy. Hegemony. There aren't even signs for those words," he added.

I wasn't sure I had the concept of hegemony, though I remembered having looked up the word on several occasions. I told him so, and he gave me a playful look, as if he knew I must be kidding. I asked him how long he had been signing, and if it had been difficult to learn.

"Six years, about," he answered. "I took a course. Very easy." He laughed. "When I first saw it, I couldn't believe anyone could learn. It looks so peculiar, and the kids sign so fast. But when it gets slowed down, it's quite simple."

I asked if it was difficult to sign and speak at the same time, and he shook his head, no. "It seems," I said, "that while you're signing and speaking simultaneously, you don't sign everything, but only certain words."

He agreed. "That's how it's supposed to be. I'm glad you brought that up. I've made a study of sign language. It has an interesting history, did you know that? Hundreds of years old, and it's always the same. Very abbreviated. For example, if I wanted to say—signing—*I'd really like to go to the movies with you on Saturday night*, I wouldn't have a sign for *I'd*, and another for *really*, and so on. I would just sign *me*, and then I'd smile—that means, *like*, then just *movies you Saturday night*."

A teacher across the table looked up from her magazine and said, "That's ASL, right?"

"No," he answered. "ASL is completely different. This is signed English. The word order is the same as English, but you never sign every word."

"We learned just the opposite," the second teacher said. "We learned that you had to sign everything."

"No. You got it wrong," he insisted. "Let me show you." He wrote it down on a paper napkin:

I want to go with you to the movies on Saturday night.
Me   you   movies   Saturday night.

"In ASL, it would be more like: *Movies. You. Saturday night. Me.* Word order all mixed up. No syntax. I think they call it free word order. In signed English, we keep the same word order. Otherwise they wouldn't learn English. They'd just use words the way they use signs, in that free order."

This description, in addition to being uninformed, inaccurate, and rude, was terribly out of date. I decided not to argue with him, and instead counted the number of signs and words on the napkin. "Look," I said, "you have only five signs here to represent eleven words. That's not good English. How do the deaf children know the words that are left out?"

"Lipreading," he said.

"They can lipread?" I asked.

He laughed. "They're all expert lipreaders," he said. "When they want to be. Which is not always in the classroom." He laughed again. "You can talk about inflation in class till you're blue in the face and nobody understands a thing. After school, say to them: 'Come on, I'll buy you some ice cream'— and they understand *that* all right. Or else they heard it. A lot of them hear more than they let on. You know what total communication is all about? It's to get around the acting. We sign so the kids can't pretend they don't understand."

"Do they?"

"No. They still complain," he said. "Actually, that's not quite true. They don't complain, they just shrug. They expect not to understand, and when they don't, they just accept it. Why should they bother?"

Suddenly, this rather laid-back, middle-aged teacher turned completely cynical. He lowered his voice slightly. "It's not so bad to be deaf," he said. "They get taken care of. If they don't feel like working, they don't work. A lot of them live on SSI. Know what that is? It's a supplemental Social Security payment just for the handicapped. They can get it and collect welfare, too. Three, four generations of people live on it.

"Look at this school. My kids don't go to such a nice school. Chicken for lunch. My kids are eating peanut butter and jelly sandwiches. Five to one; that's the student/teacher ratio. My kids go to classes that are thirty to one. Any deaf kid that wants to can go to college. Free. They can't read, that's no problem. Money, that's no problem. They have administrators here that I swear just sit around trying to think up how they can spend the money they've got budgeted."

"Are the teachers' salaries . . ." I began, but he gave me a hostile look.

"None of us are exactly in it for the money," he said. "We'd really like to help these kids." He shook his head. "You don't have any idea what it's like, trying to teach kids who can't understand, who have such low language skills. Some don't have any language at all." He shook his head again, sadly, then looked at his watch and said it had been a pleasure. "Wish you could stay longer," he said, smiled, and left.

As I was leaving the cafeteria, I saw him in the hall. "I'm glad I caught you before you left," he said. "I just wanted to remind you that all education is now geared to the individual child. Teachers no longer teach a subject, they teach a child. It's the only way to run a humane educational system, and it started here, in schools for the deaf. We have always considered the individual child and considered the limitations. You remember that." Again, he looked at his watch and said goodbye.

I found a friendly secretary who called a taxi for me, then had to wait a long time. Sitting near the front door, I watched the students, all high school age. They looked like any group of hearing adolescents, but seemed especially independent, aloof. They had contact mostly with each other, and seemed to interact rarely with the many hearing adults in the school. They signed and laughed, grabbed books from each other, shoved and ran boisterously up and down the staircases. The sounds of their movements echoed loudly off the marble walls.

A woman from public information returned from lunch and waved to me, then brought me some brochures and asked if I had any questions. I asked how many deaf teachers worked at the school. "Thirty," she answered. "No, wait a minute, there are thirty deaf staff, not all are teachers. Twenty, I think. Yes, twenty deaf teachers. There are two hundred people altogether on the staff, eighty-five are teachers, and twenty of those are deaf."

"How much does it cost?" I asked. The figure I get at most schools is $8,000 for each child. "Eight thousand dollars," she

said, then, "no, nine. Wait a minute." She went back to her office
and returned as my taxi arrived. "For 1979–80, it will be around
eleven thousand dollars per year, per child."

II

The following morning I drove up the Connecticut River Valley
to Northampton, Massachusetts, a bustling place, substantially
larger and busier than the surrounding villages and college
towns. Its broad main street sweeps past the large gates of Smith
College, and a few hundred yards to the east of that thoroughfare
is the Clarke School, perhaps the most celebrated (certainly the
most oral) oral school in the world. It occupies a large complex
of colonial townhouses, mansions, and new brick dormitories,
the most prominent and newest named for Alexander Graham
Bell. It was here, shortly after the founding of the school, that
Bell met his future father-in-law, Gardiner Greene Hubbard.
Hubbard is honored at the Clarke School as a past benefactor
and Bell is revered as a saint. "We address you on Olympus, Dr.
Bell," said a speaker in the annual Alexander Graham Bell Lecture Series, addressing a prayer to that man in that place, appris-
ing him of all the gains of oral education since his departure, and
raising an anguished cry that if Dr. Bell could but return, the
substantial problems remaining could be solved by the applica-
tion of his genius.

Clarke School Speaks is the name of the school's magazine.
At commencement, each student must deliver a speech; it is a
requirement for graduation. Inside the school, the children can
only communicate with hearing persons wearing microphones.
They cannot hear each other, the trainers they wear only receive
radio signals from the teacher's microphone/transmitter. Their
equipment is the best, the latest, it is kept in perfect working
condition; and the children's ears are always clean. The percentage of children who have truly intelligible speech at the Clarke

School did not appear to me to be any greater than at other schools for the deaf.

Again, I was assigned to a tour. About twelve people had come to visit, teachers and parents mostly, and one family: mother, father, and deaf child about seven years old. We were taken into a first-grade room with one teacher and five pupils, all boys. The teacher pointed to a sentence printed in large letters, mounted on an easel, and talked into her microphone, loudly. A staff member entered the room and sat with the visitors. (All the classrooms had space reserved for visitors.) "Don't pay any attention to me," she said, "just ignore me."

A minute later, she began shouting. "John Smith!" she cried. The woman sitting next to me cringed. The shouting continued, louder. "Larry Jones!" was screamed at about 90 decibels. None of the children made any response. It was a demonstration to prove that the children were indeed deaf, and that since they were responding to the teacher, they could hear her through their equipment. Actually, judging from their responses, only two of the children seemed to be able to follow the gist of the teacher's remarks.

All the children were concentrating very hard. They peered into the teacher's face with an extraordinary degree of attention. They leaned forward, listening, watching, straining. I've never seen that kind of attention in a hearing child. Of course, they have little else to attend to; they can neither hear each other nor any sounds, inside or outside the classroom. Their wireless receivers only pick up the teacher. Should their eyes wander, the teacher immediately summons them to pay attention. When one child began trying to talk about an event not related to the subject (I think it was about a dog), the teacher impatiently interrupted. "I don't know what you think you're chattering about, John," she said sharply.

The next class was in the Middle School: nine-year-olds. They all rose from their desks as we entered. Clarke children are well groomed, polite, respectful. The girls wear skirts and blouses, the boys slacks and shirts, and in the High School some wore neckties. Like preppies from the fifties. We seated ourselves in the visitors' section. The children, accustomed to tours, seemed perfectly poised. The teacher said: "Tell these people your name and where you are from. Not your address, and not the city, just the state." All the children were nodding. The first stood up and said: "Helen Doe. Nine years old."

"No!" said the teacher, shaking her head violently. She gave the directive again, more loudly, including: "not the *city*, just the *state.*"

The child nodded and said: "Helen Doe. Nine years . . ."

"Not your age!" shouted the teacher, throwing her arms on her desk as if in despair, her microphone rattling against the wooden surface.

The child certainly knew she had made a mistake. She either heard the teacher, read the elaborate nonverbal message, or just figured it out. "Helen Doe. Palmer, Massachusetts," she said. The child's speech was not good. There was a great deal missing from those few syllables. It sounded more like: "Ha-en Oh. Paa-er, Maa-eh."

The next child, after receiving the request, gave her name, complete address, and age. The teacher let it go. The third really tried hard. His name was unintelligible, but the words "New York" came through. "Well," said the teacher with much disdain, "everybody knows where you come from, anyway." And so on.

Last, we went to see the High School students. They would be graduating later in the spring. They looked good. Accomplished. With their short haircuts and bobby socks, they seemed even more dated than the younger children. The class was having a discussion, led by the teacher, about adoption. The teacher spoke and wrote down the question, which then appeared on an overhead projector visible to the whole class. The discussion—of a serial nature, one at a time—began at the end of a small semicircle. "Should information about real parents be given to adopted children?" The teacher repeated each answer into her microphone, and wrote it down for projection (there was no noticeable reliance on lipreading).

"Yes," answered the first student, a girl. "I would want to know." Her speech was very good.

"You say, yes, you would want to know. *What* would you want to know?" asked the teacher.

"About my deafness."

"About your deafness. Good. That would be important. You might be able to find out the cause. What else?"

"If any people in my family were bad."

"If any people in your family were bad. You would want to know that, too," the teacher agreed, and looked at each student as she spoke. "If any of them were like the people my husband works with down at probation. Remember we talked about that last week?"

The discussion rambled on, slowly, repetitiously. Before it went anywhere interesting, the teacher, was called out of the room, and I chatted with the woman beside me. She and her husband and child, who was seven and had become deaf only two years earlier, were traveling around the Northeast looking for schools. Her husband, she said, was a skilled electrician and could find work anywhere, so relocation was not a problem once they had decided on a school. Many parents of deaf children make their life plans around schools. The student who had spoken first was sitting in the semicircle almost facing us. She turned and smiled, then looked away shyly. "Oh, if my son could only talk like her. I know he can!"

I looked under the seats where the students had stacked their books. Helen Keller's autobiography was very popular; also biographies of Alexander Graham Bell. Despite claims that oral education made deafness invisible and irrelevant, deafness seemed to be the single, permanent, oppressive topic. At the American School I had found the atmosphere slack, disengaged. At the Clarke School it was stern, severe, and single-minded.

The message conveyed to the students was not that they would ever be comfortably assimilated into the hearing world, but that only by the strenuous exercise of will and intellect (and discretion) would they be tolerated by the hearing world at all.

"We all talk," said George Pratt, president of the school. "It's unlikely to me that the rest of the world is going to learn sign language just to accommodate to the deaf. The deaf have to accommodate to the hearing."

Pratt came to Clarke in 1950, from a job as a history teacher in a high school in Maryland. "My daughter is deaf. She is now thirty-five years old. An architectural draftswoman at Kodak in Rochester. She's the only woman in the office and the only deaf. If she couldn't talk, she'd never be able to have that job." He claims that in the twenty-nine years he's been at Clarke, there have been six children who have failed to learn lipreading, and none has failed to speak. "The American School kindly took them off our hands," he said. "My daughter was diagnosed at one year. The school for the deaf in Maryland was manual. I remember reading a front-page story in the *Baltimore Sun* about the valedictorian at the Maryland school who gave a talk, but didn't talk. How can you give a talk without talking? Sign language," he added in his slightly nasal, slow voice, just barely Southern, "sign language appeared not to be suitable to us.

"Manual schools use a French approach. When Gallaudet went to France in 1815, he brought back this deaf Frenchman who taught them sign language down at Hartford. It was the only method available, and it was definitely not English, it was French. It wasn't till the 1860s that John Clarke, here in Northampton, sitting beside Lewis Dudley and his little deaf girl Theresa in church one Sunday, decided he would try to help them. Eventually, he got in touch with Gardiner Greene Hubbard, who also had a little deaf girl, and they founded the school. Gardiner Greene Hubbard advertised all over New England for deaf students. That's how it started."

Students remain at Clarke School for about twelve years. Average age at entrance is four, and most leave at sixteen, having had more than three thousand hours of speech training. The object of the Clarke School is to mainstream all their students. Upon graduation they are encouraged to go on to a hearing high school. I had assumed that these graduates would enter the high schools as juniors and seniors and remain to finish the last two years. Actually, according to figures that Dr. Pratt gave me, most graduates enter in seventh, eighth, and ninth grades. Moreover, a report proudly offered by Dr. Pratt on the educational achievement of 310 graduates over a fourteen-year period shows the median reading level at 5.7—fifth grade plus seven months. Only 4 of the 310 were reading near grade level; those 4 ranged from 11.0 to 11.9.

These scores were not much different from the achievement levels claimed by the American School; they were, in fact, a little on the low side when compared to the scores I had been collecting from numerous schools throughout the country.

I tried to engage Pratt in a discussion of sign language, but he showed no interest in the subject. Clarke School students had no need or knowledge of sign language, it was never an issue, he said, and would not discuss it. Not even hypothetically. It was unspeakable. Before concluding the interview, I did manage to ask if there were any deaf faculty at the school.

"One. The shop teacher. It's good for the kids to have a deaf adult around."

From many sources, I had heard that severe penalties were imposed on Clarke students who signed. Loss of privileges, confrontations in the principal's office, parents summoned to meetings—and there were always the rumors of expulsion. I naturally wondered why such punishment was necessary for a crime that, according to Pratt, never happened. The oralists believe that deaf children sign only because they have not been taught to speak; that given speech, no matter how imperfect, and an environment free of temptation (that is, of signers), they will all automatically choose to use speech. Speech, however, is useful and necessary only in contacts between the deaf and the hearing. There is no real acknowledgment about what deaf people are to do when they get together with other deaf people. Ideally, the Clarke School expects that all their graduates will associate exclusively with the hearing. In addition to their historic hope of improving the gene pool, these associations are seen as providing deaf adults with continuous opportunities for practicing their oral skills, thus turning friendships between deaf and hearing into permanent speech therapy situations.

This preference for a hearing-only society for each deaf person is stated very explicitly, though somewhat hypocritically; they know perfectly well that the deaf seek out each other's company. The oralists seem to cherish a fantasy that when deaf people congregate, they will all be talking and lipreading the Queen's English. But few deaf people are willing or able to live out that fantasy. Moreover, the facts of twentieth-century life prevent deaf children from being sheltered in an oralist cocoon. By the time they enter middle school (at the latest), they know that the world of the deaf is a signing world.

The Clarke School pursues a busy schedule of athletic events with the deaf leagues throughout New England. Their teams (the Cougars), complete with cheerleading squads, travel to other schools for the deaf, and are visited by them. Virtually all the other deaf players sign—and have some irreverent signs for the Clarke School. By the time they are in high school, Clarke students have become aware that Gallaudet College is a real possibility for them. Many choose to go there, and an even larger number go to the National Technical Institute for the Deaf (NTID) in Rochester, a manual institution.

The gap between oral and signing institutions seems to dissolve at the higher, more heavily funded levels, and the same people are actively involved in running both. Dr. S. Richard Silverman, who apostrophized Dr. Bell on Olympus, served on NTID's original planning board. He is also chairman of the NTID National Advisory Group, and a member of the Board of Fellows of Gallaudet College. In his lectures at the Clarke

School, Silverman characterizes advocates of sign language as those who would have the deaf become "contented members of a subculture secure in its mores, its sanctions, its modes of communication, and its opportunities for social expression." He contrasts manual communication with the idea that there is something else, "something right ... and if it is done early enough and properly, deaf children need little if any specialized instruction." At NTID, with an interpreter at his side, he talks of costly specialized instruction to an audience that is more mundane than Olympian.

A few days after my visit to Northampton, I encountered a group of Clarke School students at the Springfield bus terminal. They were all enthusiastically signing to each other.

III

"Most teachers of the deaf think of their pupils as non-functioning talking machines."

Ray Stevens is principal of the Austine School in Brattleboro, Vermont. The school is beautiful, built on the side of a hill overlooking a lovely valley with a background of green mountains. The principal's office is small and cluttered and overlooks the back of another building, but is strategically located in the center of all the comings and goings of the school community.

Stevens is a committed teacher, extremely hardworking, cranky, intelligent, savvy, and essentially masochistic in the pursuit of his profession. And he has a nice school to show for it. High reading scores. "Relatively," said Stevens. "Last year we averaged eight-point-two—eighth grade plus two months. Only one school in the country had higher, St. Rita's in Cincinnati. Of our fourteen graduates last year, three were reading at the twelfth-grade level. But one," he added compulsively, painfully, "scored just a little better than third."

The school is very small; 120 students from preschool through high school, and all the staff agree that it's a perfect size.

Most schools for the deaf are essentially ungraded, but Austine has a real secondary program and offers actual high school subjects. All upper-level students take four years of math, science, social studies, and English. There is strong emphasis throughout the school on reading and writing. Every day, each teacher has a writing class of four students. The day I was there, Stevens was working on embedded clauses.

"If you ask a deaf child—and possibly a non-native speaker—who is sick in the sentence *The man who saw the dog was sick*, they're likely to answer, 'The dog was sick.' See, it says so right there, *the dog was sick.* They never heard it, they're just looking at it. They sometimes get confused about how the constituents within sentences work."

The school also seems to have a positive attitude about ASL. Relatively, as Stevens would say. I saw teachers at Austine correct children for using the wrong sign, a correction considered not worth making or even noticing at most other schools. Also, I saw a teacher go to some trouble to find out a correct sign. She stepped into the hall as Stevens was passing and asked him. He sent her, with her class, to find and consult one of the older kids. "ASL is a language," he said. "We respect it. Of course the teachers ask the kids for a correct sign. Who else would they ask? I guess," he added, "that not all the teachers here feel that way about ASL."

A few years ago the high school put together the Austine Idiom Project. They listed 150 common idioms of English and translated them on videotape into ASL. "*Kick the bucket,*" said Stevens. "*On the fence.* That kind of thing always gives deaf readers a lot of trouble. They just never heard them in ordinary conversation. Reading is always difficult and most deaf kids read rather literally. An idiom like *playing the field* causes quite a lot of anxiety the first few times it's encountered."

Stevens is thirty-seven, pale and bearded. He seems both young and old. He is tall but walks with a bad stoop; he suffers from arthritis. One afternoon I saw him walking across the grounds with three of his students, and all three had listed forward into a sympathetic stoop. At his office door, Stevens straightened them into an upright position before letting them go.

Stevens grew up on a farm in South Dakota. "They spoke Norwegian at home." When he was seventeen, and looking for a college, he visited a small Lutheran institution in Sioux Falls and was told they had a program in deaf education. "I went back to the farm and thought about it very seriously." He nodded, seriously. "Seemed like a useful and interesting thing to do. So, in the fall, I enrolled." He graduated in 1964 with a major in history and psychology and a minor in deaf education. His first job was with an oral school in Minnesota. "It was awful," he said. "I remember the day I realized that I couldn't stand it. There I was, in front of the class, trying to tell them about George Washington." He got up and faced me, becoming a teacher, and consulted an imaginary book. "*George Washington was a tall man.* I looked at the kids and they were looking back at me, not understanding. *Tall,* I said." He raised his hand over his head and smiled, expectantly. "*Tall. George Washington was a tall man.* Then I'd look around the classroom and ask the kids, *Got it? Tall. O.K.? O.K.?* And they'd just look at me. When I got eye contact, they'd nod. These kids were twelve or thirteen years old. We were nowhere near George Washington was the father of our country, or the first President of the United States, or even the cherry tree. All I could say to them was *George Washington was a tall man.* Can you imagine it?"

I had to laugh. I had sat through a lot of classes just like it. "Finally," Stevens said, "one of the big kids got up and said, 'I understand. You and me, we understand, but they don't understand. They're stupid.' But he didn't understand, either. That was the terrible part of it.

"I realized what a foolish waste oral education was. The next year I went to Gallaudet and learned sign language. Learned

ASL." He smiled. "That was 1965. A lot of people were interested in ASL. I took linguistics courses with Stokoe. He was just finishing the dictionary. My ASL was considered pretty good. I have a Norwegian accent.

"I became engaged to a deaf girl in Washington. Got excellent instruction from her. Every night. For a long time. We broke up eventually. I don't know exactly why. The deaf/hearing thing is complicated. Most of the deaf/hearing marriages I'm familiar with, the man is deaf. Deaf society is strongly male-dominated, but the women set the social tone. Maybe if either of us had been a more outgoing or adventurous individual . . . but we were both very quiet people. Homebodies.

"I worked at Kendall, the elementary school at Gallaudet. It was very interesting for a while. Developed lots of new things, and had lots of ideas. Washington is terribly political, though. The principal was one of the good people—he's with HEW now—and somehow, I always thought it was through no fault of his, the politicking got out of hand. The place went downhill instantly. I came here to Austine in 'sixty-nine as a teacher, and became principal the following year. In 'seventy-four, I took a leave and went to Syracuse to get my Ph.D. Came back in 'seventy-seven again as principal."

The school uses a large amount of material that the staff itself has designed, developed, and produced. Stevens constantly complained about the shortage of good classroom materials for deaf children. "I went to Norway last summer and visited schools for the deaf. They've only got around five schools in the whole country." He laughed. "They argue about whether to use Signed Norwegian or NSL, you know. But they're really very well organized. The deaf social clubs have assumed the responsibility for teaching sign language to all the hearing parents of all deaf children in the country. The schools have books specially written for deaf schoolchildren. They've got a history of Norway. They've even got a history of the United States. I was thinking of trying to get it translated. We've got nothing like

that. Their attitude recognizes that deaf children who are reading at a fourth- or fifth-grade level might be very intelligent; they
can understand more than they can comfortably read. Interesting information can be written in short, simple sentences, too.
But if our kids are reading on a low, fourth-grade level, all
they've got to read is fourth-grade books—*The Little Engine
That Could.*

"We've adapted some readings for our kids here. Just edited
them. Changed complex sentences to shorter ones; avoided the
passive voice and embedded clauses. That sort of thing. *The
man who kissed the cheerleader with the big blue eyes is the
football coach.* Too involved for people who have never heard
English and have trouble reading. They can pull it apart, and
look things up, but it's no fun. They lose interest in finishing the
story. We need interesting books written on simpler levels.

"Deaf children are starving for information. Almost everything they learn is new to them. But in most deaf classrooms
they talk about the same things every day. What they had for
dinner last night, and whether or not it's raining. They keep
saying how important incidental learning is, but in most deaf
schools incidental learning is only about stringbeans and mittens
and socks."

Stevens thinks the ideal classroom would be a large station
wagon with a deaf teacher who would drive the children around
the countryside, exploring.

"Materials are one of the biggest problems. When I go to a
conference of teachers of the deaf, I like to run a materials display. Teachers actually line up to get a look, and usually, I have
the only display."

I asked about the media products that were designed for the
deaf: captioned films, slides, videotapes. Stevens laughed. "The
bureaucracy is terrible. The Bureau of the Handicapped has set
up several media centers across the country and each specializes
in one kind of thing. Slides in the East; films in the West. It's so
complicated that it's almost impossible to get, say, a videotape

because it's produced in a different region. Once in a while I get hold of some good materials, like captioned films. Friend of mine got some for me. I didn't want to ask too many questions, but who knows where he got them."

Lunch at the Austine School was very pleasant, the food good: a strictly Yankee version of chicken chow mein with lots of fresh vegetables. A bowl of fruit was on the table, and there was marvelous home-baked nut bread, also very New England. The food at all the schools for the deaf is excellent. I think there is a sensitivity left over from the time when the schools were asylums, institutions run by state charities on budgets so small that the diet was dependent on deforming porridges. The new institutions, no matter how else they might be found wanting, are highly successful in providing physical amenities. We sat at a large round table and were joined by other teachers, and by Richard Lane, the headmaster. Stevens as principal is responsible for the academic program; Lane handles all the other aspects of running a residential school.

Lane was expressing cheerful irritation at the soccer coach of another school who had been trying, by phone, to cancel a match scheduled for that afternoon. "I told him it wasn't raining here," Lane said, looking out the large windows. I would have described the downpour as relentless. "I'm sure it's going to clear up," Lane said, as he was called to the phone again.

Looking around the dining room, I thought of all the cafeterias in hearing schools and all the teachers I knew whose only wish was to brick them up. This one was quiet and serene. The children were eating and signing, and that took some tricky coordination. There wasn't any shoving, stomping, yelling, spitting, talking with mouths full, or other expressions of oral aggression. Several older students were working in the kitchen, happily. Stevens said they got paid for their work.

The teaching staff was young. Most seemed in their late

twenties or thirties, and impressed me as gentle and somewhat introverted. They were all very quiet. The senior teacher was Mr. Igleheart. When he wasn't teaching, he could always be found in his office, correcting papers or editing stories for classroom use, and listening to classical music at very low volume. While the principal had spent the summer in Norwegian schools for the deaf, the senior teacher had taken his wife on a trip to Iceland to "escape the terrible Vermont heat."

Dick Lane appeared to be the only real extrovert among them. White-haired, urbane, and optimistic, he was also a facile and witty signer, and seemed on especially good terms with all the children (they smile at him slyly when he greets them, they beam and giggle, and as often as not go into hysterics). Lane grew up close to a deaf community; his mother was a social worker at the Illinois School for the Deaf, and he learned ASL there, as a child, from his playmates. He trained at the Lexington School in New York when it was in Manhattan, at Lexington Avenue and 67th Street.

"New York was wonderful in nineteen forty-nine," he said. "Central Park. Columbia. It was beautiful. A wonderful time to be a young man in New York. The Lexington was very famous. All oral, of course. They used the 'natural method.' Margaret Groht. Nobody had the results with it that she did. A brilliant teacher. She did it, that's what the whole method was, it was her. She was the glue.

"You should have seen the hearing aids then, thirty years ago. A and B batteries, printed circuits. Like a grand piano kind of thing with the high strings cut. Lost most of the consonants."

He had to renegotiate the soccer game again, and when he returned we gossiped about various schools. Rivalry is keen among them, and speculation always wide-ranging. Lane said that the rumor in the field was that MSSD, the model high school at Gallaudet, costs around $33,000 per year per pupil. (I had checked out budgets, and MSSD did, in fact, cost exactly that in 1978–79. In my opinion, MSSD is one of the supreme

comic-tragedies of deaf education.) I told him that I had estimated that the cost of educating a deaf child through college was
between $200,000 and $300,000—unless they went to MSSD, in
which case it would be more. He didn't like to hear such big
numbers coming from an outsider, and immediately took umbrage. With pencil and paper, he tried to prove to me that a deaf
classroom costs no more to run than an ordinary classroom in a
hearing public school. Chastened but amused, I left him to visit
some classrooms.

Few of the teachers displayed the ability or the outlook of
Stevens and Lane. Maybe they were too young, or too serious.
Only a few were really good signers, which was a terrible disap-
pointment. It seemed to me that the whole point of using signs
was to give the kids a language they could understand. I asked
Stevens about it. "Do you do anything here at the school to improve the signing of the staff, or evaluate them?"

He looked pained. "It's something we talk about a lot. It
takes years for some people, I'm afraid. Like any language," he
said. "They're all good teachers, though."

They did seem like very good teachers, and they all appeared
to approach teaching as an active profession, an active process.
They worried about material to cover, tests to pass, subjects to
teach. (I wonder when the idea of teaching the child instead of
teaching the subject became fashionable? Is that when the decline set in?) But I couldn't tell what the staff's attitude was toward deafness, or what sort of personal relationships they had
with their pupils outside the classroom. Their concern was education—at a staff meeting, one teacher described a disappointing
student as "just lacking education." They were an unusual collection of authentic teachers; and I left Brattleboro exhausted,
with the singular impression that everybody up there works
very hard.

I had begun my search believing that sign language was out of
the closet and that oralism had dwindled to a small, compara-

tively ineffectual force. Two years later, I was still looking for good signs. The total communication schools still emphasized the same shop-worn oral methods, and still avoided ASL. There were many reasonable arguments to support the use of signed English in the schools—but the schools weren't even using good signed English. Only a small number of teachers were skillful, sympathetic signers. On the hands of most, sign language fitted the derogatory description of the oralists: it was a rough, rudimentary, incomplete system with no grammar. Nevertheless, total communication was a tremendous improvement in deaf education. The children were apparently able to make use of any signs they were offered, and their own signing was encouraged in the classrooms.

IV

The New York State School for the Deaf (NYSSD) in Rome, New York, is one of the great old residential schools; the original building went up in 1875. It was the first school I visited, and my first contact with deaf education.

In 1977, I had been told that NYSSD had a fairly large deaf staff, including several classroom teachers. Two years later, in 1979, when I called to arrange a second visit, I learned that all but one deaf teacher, Andrew Wallace, had left the school. I made an appointment to see him.

Though I had said I would need an interpreter, he met me in the school lobby alone, introducing himself in sign and in perfectly modulated speech: "I'm Andy Wallace." He talked comfortably as we walked through the halls and into a quiet room where we sat at a table.

"Can you hear me?" I asked.

"No," he answered. "I am profoundly deaf. I'm speechreading you. I lost my hearing when I was two, from meningitis." At age twenty-nine, he was beginning his fourth year of teaching in Rome. A few weeks earlier, he told me, he had gotten married to another teacher at the school, who is hearing. Both families, he said, were very pleased.

Wallace comes from Cleveland, the second child in a family of four children and the only one who is deaf. His father is a physician, and his mother is a nurse. He went to the Millridge School, an oral day school in Cleveland, then to Allegheny College in Meadville, Pennsylvania. He had notetakers in college, but no interpreters. After graduating from college, he took his teacher training at Case Western Reserve. Before coming to Rome he ran a community program for deaf infants in Cleveland that advised families trying to make plans for their children and offered home-based instruction.

Wallace worked toward a Ph.D. at Syracuse for several years while teaching at Rome, but decided to remain a teacher and left graduate school before beginning a thesis. "It seemed that everybody expected me to go to Washington when I had the degree. They guaranteed that I'd be a bigshot in HEW as soon as I finished." He shook his head. "Turned me off. I doubt anybody ever helped people from Washington," he said. "I wanted to stay with the kids. Couldn't stand the idea of being a bureaucrat. I'm taking some courses at St. Luke's Hospital now, and I'd like to set up another baby clinic in the future."

He was, without question, the best speechreader I had ever met, and I told him so. He accepted the remark with equanimity. "I went to a speech pathologist for three hours every day after school for oral training. For years and years. God, was it boring!"

"Are you sorry?"

"No, I'm not sorry. I think it would have been better if I had had sign language earlier and had been able to use it."

"Where did you learn?"

"At school. You know, we all used it. When the teachers weren't looking." He said he considers sign language essential. "It helps skilled deaf people to improve their English, and it helps deaf people who aren't skilled"—he shrugged—"to become smart deaf people."

When I asked him about the signing of the hearing teachers, he made a sour face. "I'm head of a committee to study and improve signing. It's a very political issue. Evaluations . . ." He shook his head. "They don't like it. The union won't stand for it. We offer courses and demonstrations and discussions. Try to tempt them rather than forcing it. Some of the teachers are very good signers. My wife has beautiful signs." He looked at me. "It really is a problem."

"Who gives the courses?"

"There are several deaf people who work in the after-school programs and in the dorms."

"Do you sign English in your classes, or ASL?"

"When I'm teaching from a book, I use signed English and follow the English word order," he said. "Of course, when I want to explain something to the kids that they don't understand, I use ASL.

"Having more deaf teachers would be good. Not many deaf teachers want to move to Rome, I guess. Small deaf population."

"Is there a deaf club here?" I asked.

"Deaf people around here," he sighed, "they're country deaf. I don't like to be around them very much. Most of my friends are hearing, and deaf people from the school. Oh, in Cleveland, it's different. When I'm home, I go to a deaf club. Lots of interesting people there. I have a good friend in Cleveland who's in medical school. He's in his second year. A very smart person."

After we had talked for about forty minutes, Wallace seemed fatigued. Speechreading takes concentrated effort. I had not consciously altered my questions to provide him with easily read words, and at first, he had no trouble with terms like "sibling position," and "linguistics"; nor did he show any stress over changes in topic. Later in the conversation, though, he began to miss some words and asked me to repeat or paraphrase.

When I told him I'd like to meet his wife, he rose immediately and looked at his watch. He said she'd be free in a short time and invited me to his classroom until then. On the way, he told me about his pupils. They were kids with special problems, he said, and learning disabilities. ("They always give the worst kids to the deaf teachers," Bill Stokoe had once observed. "The ones with the most severe problems. If they gave those teachers the best kids, or even just the normal kids, something interesting might happen in deaf education.")

"We have a new girl from Albany," said Andy Wallace. "She's not deaf, she's autistic. I was worried about her, but she's making good progress. Doesn't seem too bad to me. She's learning signs. Makes eye contact." He shrugged again. "Maybe she just needed a deaf environment."

The last time I was at the school, the principal (who has since left) told me that the children's affection for the deaf teachers was extreme. He had shown some embarrassment in telling me about it. "Their love is so real, so happy, and so intense," he had said, gravely, "frankly, it's hard on the hearing teachers. They wouldn't be human if they didn't feel it. A little jealous, I mean."

In the corridors at Rome, Andy Wallace was a celebrity. Hands waved to attract his attention. Small bodies jumped up from the floor. When the children saw him coming, they stopped and waited like a reception committee; then they tagged after him for as long as they could, till he sent them away. After class, we walked to the high school building to meet Sue Wallace, and the big boys ambled over and elbowed their way into Andy's line of vision. While we waited, Andy had several spirited conversations, silently, in ASL. Sue Wallace stuck her head out into the crowd that had formed outside her classroom door and suggested that I wait in the teachers' lounge.

Susan Wallace had been teaching at Rome for three years. "I came six months after Andy," she explained. She is in a new experimental program called STEPS—Steps Toward Educating People for Survival. There are only two children in her class, both boys, fourteen years old, mentally retarded, and deaf. Until this program began, two years ago, the school did not take children with such severe retardation. She is with them from 8:30 in the morning, through lunch (they cannot be left alone), and all afternoon until 3. I talked to her on her after-lunch break when an aide took over the class.

Sue's two students live in a sheltered institution, the Rome Developmental Center (RDC), and are bused daily to and from the school. They have no language—Sue is trying to teach them signs, and printed words, and how to count. One of her pupils, she says, is doing well; the other has shown no spark. Both boys are taller and heavier than she. "I took a behavior management course. Simple things like how to block a blow, what to do. Just in case." She thinks that one of the boys—the one who has learned some signs, some words, and some numbers—might possibly have been misdiagnosed, might not be as seriously retarded as they think at RDC. "RDC may have caused a lot of their problems. Some of those kids over there haven't been home in years. It's too bad they can't stay here at the school," she said. "I think they'd learn a lot from dorm life. They might learn sign language." Sue Wallace is presently trying to develop a new curriculum.

Sue herself learned sign language at college, she said. "I went to a small college called McMurray, in Ohio, that gave a bachelor's degree in deaf education. Basically, it was all deaf education. I graduated in December and came here in January. Taught a class of bright sixth graders, and really it was they who taught me sign language." She is just twenty-two years old.

I told her that Andy had said she was a beautiful signer. "Oh, that's a compliment," she said. "I was worried about going out with him at first, but I'm pretty good now. I do some interpreting. I interpret for Andy in his classes. When we started dating, my brother learned sign language. Guess he knew it was going to be serious."

Later, we went to the gym with Sue, whose two pupils were

scheduled for the pool. The gym, in a separate building, was impressively equipped. A large, pale girl wearing gym clothes rushed up and put her arms around Sue's neck, then turned and stared at me. She seemed spacy. She wanted to know who I was and Sue tried to explain. Disengaging herself from the girl's embrace, Sue sent her to line up on the gym floor with a small group of other children, all in matching suits. I asked if the child was on medication.

"Yes," said Sue. "I think so. Quite a few of the kids on the STEPS program are. That's Nina. I worry about her. Some days she seems like a zombie. She makes a little progress, then falls back. I don't know how she'll make out. She doesn't have enough room to regress, really."

The two gym teachers were giants. Great, strong, towering men. While one shaped up the kids on the gym floor, the other passed through leading three of the very smallest children into an adjoining room. They were so tiny they barely reached his knees. Through the door, we could see them doing setting-up exercises on floor mats. Then we went to the pool.

A large aluminum canoe was propped against one wall. The pool was big enough to provide a decent amount of canoeing space. Sue's boys were in the water, each with a teacher, thrashing around, screaming, submerging. Only the teacher's muscular efforts kept every head above water. I found the scene very disturbing, and left to find the new principal, Dr. Frederick Volp. He was quite young, very tall, exceedingly voluble, and a little manic. "Hi," he said, "I'm Rick Volp. Sit down." He had been principal for less than two months. Immediately, he began talking about all the exciting things that were happening and about to happen at the school. He didn't seem to know anything about its history prior to his arrival.

"How old are you?" I asked, politely.

"Well," he answered, "I'm thirty-two."

Volp had no experience with deaf education at all, and had never been to a school for the deaf until he decided to apply for the principal's job. He has a Ph.D. in education from Penn State, and characterized himself as a generalist. "I spent eight years with the great Burt Blatt," he declared, and looked at me eagerly, but I had never heard of Burt Blatt. "He's one of my heroes. After I got my doctorate, I stayed at Penn State as associate director of the Teachers' Corps." Just before coming to Rome, Volp was principal of the Skytop School, a demonstration school at Syracuse, part of the Syracuse City School System. "It was for primary-age kids, multiply handicapped and developmentally delayed. Until Skytop," he explained, "these kids were clinically homeless. They spent a half-day at Skytop, making up the developmental stuff, and the other half mainstreamed in a regular Syracuse school." He lit up at the word "mainstreamed."

I had found many changes at Rome since my last visit, and had been cataloguing them all day. Before Rick Volp's appointment, the school had been without a principal for an entire year. It was no great hardship for the students, apparently, for as Volp told me with great enthusiasm, "For the first time in history, graduates of this school received a New York State diploma!" What he meant was that all sixteen graduates had passed the state minimum competency requirements in reading and math. I was impressed. "Next year," Volp said, smiling, "I want to go after the Regents basic competency. The one they passed last year was tied to a seventh- and eighth-grade level. Next year, the Regents will peg it to a *ninth*-grade level.

"What makes a good school?" he inquired. "Did you ever ask yourself that?" He sat back, folded his hands. "Just think about it a minute. What makes a good school? I know very intelligent and able educators who have been asking just that. What *does* make a good school?"

He seemed to be waiting for an answer. "Good teachers?" I ventured. Wrong.

"A good school sets high standards for itself. That's what we're going to do here. Set high standards. We've changed the schedules. Instituted more teacher-contact hours, eliminated study halls that were really just recess, and given the kids more actual study time."

It didn't sound bad to me; but it did seem to fly in the face of tradition. Deaf education, by definition if not by design, has had a long history of low standards.

"The way I think about it, deaf kids are just like hearing kids. They just can't hear so good. Well"—he smiled again—"maybe not quite that, but close. Let's give it a try. This is a lighthouse school, perhaps our beacon must burn brighter," he said, then added cheerfully, "That's a metaphor." I nodded and dutifully wrote it down in my notes. "Lighthouse," he said. "Beacon." I nodded. "We are going to set high standards, and we are going to put it in writing. Spell it all out in the IEPs."

The IEPs are the Individualized Educational Programs: the written contract between the school and the parent that specifies what the school will undertake to teach the child, and what services will be provided during the coming year. At all the schools I visited, teachers and administrators were moaning over the IEPs, and over the new bureaucratic nightmare Public Law 94-142, the federal legislation that has probably changed the entire nature of special education. It's the mainstreaming law.

"We are mainstreaming, now. In this school," Volp said.

"What do you mean?"

"Our auxiliary activities, like athletic programs at the Rome Y, are already mainstreamed. We could possibly mainstream the Boy Scouts too," he said. (The Rome school has the oldest deaf Boy Scout troop in the country. They have been invited to merge with hearing troops many times in the past, but felt great pride in maintaining the oldest charter.)

"We have hearing kids mainstreamed in this school," Volp said emphatically. "*Hearing* children."

"Do you mean the mentally retarded children from the Rome Developmental Center?"

"Yes," he said. "Some of them are not deaf."

"That's mainstreaming?" I asked.
"Certainly," he replied. "What else is it?"

V

The Education of All Handicapped Children Act, PL 94-142, was signed into law in November 1975 by President Ford, and became fully effective two years later. It extended to handicapped children the concept of equal educational opportunity as argued in *Boston* vs. *Board of Education* in 1954. It mandated the right to free education at public expense; appropriate education (if the child did not fit the program, a program must be designed to fit the child); the right of due process, and nondiscriminatory evaluations—and all this in what the law described as "the least restrictive environment." State and local educational departments were made responsible for implementing the new law, cost to be covered by the states but aided by large federal monies to be awarded according to the number of handicapped children served. Noncompliance would result in the withholding of federal funds, not only the funds promised by 94-142 but also all funds covered by the separate Elementary and Secondary Education Act.

"Mainstreaming" is not defined in the law's text, but "least restrictive environment" was widely interpreted as meaning local education in home districts. Residential schools were regarded as institutions, and therefore, highly restrictive.

The legislation came at a rather good time for the public schools. Faced with declining enrollment, reduced budgets, school closings, and high levels of anxiety among teachers because of imminent unemployment, the local schools diversified—tooled up to receive the handicapped. It was a drastic change of direction. As educational instruments (tests on paper) became more refined over the last decades, larger and larger numbers of children were diagnosed as minimally brain-damaged, perceptually handicapped, and learning-disabled. Because of depressed test scores, these children have been taken out of their classrooms. Now, with 94-142, children with real and serious physical handicaps are being mainstreamed—integrated into regular classrooms—all over the country.

The law was a direct result of legal action initiated by parents and organizations on behalf of a group of retarded children. None of the original cases concerned children who were deaf, and throughout the deaf educational system mainstreaming was considered irrelevant. The law seemed to be intended for two types of children. The first were those excluded from neighborhood schools because of some physical or mental handicap. Many had orthopedic problems—were in wheelchairs, perhaps, and unable to get around ordinary school buildings. For a number of these children, all that was needed was an extra teacher's aide, the removal of barriers, or the construction of ramps. Others in this category had mental or emotional difficulties that prevented them from keeping up with their classmates. Frequently, children with physical handicaps and children with mental problems had been assigned to the same classrooms, in random locations, that were merely holding operations and provided no particular education at all.

The second kind of pupil that 94-142 seemed intended to serve was the more severely retarded and multiply handicapped, already confined in custodial institutions. It was suspected (with reason) that many of these children had been diagnosed incorrectly, with unnecessary harshness, or despair. There were certainly deaf children in both groups.

By 1980, the concept of mainstreaming was expanded to include all deaf children: those with moderate impairments, some of whom were already attending public schools; and those enrolled in residential schools for the deaf, on the grounds that residential schools constituted a restrictive environment. The most obvious question to ask about mainstreaming is: How can

American education, which has failed so many hearing children, hope to succeed with the deaf?

It was not easy to find or arrange to visit mainstreamed class-rooms. The larger and more centralized the institution, the more accustomed it is to being observed. The state schools were open, and for the most part hospitable; the local schools, much less so. I had to go from local school principal to district administration to special education department to coordinator of hearing-impaired (H.I.) programs. In one district, when I found the H.I. coordinator, he told me that there were no hearing-impaired children in the district, though I knew two of them personally.

In one large Eastern city, I left detailed messages and wrote letters, and eventually received a telephone call from the office of the director of handicapped services. I was given the phone number of a school, and the name of a teacher (I will call her Miss King). If she wanted to make an appointment with me, it was all right with the director, I was told. I telephoned Miss King at her school, a junior high school, and we made an appointment. She seemed to have a slight German accent.

All the mainstreaming situations I've seen are organized around a special room, usually called something like the Hearing-Impaired Resource Room, and the deaf children spend most of their time there. Ideally, the room is looped for radio transmission and the children wear hearing aid/amplifiers. The kind known as the Phonic Ear was very popular in schools I visited throughout the East.

Typically, deaf children get all their schooling in their resource rooms, and are mainstreamed (with hearing children) for lunch and recess, and sometimes gym or art. Theoretically, they can attend classes with hearing children either with or without an interpreter, when they are ready, if they have progressed sufficiently to keep up with the class at grade level and have no other problems. A few children, usually those who have a mild or moderate hearing loss, are mainstreamed for everything except reading and language arts, which they continue to take in the resource room. Many, however, only leave for appointments with a speech therapist once a week.

Miss King's accent turned out to be the product of twenty years of speech therapy: she was hearing-impaired. "I have a sixty-five dB loss in both ears. It's in the moderate-to-severe range, I think. Without my ear molds I'm lost, but I manage quite well with them." A small woman, blond, dainty, and neat, she gave her age as twenty-seven and a half. She was working with two students, a strapping, six-foot-tall sixteen-year-old boy named Johnny, and a chubby thirteen-year-old girl named Debbie, who was intensely shy and cringed under my gaze. Both were black. It was June, near the end of the school year, the end of Miss King's first year of teaching, and the end of the first year of mainstreaming for both students. Until being assigned to Miss King, both had been in classes for the retarded. "Johnny wasn't diagnosed until he was thirteen. Debbie was ten or eleven. She was in a class for MRs [mentally retarded]. They never went beyond reading readiness books."

Johnny was reading at about the third-grade level now, and his speech was good. Work was displayed on the walls, and I walked around the room looking at it. There were drawings of Americana, with short paragraphs printed beneath. "That's mine," Johnny called to me. "I did that." I turned and said it was good work. He looked embarrassed. "I did all those," he said, then lowered his head to his book and looked busy.

"If we can keep him in school," said Miss King, "he'll probably do O.K. He had such a late start, and he's so big, I'm afraid he'll drop out." She sounded doubtful. For the other student, Debbie, she felt more confidence. "Debbie's really bright. I mean really bright. She learned cursive writing in two weeks. She has beautiful penmanship and her spelling is excellent. How they had her in a class of MRs is unbelievable. The system certainly failed for Debbie." Miss King had no idea how Debbie and Johnny found their way into her classroom. Both youngsters just turned up assigned to that school.

Miss King was raised in upstate New York. She had been educated in public schools before there were special programs and resource rooms, and had been the only deaf person in her elementary and high school. "I had speech therapy three times a week. I hated all my speech therapists. *Hated* them," she said. She attended a small college near her home, then took an M.A. in deaf education at Gallaudet. Mainstreaming had created a demand for teachers of the deaf, and when this district advertised, she applied and got the job. "The administration doesn't know anything about deafness," she said. "Nothing. They pay for the hearing aids, that's it. Phonic Ears cost fourteen hundred dollars apiece, incidentally. The room isn't even looped.

"I work here completely alone. I think all the teachers of the deaf in this city do. I have no supervisor, and I'm never evaluated." She laughed. "I kept calling up central administration asking for someone to come over and see the classroom. They acted like I was wacko. This is my first year of teaching, and I wanted some contact with—someone. They sent a teacher, finally, who sat right there for an hour. When I got her report, all it said was, 'Repeats too much.' I gave up.

"I can laugh about it now, but it upset me a lot at first, in September. There's just no plan. Nobody knows who the students are who might be here next year. Or where these students will go next. Maybe they plan to leave them here forever? It's possible. There's no program, no coordination. I never talk with any other teachers of the deaf. There are never any meetings. I have no one to talk to.

"I talk to my boyfriend," she went on. "And sometimes I talk to the people on my other job. I work as a medical technician at the hospital. Just one evening a week, and I usually work during school vacations. It's nice to be around people. I've been offered a job in a real mainstream program in Virginia. A real program, with twenty children. I'm thinking about taking it."

Some mainstreamed programs are terrific. In one school in Pennsylvania, I thought the deaf children were getting a better education than the hearing kids. There were eight children in the resource room, a teacher who was intelligent, kind, imaginative, and efficient, and a busy teacher's aide. After spending the morning with the children, I followed them into mainstreamed classes. There were two groups. One went to science, the other to art. Two excellent interpreters accompanied the children. In the fourth-grade science class, there were thirty-five other pupils, and what the teacher was demonstrating seemed hardly worth interpreting. It was an experiment suitable for pre-schoolers.

After science, I looked into the art room. The teacher, with close to forty children, whispered that she was having a discipline problem. For an hour the children had to sit in silence, and were not allowed even to pick up a pencil. The deaf children sat with their interpreter, waiting, sharing in the discipline (mainstreaming for discipline). At the end of the hour, they joyously returned to their resource room.

The object of mainstreaming is to integrate handicapped children into the larger society of children during their school years, and to give them an opportunity to make friends. But deaf children find few friends outside the resource rooms. They cannot communicate with hearing children: they cannot hear them, they cannot speak. The hearing children do not sign. Deaf children are transported to their schools from widely scattered areas, and the likelihood of any two living in the same neighborhood is almost nil. After school, they ride the bus home, and lead solitary lives. Their social contacts are restricted to those with whom they can communicate at home, and to those with whom they can communicate in the resource room—often their only friends.

Instead of restricting deaf children to the buildings, grounds, and playing fields of a residential school, mainstreaming often restricts them to a single room in a public school. Without speech and hearing, their participation in the world of hearing children is essentially unchanged, and their needs remain unfulfilled.

It wasn't until I visited an inner-city day school that I realized the extent to which a deaf child's needs can be left unfulfilled.

For more than a century, the reported incidence of deafness among blacks has been lower than among whites. The reason usually suggested is that because of better food, housing, and medical care, white children have a higher survival rate; diseases that are fatal to black children merely deafen white ones. This hypothesis might account for environmentally caused deafness, but it does not concern those in the population who inherit the genes for deafness, which are not life-threatening and not linked to infant mortality. If there are fewer black deaf people in America, it is quite possible that there are fewer genes for deafness in the black population. It is also possible that many black deaf children are not being classified as deaf, but are classified in some other way that places them outside the deaf educational system.

One Eastern city I visited had, within its boundaries, a large residential school run by the state, a variety of mainstreamed programs throughout the metropolitan area, and a day school for the deaf operated as one of the city schools for more than forty years.

The inner-city day school was located in a borderline neighborhood between an enclave of half-million-dollar townhouses and a respectable working-class area fringed with rubble. Obliquely across from the school, behind fortress walls forty feet high, was an abandoned penitentiary that gave the neighborhood a depressed look psychologically as well as economically. The streets seemed oddly lifeless. Inside the school building the wide halls, varnished doors, and old-fashioned layout reminded me of the schools of my childhood, but this was much quieter. It seemed deserted.

An administrator from Special Ed was waiting to give me a

tour. She was a pleasant young woman; we had visited another city school together. She was, however, completely unenthusiastic about my purpose, and nervous. "It might seem," she said, then smiled and began again, "It might *seem* that all the black children are sent here, and that none go to the mainstreamed schools; but that really isn't the case. Districting just worked out this way."

I had, of course, noticed few black children in the other programs. "How many black children do you have here?" I asked. "Oh, I don't think we keep records according to race," was her answer. Walking around the deserted halls, looking into the quiet classrooms and out into the completely paved-over playgrounds, my estimate was something between 80 and 90 percent.

"Do the children live in this neighborhood, then?"

"Oh, no. They come from all over."

In a fourth-grade classroom, there were six children. The teacher told me that she had eighteen years' experience teaching the deaf. The class was doing drills from the Fitzgerald Key, a textbook published in 1926.

The Fitzgerald Key (the book's actual title is *Straight Language for the Deaf*) attempts to teach reading by breaking down English sentences into formal grammatical units, and providing lots of drill. The book is accompanied by yellow drill sheets, seventeen inches wide, with headings across the top:

Subject:	Verb:	Indirect Object:	Direct Object:	Where:	From: For: With: How:	How far: How often: How long: How much:	When:

Deaf children spent years diagramming the sample sentences given in the book, and identifying each of the parts with special symbols. The Fitzgerald Key was the triumph of oral education and was used in three-quarters of all the schools in America for more than fifty years. The reason for its vast popularity was that there wasn't anything else; it was almost the only book in the field that attempted to teach reading. All other textbooks taught "language"—that is, speech. Fitzgerald's method was designed to give deaf children a better idea of what a particular sentence was about by pointing out the key words—the who's, what's, and how's. It was a great improvement: oral schools considered reading unnecessary and possibly harmful to speech training. Mrs. Fitzgerald's Key was accepted because its heavy emphasis on grammar was supposed to encourage a general knowledge of the English language. Unfortunately, the children rarely went beyond the ninety-seven-page text, and rarely read anything except the isolated sample sentences it contained.

The teacher I observed didn't bother with sentences at all. For the entire half hour I was in the room, the class did verb drills. The teacher wrote infinitives on the blackboard, and asked the children to supply the correct tenses: *To see—present as a question*, she wrote. *To eat—present progressive.* The class (and I) had a hard time with that one. The teacher wrote *is eating* on the board, and the kids filled in their yellow sheets. In an aside, the teacher said that her class was the brightest in the school. I asked if they were reading at grade level. "I wouldn't know," was the stiff reply.

Next, I was taken to the telecommunications center, a vast room on the ground floor that contained about a dozen IBM electric typewriters attached to television monitors. Messages typed on the typewriter are displayed on the screen. New telecommunications devices being developed for the deaf may look something like this in the future, with hook-ups to computers. These machines weren't hooked up to anything, they were just for training purposes. Both the administrator and the teacher who ran the center seemed proud of their equipment, and said that no other school in the state had such wonderful technology or was preparing deaf students to use TTYs.

The class ended shortly, and the teacher, a young man, joined us at a table and lit a cigarette. He had a few minutes free,

he said, and could talk. He had a breezy manner; his high tenor
voice tinged with hysteria. He asked immediately what my interest was in the school, and how much I knew. Specifically, he
wanted to know which other schools I had visited. He had come
to work here after several years at a famous residential school
and considered his present situation a come-down. "This is just a
gimmick," he said, nodding toward the machines. "You gotta
have a gimmick. So what? I mean, the kids would learn to use a
TTY without all this."

I asked about the students' reading.

"Off the top of my head, I'd say the average for the whole
school, I mean the *whole* school," he shrugged, "second grade.
Tops. And you know what that means? A lot of the kids can't
read at all."

"How can they use a TTY if they can't read?"

"You've got a point," he answered, and blew smoke into the
center of the room. "This place is the pits," he said. "Nobody
gives a damn. What a place to bring deaf kids. Look at it. No rugs
on the floors. Those hearing aids pick up everything, every foot-
step." He shook his head. "We can't teach them anything. We
can't even communicate with them. It's supposed to be a total
communication school. I doubt that even a third of the teachers
know how to sign the barest minimum."

The administrator grimaced, cleared her throat, and finally
said, "Don't talk to a reporter like that."

The teacher grunted. "She knows," he said. "She's been
around. I'm not telling her anything." The administrator sput-
tered, and looked into the yellow pad on my lap. The teacher resumed his dismal recitation, and the administrator alternated between trying to restrain him and trying to laugh the whole thing
off. Soon the teacher announced that he had to go and interpret
at assembly. Before leaving, he gave me his name. He spelled it
and waited for me to write it down. Just to upset the administrator, I thought.

She *was* upset, and seemed discouraged as well. She asked

me if I wanted to go to assembly, and we began walking toward the other end of the building. Suddenly, she brightened. "Wait," she said. "There's someone I want you to meet. Someone nice. The school nurse."

We reversed our direction, and found the nurse's office. She was indeed nice; a straightforward, good-hearted person, trying to do some kind of professional job, without knowing exactly what it should be. "I do triage on these kids," she said.

Triage is a French word that originally meant a simple sort into three parts. It became a medical term for a technique used by military doctors on the battlefield for deciding which of the casualties would be treated immediately, which could wait for later attention, and which must be left to die.

"I honest to God do triage on these kids." She explained the difficulties of getting medical treatment for the children at the school. Some of them, she said, had severe problems. She led me to her desk, and opened a folder for me to inspect. Spread before me was a young student's entire family medical history. His age: eleven; his race: *B*. She pointed to specific entries she wanted me to read. His hearing loss. The notation that he may have diabetes. He had no language, the chart said, and his IQ was listed as between 70 and 80.

The most interesting thing on the chart was the diagnosis: conduction deafness—middle-ear deafness. "Conduction deafness," she said, "is sometimes treatable. Often. It's the only kind that's ever treatable." She had sought a referral for the child; had sent his chart to an ear, nose, and throat clinic requesting an examination to investigate the possibility of surgery to correct the deafness. "It was refused," she said. "Referral denied." She pointed to a notation on the chart. "Why?" she asked, and pointed to the IQ score. "Because he was retarded anyway."

I looked at the chart. "What's going to happen to him?"

"If he does have diabetes," she said, "that could have caused his deafness, I think. Diabetes unchecked does a lot of damage. And if he has it, he'll get worse. Maybe I should try to send him to a diabetes clinic. I'll try, but they'll probably turn that down too. What's going to happen to him? He'll probably wind up being diagnosed deaf/retarded, and eventually be taken out of school and sent someplace else.

"The thing is," she went on, "I don't think he's a so bad. He might even be a pretty bright kid. The reason he has an IQ of seventy to eighty is because he doesn't have any language. That's not a bad IQ for a kid with no language. If he had language, his IQ would be normal. It figures. Doesn't it? Doesn't that make sense?" She closed the folder on her desk and filed it in a rack. "That's the sort of thing I do here," she said.

Information

What the deaf want is information. All their efforts, and all their demands on the hearing world reflect their desire for direct access to information. As a group, they have rarely demanded to be taught speech; their interest in hearing aids is guarded; they don't spend much time or energy trying to invent a better lipreading system. Speech training, amplification, and lipreading are all inventions of the hearing, useful but limited. For the past twenty-five years the deaf community has consistently requested, lobbied, and worked for three things: a telephone they can use; captioned television; and a wider use of sign language interpreters.

In 1964, after years of halfhearted and unfulfilled promises from the communications industry, a deaf man in California named Robert Weitbrecht invented an acoustic coupler that made transmission of typed messages possible over regular telephone lines. There are several models of TTY on the market; the most popular are compact and portable, and look like miniature typewriters with a cradle on top to accommodate the handpiece of a telephone.

Anyone with a TTY, and telephone service, can dial a number, place his handpiece on the cradle, and type out a message to someone with similar apparatus on the other end. The message can be a paper printout, or may appear in a ribbon of electronic type. The system is expensive when compared to the telephone; a TTY costs in the neighborhood of $500, and because typed messages take longer to transmit than spoken ones, deaf people have higher phone bills. At present, government offices, local health facilities, railroads, airlines, and even brokerage houses have installed the devices, and a large proportion of the deaf population is expected to be using this means of communication in the future. Without a TTY, all the things that are done by hearing people over the telephone—making appointments, seeking services, booking travel reservations, keeping in touch with friends and relatives—must be done by the deaf either in person or by mail.

Captioned television became a reality toward the end of the 1970s. News programs and a small number of shows on educational and local stations were captioned. These used a system known as open captioning: the captions were added at the local stations and appeared on all the television screens in the viewing area. Beginning in 1980, largely through the efforts of the Bureau for the Handicapped, a system of closed captioning began: captions added to a large group of commercial programs could be picked up only on television sets equipped with special decoders. The decoding device can now be purchased throughout the country and is easily installed on a home set. It costs about $300 (plus the cost of the set). In addition to other advantages, it's still a lot cheaper to be hearing than to be deaf.

Sign language interpreters come from within the deaf community itself. Traditionally, they have been the hearing, bilingual children of deaf parents, and also interested professionals who learned the language naturally, by association, usually in the residential schools: teachers, ministers, social workers—and *their* children, who grew up in a signing environment. The last decade has seen a new group of interpreters emerge from the ranks of the ASL linguists, and it's not unusual to observe a young academic with a Ph.D. leave the research laboratory or classroom to meet an interpreting commitment to a deaf colleague.

Sign language interpreters are a highly self-selected group. Those who use their bilingual skills professionally are likely to be those who have positive opinions about deafness, who feel respect for and pleasure in using signs. Good interpreters are manually as well as verbally dexterous individuals who are comfortable playing the minor, often self-effacing role of helper. Until recently, interpreting arrangements were informal and rarely included payment. Even when modest fees were established, interpreting offered only the most occasional, part-time employment. Most interpreters for the deaf are women.

In the mid-1960s, interpreters began to get together to set standards, train new interpreters, and establish fees. Interpreting was recognized as a profession at about the same time that ASL was recognized as a language.

The Center on Deafness at California State University, Northridge (CSUN), is the largest employer of sign language interpreters in the world. Two hundred deaf undergraduate students are enrolled along with 25,000 hearing students. The Center grew out of something called the Deaf Leadership Training Program, which was set up in 1964. The first year it enrolled ten hearing graduate students studying school administration. Before the semester was over, everyone working with the program agreed that something was missing. The second year, interpreters were added to the staff, and two deaf graduate students were admitted for training. The same year, two deaf undergraduates applied to the college, and the Center agreed to provide interpreters for them in all their classes.

Since then, the Center has been expanding. It employs and trains interpreters, and has initiated research, results of which show steady and rapid success. The attitude of the hearing students as well as the university faculty toward the deaf undergraduates has been very positive; at present, 80 percent of the interpreters used in the classrooms are themselves CSUN undergraduates who have been trained at the Center.

Ray Jones, director of the Center, walked me around the

campus, and we sat in on a seminar in the leadership program. It
was a large group, all graduate students. About one-third were
deaf. Jones is a tall, lanky man in his fifties, a Mormon from
Utah. He was dressed rather formally for southern California
in a blue business suit, but still looked very Western. When I
asked Jones how he had gotten into the business of running the
Center, he told me he had come to Northridge to replace someone else for a short time, temporarily, and somehow he was
still there.

He was less vague when he began talking about the program.
Without a great deal of theory about educating deaf college students, he explained, they had just begun doing whatever seemed
appropriate and logical, and things had turned out pretty well.
The entire program was built on interpreting services.

Jones complained bitterly about Gallaudet College. Gallaudet got all the publicity and all the money, he said, but in his
opinion was not doing its job of educating deaf students. He referred to Gallaudet as a segregated institution, and Northridge as
integrated. Jones had tried to arrange an exchange of faculty between Gallaudet and CSUN. "We offered to provide interpreters for their professors, hearing or deaf," he said. "We were very
interested in having more deaf teachers here. But Gallaudet
refused to provide interpreters for *our* faculty. They insisted
that our professors take one of their short, crash courses in
signing.

"Can't give a college lecture in a language you just had a
crash course in," said Jones. "That's just dumb. It wouldn't be
the same material. Here at Northridge, with interpreters, the
deaf students get exactly the same education as the hearing students. A real college education. The extra help they get is in the
support services—notetakers, counseling, and advising. But the
most important thing is the interpreters."

Despite lower test scores at admission, and despite the generally poor quality of deaf education through elementary and
high school, the deaf students at CSUN maintain a grade point

average equal to that of the hearing students. According to a survey taken by the Center of faculty and hearing students in classes with deaf students, the deaf students were perceived as more highly motivated than their hearing peers, had better work habits, and came to classes better prepared. "They work harder than the hearing students," said Jones. "They work much harder." (Deaf students have told me that they never feel comfortable about their classes unless they have done *all* the reading beforehand.)

Dr. Jones gave me an office where I could talk to some of the Center's staff. Sharon Carter, director of support services, was waiting for me. She is deaf, and told me she had become deaf during childhood, well after speech acquisition. She is a large, colorful woman with a large, booming voice. She didn't lipread at all, and while we waited for an interpreter, she spared me the embarrassment of a long awkward silence by talking continuously.

A tall, handsome, pregnant young woman came into the room, out of breath, sat down beside me, and said: "I'm Sharon Newmann Solow, but I'm not here as myself. When the interpreter comes, I'll be Sharon Newmann Solow. But for now, I'll interpret. Is that O.K.?"

I had no idea what she was talking about. She seemed keenly interested in the interview, eager and enthusiastic. Even though seated and motionless, she seemed bouncy. I turned back to Mrs. Carter, and the newcomer interpreted my questions into sign. Shortly, another woman arrived, wearing an interpreter's smock, and apologized for being late. (The interpreters at Northridge all wear dark blue smocks. These garments provide a good background for signing and also make the interpreters highly identifiable.) Finally, I realized what Sharon Newmann Solow had been saying: she had been sent by Dr. Jones to give me information, but since no other interpreter was present, she would step out of her role as faculty member and become my interpreter. When the scheduled interpreter arrived, she was free, as she put it, to be there "as myself"—and step out of the anonymous interpreter's role.

In the ethics of interpreting, the interpreter is present as little as possible and sometimes seems not to be there at all. The exchange is considered to be between the deaf and the hearing individual, and is conducted like any face-to-face conversation. All questions are addressed directly to the deaf person: "How old are you?," for example. It is a breach of etiquette to address questions to the interpreter: "Ask him how old he is." A hearing person who persists in talking to the interpreter might well be chided. ("Why are you talking to me in the third person?" I once heard a deaf man inquire.)

There is almost no reason for the hearing individual in a conversation to look at the interpreter. The deaf partner in the dialogue watches the interpreter's signs, of course, then looks back at the speaker in normal conversational fashion, maintaining eye contact while signing a reply. I like to watch my words being signed, and sometimes look at the interpreter, but there is no necessity for it. Interpreted exchanges are pleasant, efficient, and interesting. It took me one or two trials before I was entirely comfortable. Seeing the pain on an interpreter's face while trying to express my excessively worded observations was humbling. I quickly learned to phrase my questions more concisely, and my own fluency in English has certainly improved because of my conversations with the deaf.

The two Sharons—Sharon Carter and Sharon Newmann Solow—gave me a good idea of the deaf students' experiences at Northridge. The blue-smocked interpreters have become a symbol of the deaf students' permanent presence on campus. A substantial number of hearing students make inquiries at the center each semester, offering help as volunteers and expressing interest in ASL classes and in interpreter training, which are a regular part of the college curriculum. Since 1972, the number of hearing students taking ASL classes has been larger than the number of deaf students. (Deaf students take ASL classes the way hearing students study English, and there are offerings at the upper levels in theatrical signs, poetry, and song in ASL.)

Hearing students who wish to become interpreters work their way up. After completing basic courses in ASL, they may work for the center as notetakers. A good record as notetaker (good attendance, well-organized notes) and some proficiency in ASL make them eligible for interpreting assignments. At first they are assigned to lab sections where a minimum of verbal information is exchanged. They continue to take more advanced interpreting courses, and are evaluated regularly, their skills upgraded from one level to the next. Videotapes are made in the classrooms, played back, and analyzed. The regular professional interpreting staff also runs workshops, practice sessions, and meetings for the student interpreters.

Sign language interpreting in the classroom—like almost all public interpreting—follows the English remarks of the speaker, word for word, as rapidly as possible. Though the signs are ASL signs, their use in English word order and with the addition of some English grammatical conventions violates the particular grammar of ASL, and is not really ASL. (If French words were merely substituted for English words, the result wouldn't be French, either. No two languages can ever be transliterated perfectly, with one word the exact equivalent of another.) In this kind of sign language interpreting, the interpreter is attempting to give a signed representation of the English used, but strictly speaking, it's not really good English, either. The language of interpreting is what the linguists call Pidgin Sign English: a blending of the two languages.

Pidgin languages occur naturally all over the world. According to some definitions, English originated out of a pidginization

of Anglo-Saxon and Norman French following the invasion of
1066. (Anglo-Saxon had developed centuries earlier, when the
Angles came to terms with the Saxons.) Pidgin languages are
created when speakers of two mutually unintelligible languages
meet regularly and wish to work out a means of communicating and of transacting business. Pidgins are simple languages at
first, using only key words from both languages, omitting function words, articles, inflections, elaborations. If the situation is
prolonged and the two language communities continue to
mingle, and if new generations grow up learning the pidgin as
their native language, it changes: takes on elaborations, and
becomes a new language, a real language, which is known as
a creole.

Some linguists and educators believe that ASL is undergoing
a pidginization process and will someday be completely replaced
by an English-based (creole) sign language. Attempts to make
the sign language of the deaf resemble the spoken language of the
surrounding culture have been going on for centuries. L'Épée's
methodical signs were an attempt to make sign language something closer to spoken French. While there is a great deal of disagreement about whether or not these artificial languages are
useful for teaching, it is certain that no signed version of any
spoken language has ever become the ordinary, everyday language of a deaf community. The most obvious reason is probably the difference in mode.

Spoken language is received by the ear in a stream of sound
signals, one after the other, in sequence, over time. The ear is
specialized for receiving this kind of information, the eye is not.
The eye is adapted for picking up information in the environment, not only sequentially over time but also simultaneously.
The eye picks up large chunks of information: sees many things
in the visual field, simultaneously occurring as well as ongoing
events. Manual languages of the deaf evolved to take advantage
of the visual mode, and are based on a positive use of vision
rather than on a negative functioning of the ear.

Pidgin Sign English produces a rather bare English sentence adorned with ASL signs and a large number of fingerspelled English words. It is not comparable either with natural pidgins (where neither party knows the other's language) nor is it comparable with standard foreign language interpretation (where neither party knows the other's language, but the interpreter knows both). In sign language interpretation, the interpreter may know both ASL and English, but the deaf client *must* know English. It is the only kind of language interpreting that assumes the client is competent in both languages.

"It's really the deaf students who do the interpreting," said one of the senior interpreters, a native signer. "What they get doesn't make much sense unless they do some translating."

"What do they translate into? English or ASL?" I asked.

"English," she said. "If they're given a good interpretation, close to ASL, they don't have to do anything, they just understand directly. Go right to meaning. But if they've gotten a garbled English sentence, they have to try to put it into English, and sometimes translate it into ASL in their heads before they get any idea what it means.

"Most of them are pretty good with English. They're all college students, they read English well or they wouldn't be in college. A few don't know ASL, they learn it here. They've never had an opportunity to learn, never been around other deaf people before. They take ASL courses, and they learn it in a snap, too. The English teachers say that the deaf students' writing is quite respectable. Nothing fancy, but simple and clear. All the professors here seem to think that the deaf students were taught English in the most abominable sort of way, and there's nowhere to go but up. They all improve during college.

"All our interpreters are familiar with ASL. Many interpreter training programs only teach Pidgin Sign English and the interpreters never learn ASL, and never even have any idea that they're not learning ASL. It's really terrible. All our interpreters can carry on a conversation in ASL—and can understand ASL.

It's essential. I'll give you an example: A classroom with an interpreter. About five minutes into the lecture, a deaf student stands up and begins signing: *You said today would be the transportation revolution. I read the transportation revolution all weekend. Why are you talking about Andrew Jackson? Andrew Jackson is not till March.* O.K. He's upset, and he's signing in ASL. If the interpreter can't read the signs, it'a a very bad situation, with everybody unhappy."

"Why isn't ASL used in interpreting instead of Pidgin Sign English?"

"It's harder," she answered. "Some students say they prefer to have the interpretation in English because they don't really trust the interpreter to do it correctly in ASL, it gets too simplified. Baby talk. They'd rather have it in approximate English and be sure it was what the lecturer was saying, then figure out what it means. Teachers of the deaf used to say that signing in English to deaf students was good for them because it actually taught them English, but then they took a good look at it and saw it wasn't English at all. That's when everybody started to make up those other systems, with signs for *-ing*, and *-ed*, and suffixes and affixes, and it got very complicated.

"There are other reasons for not using ASL, too, that have to do with platform styles and the flow of the lecture. The interpreter begins signing a few seconds after the speaker begins, and ends only a few seconds behind. There's no waiting, no delay. In ASL, it doesn't take longer, but the rhythm is different. The interpreter has to wait before beginning to sign, to get a sense of what is being said—a whole phrase, if not a whole sentence. The message is out of synchrony. The hearing students are laughing in different places. Not necessarily later. Sometimes the punch lines come earlier in ASL, but it's embarrassing and somehow, in a subtle way, disruptive. With some speakers, everybody better be laughing at the same time!

"When they agree to having an interpreter, the professors have to be pretty well convinced that the pace of the entire lecture will not be changed. Some of the hearing students complain that the interpreter is distracting. We don't pay too much attention to that, but if a professor should complain, that would be more serious. We plan where the interpreter will stand just for that reason, so the signing won't bother the lecturer.

"Then there's feedback, or something like it. If the interpreters are going from English to ASL, they must delay signing until a whole phrase is understood. Then, while signing, they must remember the phrase and listen for the next phrase, all at the same time. I've seen interpreters who are good ASL signers, even native ASL signers, close their eyes to help their concentration while trying to take in English and produce ASL. With interpreters who aren't absolutely comfortable with ASL, it's harder. Sometimes they hear a word or a phrase in English while they're in the middle of an ASL sentence, and it just throws them off completely. Drives everything out of their heads. They're helpless.

"Interpreting from English into ASL has been done for years. I've done it for years. It's no great problem when it's your native language and has become pretty much automatic. But ASL is a very difficult language, and few hearing people who didn't learn it in childhood are really good at it. We give our student interpreters as much ASL as we possibly can. Even Pidgin Sign English is going to be better if the interpreter knows ASL. Incidentally, deaf people sign in English better than hearing people. They sign in anything better than hearing people. Let's face it, the deaf are the very best signers. The next best are their bilingual children. But there is definitely a shortage of bilinguals, and some of the college students have become very good indeed. A few have been good enough to become certified interpreters, though not many. I'm sure it's comparable to any other kind of language interpretation. Very few people could study, say, Turkish, for three or four years in college and then get a job at the UN.

"We schedule the classes very carefully. The less experienced interpreters only do lab courses, and the relatively simple courses. We try to make sure they understand the material they're going to be interpreting—in some cases, the interpreter has already taken the course and has the advantage of knowing what the professor is going to say.

"The deaf students don't complain," she went on. "Not often. Not as often as they might. They know they probably wouldn't be going to college at all without interpreters. Sometimes I think they should complain more. They're really marvelous at making do with interpretation that isn't all it should be. Maybe it's not all that bad considering what they had before. Even our inexperienced interpreters are better signers than most teachers at schools for the deaf. We keep trying to attract more native signers. The more good signers on campus, the better all the interpreters will become."

High school seniors who already have bilingual skills are encouraged to apply for admission to CSUN. Hearing children of deaf parents are contacted through deaf clubs and are offered a small stipend if they decide to attend the college. These stipends are not in the university budget, but are raised in the deaf community—often by the deaf club in the prospective student's home town, or by the Northridge college community. CSUN's deaf students hold an annual fundraising banquet for the purpose. Like all money actually controlled and disbursed by the deaf at the grass roots, the amount is small, between $300 and $500, depending on how much has been raised, and is awarded only once, to incoming students. It's a large incentive. Deaf families are typically employed in the poorer-paid occupations and can rarely afford college expenses. The stipend, combined with the prospect of the students being able to work their way through college as interpreters, and the knowledge that their signing skills are valued by the college, often makes a difference.

Of all the deaf people, I know, Ted Supalla has had the most experience with classroom interpreters, having gone through col-

lege and graduate school with interpreting services. I asked him
to tell me about his experiences.

"It can be hard work," Ted informed me, "and kind of
nerve-racking. Of course, interpreting would probably be better
in ASL, but they hardly ever use it. They always want to be finished signing at the same time the speaker finishes talking. Sometimes they sign so fast that they lose all expression, and all into-
nation. The sentences just run together, and it's hard to tell
whether something goes with one sentence or with the next.
They fingerspell too much, I think. Not only words that have no
signs, but many times they fingerspell words that have perfectly
good and well-known signs, but they're going so fast they can't
stop even for a second to think what the sign is, so they just bar-
rel ahead with the fingerspelling. Their spelling is not all that
great, either.

"It's exhausting," he said. "I often feel I'm working very
hard. It's an active process most of the time, reading the interpreter's signs and trying to figure out what they mean. I always
make allowances for the interpreters and try to figure out what
mistakes they're likely to be making. After a few classes with the
same interpreter, I know what to look for. Sometimes, in small
graduate courses, sitting at a table, I was able to control some of
it. Sometimes I could slow down the speaker, mostly by eye
contact, if he was going too fast. I couldn't do that in large
classes, of course. Seminars were the hardest, where people all
around the room were talking and sometimes several at once.
After some seminars, I'd feel really exhausted. Drained. And
have a terrible headache.

"You're not supposed to complain," Ted went on. "You're
supposed to be happy with whoever you get. Most hearing people cannot understand the idea that there could be a difference
between interpreters."

Ted said he remembered having some really great interpreters, and most of them were native signers, children of deaf parents. One of the interpreters he remembered was Sharon Newmann Solow. Ted and Sharon were exact contemporaries at

Northridge; they had both been undergraduates, and Sharon worked as an interpreter as well. Several years later, it was Sharon who accompanied Ted on interviews with faculty at San Diego when he was negotiating his admission as their first deaf graduate student in experimental psychology.

"The interviews went extremely well," Ted told me. "I explained how interpreters worked, and Sharon was right there interpreting. The professors could see how it worked. At the time, there was a possibility that Sharon would stay in San Diego, and I thought she might be able to interpret for me, but she decided to go back to Northridge. After I was admitted to grad school, I never had such good interpreting."

It took me days to make an appointment to see Sharon Newmann Solow as herself. She was all booked up. She was either interpreting at the Jewish Community Center all evening or had promised to stop by the drama club and coach their signs; she was teaching classes all day, or was scheduled to give a demonstration. Finally, we found a good day with a couple of hours free. She picked me up late in the afternoon and brought me to her home in Van Nuys. The house was cheerful and cluttered. Sharon's husband is an audiologist—a signing audiologist, she told me. Electronic equipment and pieces of electronic equipment were laid out on every table. There were books everywhere, and articles, manuscripts, toys, memorabilia, gadgets.

In addition to her reputation as one of the great interpreters, Sharon is known as something of a clown. She signs in several regional variations of ASL, and frequently amuses her deaf and hearing friends with satiric monologues in ASL dialect.

Sharon Newmann Solow looks like a big, precocious California kid. In an instant, she turns into a stately, unsmiling professional. The second daughter of two deaf parents, she was born in Tucson, where both her mother and father were teachers at the Arizona School for the Deaf. "They didn't use speech," she said, "and were super-conscientious about providing me and my sister with lots of oral input. Both of us talked real young. They bought story records for us, brought the neighbors in to talk to us. They took us everywhere. I remember meeting lots of kids of deaf parents. They were all signers, and all hearing. Hardly any were deaf. We used ASL at home all the time and I played with the deaf kids at the school. I don't remember learning ASL or learning English. We just grew up with both and I guess I interpreted for my parents a lot, but it was all part of the same thing, talking and signing." She smiled.

"I became professional at a very young age, fifteen. A man named Vic Galloway was enrolled as a doctoral candidate at the University of Arizona, with an interpreter, but it wasn't working out. He was shocked at the kind of interpreter the college gave him, so he decided he'd find someone better. He knew my father had daughters, and he came over and asked if one of us could interpret for him. My sister was older, but didn't want to do it. She didn't think she was temperamentally suited to standing in front of a class and having people staring at her. So I went.

"I loved it. Got out of high school one period early to interpret. Later, other graduate students came and asked me to interpret for them. Shortly after Vic got his degree, he went to Rochester, to the National Technical Institute for the Deaf, and not long after, I got an offer from NTID too, for an interpreter's job.

"I had just graduated from high school and couldn't afford to go to college. I thought I'd go and work for a while, save my money, and think about college later. That was 1968. I was eighteen, and the first interpreter at NTID. I stayed for the whole year and through the following summer.

"It was a strange experience. I was pretty young, and it was my first winter in that horrible climate up there. I hardly knew a soul and was quite lonely, frankly. It would have been natural for me to go out with the deaf students—they were my own age, and we didn't have any language problems. But it didn't seem very professional of me to be having dates with my students.

"During that year I met Ray Jones, who was visiting from the Center on Deafness here. *What's a nice Jewish girl from Tucson doing here in all this snow?*" she said in a Western drawl. "Mostly, he just told me that I should be thinking about my own education. He was very kind and concerned, and sometimes I think he rescued me from NTID. He worked it out that I could come back to California, go to college full time and work half time as interpreter. It was perfect for me. I got my B.A. in English in four years, and then I went to Salk to work with Ursie [Bellugi] on ASL research, and started graduate school in linguistics in San Diego. That was dumb. Well, it was smart to work with Ursie, but dumb to go to graduate school. Linguistics," she grimaced, then shuddered.

"I came back here to teach advanced courses in ASL, and also to work on interpreter training. I worked organizing the National Interpreter Training Consortium, of which I am still consultant from CSUN. I trained interpreters all over the West, Oregon, Washington, Nevada, California. Alaska," she said. "I was the first interpreter to visit Alaska, and helped them set up a training program. It was interesting and cold. Worse than Rochester. There were only fifteen deaf adults in the community. When I was getting ready to leave, they gave me a party and thirteen came. Two were sick. I felt quite flattered.

"The Alaskans were much different from any deaf people I'd ever met. All the deaf people I knew were like my parents, starved for information. They spend their whole lives fighting off isolation, trying to find out what's going on. But in Alaska, the deaf people had gone there *looking* for isolation—to get away and be by themselves. But they were still worried about the deaf children up there, wanted to do right by them, and wanted to give them whatever they needed—interpreters and a good education. I trained about twenty interpreters."

II

By definition, interpreters are never famous. Only one, I believe, has become a truly historical figure who continues to arouse the biographer's attention, the dramatist's regard, and the educator's curiosity: Anne Sullivan, companion and lifelong interpreter for Helen Keller. Though famous as a teacher, most of Miss Sullivan's teaching was accomplished during the first dramatic years she spent with her deaf and blind pupil at the Keller home in Tuscumbia, Alabama. In 1887, when they met, the child was seven, the teacher not quite twenty-one. Using the manual alphabet, Anne Sullivan spelled words into her pupil's hand, and the famous scene at the water pump occurred barely one month after her arrival.

The following year, Helen Keller was in Boston with Miss Sullivan, meeting Oliver Wendell Holmes. They took up residence for a time at the Perkins Institution for the Blind, where Helen learned to use the Braille library and other facilities of the school. When she was fourteen, she was enrolled in a school in New York City, and two years later went to a second school in Cambridge. In 1900, Anne Sullivan accompanied Helen Keller to Radcliffe and fingerspelled a college education into Helen's palms. She interpreted every lecture, and because few books were available in Braille, she read the books, letter by letter, into Helen's hand. She described the classroom scene, interpreted conversations with other students, made observations on the teaching style of various professors, and transcribed Helen's papers. The college was so nervous about having her there, and so frightened at the possibility of fraud, that they barred her from all examinations.

Anne Sullivan was the first interpreter ever to sit in a college classroom with a handicapped student. She had no status whatever at Radcliffe, and received no recognition for her difficult work. The notion that she was capable or worthy of higher education never entered their minds; but the idea that she was capable of perpetrating a fraud against higher education was never far from their consciousness.

During their early life together, there was a tendency to confuse their two identities and to think of them as a single person. "For it took the pair of you to make a perfect whole," commented Mark Twain—not the most tactful thing to say about two human beings painfully struggling for autonomy.

When Helen Keller's early and outstanding intellectual accomplishments became known, Anne Sullivan was acclaimed as a miracle worker. But Alexander Graham Bell insisted that no miracle had been worked at all; a good method had merely been employed by a competent teacher. At the Perkins Institution, there was a general opinion that any college-trained girl in America could have had the same results. Anne Sullivan had been blind as a child; a series of operations left her partially sighted for the rest of her life. She had, in fact, been trained at the Perkins Institution.

Anne Sullivan got the best education for herself that a half-blind, orphaned, and impoverished child of immigrants could get in the nineteenth century. It began when she entered the Perkins Institution at the age of fourteen. Six years later, shortly after her graduation, she was in Tuscumbia, recommended by the Institution as a tutor and companion for the deaf-blind child whose family had sought their assistance. The personal letters that Miss Sullivan sent back to Boston during the first difficult and lonely weeks in the Keller home were later published as models of pedagogical wisdom. Her most recent biographer notes (rather meanly, I thought) that errors of spelling and punctuation had to be corrected before publication.

A precedent already existed for the education of a deaf-blind child. Samuel Gridley Howe, first director of the Perkins Institution, had personally educated Laura Bridgman, who came to the school in 1837. She was eight years old and had been deaf and blind since the age of twenty-six months. Howe began by using labels in raised type attached to familiar objects. After several months of slow but certain progress, he sent one of his teachers to a deaf person to learn the manual alphabet. When Laura Bridgman had also learned it, the manual alphabet became the means of communicating with her. Joseph Lash, in his book *Helen and Teacher*, characterizes Laura Bridgman as having a "trite" mind. She seems to have suffered even more from an institutional personality. She spent her entire life at the school in essentially institutional pursuits, praying and sewing. She was said to be conventionally, narrowly, religious, and an accomplished lacemaker.

Howe devoted a few hours each day to his pupil, and, having a scientific turn of mind, kept notes. After the first two years he turned the child over to regular teachers on his staff, and made his notes from the diaries that he instructed them to keep.

When the call from Tuscumbia came, Anne Sullivan prepared herself. She read widely on the general subject of education and "mental development." She studied Howe's notebooks closely, became skilled in using the manual alphabet, and spent a great deal of time with Laura Bridgman, who was still living at the Perkins Institution and was then fifty-seven years old. When she went to meet her pupil, Miss Sullivan had some well-formed ideas about how to proceed. She would avoid fixed hours of instruction, would make teaching and learning an ongoing, continuous activity. She would teach her pupil language, and then talk to her about everything.

She found Helen Keller a bright, sturdy, strong-willed child; ferociously resistant, and prepared to stand her ground. Anne Sullivan moved her. Not in the slow, painful pace typical in the education of handicapped children, a steady accumulation of small skills, but in a most dramatic, instantaneous leap: a revelation. Helen Keller's moment of understanding has mythic overtones—it fulfills a deep and ancient human hope that knowledge comes in a bright, shining flash and changes everything.

On this meaningful event, the two very young women built their relationship and their future.

After the death of Helen Keller, the tendency to merge the two personalities into one began reversing itself, and it has now come almost full circle. Today the two are portrayed as having opposite, if not opposing natures, Helen with a luminous intelligence, Anne with dark cunning. "There were also genetic forces at work," writes Lash, developing this theme in his massive biography, "producing difference in temperaments, so that one always viewed the world 'through a glass darkly,' while the other, though sightless, surrounded it with sunshine and gaiety."

Helen Keller developed a personal style of great charm that unfortunately verged on excessive sweetness. Anne Sullivan was not the least among Helen's admirers to be captivated by it. Her loyalty and protectiveness toward the child, her willingness to free Helen for high intellectual attainments, left her vulnerable to criticism. As an interpreter, she ran all the risks to which interpreters are subject: charges of misrepresentation, distortion, censorship, self-interest, manipulation. A great deal of hostility was expressed toward her simply, I think, because she was an interpreter.

Communicating with Helen Keller was always extremely difficult. Though she was determined to learn speech and took speech training for years, practicing endlessly, painfully, and with great difficulty, each public appearance had to be carefully planned, coached, rehearsed—and was usually brief. Speech was tremendously useful to her for platform appearances, but for personal communication it fell short of making ordinary discourse possible. In a foreword to Helen Keller's autobiography, Eleanor Roosevelt wrote in 1961: "I find it hard to understand Miss Keller's speech today but many people understand her quite easily and sometimes I think one does not actually have to understand her words because her spirit shines through the expression of her face and her eyes that are so full of beauty."

Helen Keller's conquest over her handicaps has not been exaggerated, but is often inappropriately stated. Her victories were unquestionably real, yet they were intellectual, literary, and spiritual victories; her physical limitations remained formidable. She needed an interpreter as well as a guide all her life. Here is a description of a stage appearance from the Joseph Lash biography:

> Teacher went on the stage first and spoke in her musical voice about the education of Helen. She then led Helen onto the platform. To accustom the audience to the strangeness of Helen's voice, she had Helen repeat slowly sentences that Helen read with her fingers on Teacher's lips. Then Helen repeated the lines of *Abide With Me.* The audience thus prepared, Helen launched into what she called her "Message of Happiness," a series of epigrams, mottolike statements counseling hope, cheerfulness, and good works. The audience followed the high-pitched, strangely inflected voice with difficulty, but there was always an ovation at the end because of admiration for the courage behind the effort.

Her only comfortable and natural mode of communication was the manual alphabet. Anne Sullivan spoke to her in this way, interpreted conversations with other people, and relayed Helen's fingerspelled replies. Through years of this kind of conversation, both had become remarkably skilled and extremely fast. Certain of Helen's friends also learned and used the manual alphabet, and Miss Sullivan encouraged them, not only to relieve herself of the responsibility of continuous interpreting but to foster those relationships. There were always a few people significant to Helen who could communicate with her directly, but the number remained rather small. For people lacking the manual alphabet, the only way of avoiding an interpreter was to write a letter in Braille. Helen was said to be able to lipread by placing her fingers over the lips of a speaker, but in most accounts and photographs of her doing so, she was reading the lips of Anne Sullivan.

Anne Sullivan was a brilliant teacher, for which she has become justly famous. She continued to have interesting ideas about education all her life. She both sought and valued recognition as a teacher, and Helen Keller insisted on it. However, ignoring her role as interpreter implies that deafness and blindness are purely intellectual problems that have educational solutions; that the combination of a brilliant student and a brilliant teacher (or merely a competent teacher with a good method) will compensate for these monumental physical handicaps.

Helen always called her, reverently, Teacher. It was the name Anne Sullivan taught her as they stood beside the well. Psychologically, both women remained tied to that moment and that experience. Anne Sullivan remained a teacher to Helen Keller only in the sense that all lifelong and loving friends are teachers, and in the sense that all great interpreters are teachers. Anne Sullivan taught Helen Keller about the world by interpreting it into her hand—slowly, daily, piece by piece, letter by letter. It was not the same kind of knowledge that comes in a shining flash and changes everything, but a slow accumulation over five decades, and two remarkable lives.

III

Rochester, New York, is located on the south shore of Lake Ontario, on a plateau creased long ago by the northflowing Genessee River. Once an important Great Lakes port, it was a beautiful city—the parks along its waterways, lakes, and waterfalls were designed by Frederick Law Olmsted. For more than one hundred years it has maintained a large university, a music conservatory, a symphony orchestra, a mechanical and technical institute, and an international optical and photographic industry. Like so many American cities that rose in the middle of the nineteenth century, it began to decline in the middle of the twentieth, and Rochester in 1980 appears to lack a center, a downtown. Driving through, it is clear where downtown used to be—a circumferential highway loops around the urban renewed remains within view of the great lake. Rochester has staggered southward, filling up abandoned wheat fields with treeless highways and tacky shopping centers. In one of these areas, in a newly landscaped flat plane adjoining the Rochester Institute of Technology, stand the new buildings of the National Technical Institute for the Deaf.

NTID has a complex and confusing relationship with its parent institution, the Rochester Institute of Technology (RIT). Deaf students enroll at NTID in specific career programs awarding certificates, diplomas, or associate degrees. About 12 percent of the deaf students go on to RIT and receive baccalaureate degrees. The two institutions are fairly separate, with only a small overlap in faculty, administration, and students. I met with two deaf faculty members, Loy Golladay and Robert Panara. Both are members of the NTID Support Team and teach courses at RIT. They are both English professors.

Golladay is sixty-five. He has white hair, a trim white mustache, a cheeky Gallic face, and long, expressive, poetic hands. He is a native speaker of English. When he lost his hearing at the age of eight, he was already in the fourth grade and an addicted reader. "I was the only deaf person in St. David's Church, Virginia, in the Shenandoah Valley." Because his father, a lawyer, was reluctant to send him away to "an asylum," the family and the child were pretty much resigned to his being educated at home, where he was already making inroads into the family library and casting an eye on his father's law books. At a sporting event between a local junior college and the West Virginia School for the Deaf, Golladay saw sign language for the first time. His father was so impressed with the deaf students' intelligence and demeanor that he decided to enroll his son the following fall.

At school, Loy Golladay continued to read. Few of the teachers were college-trained; the few who had been to college were usually the deaf teachers. His speech teacher was "a New England lady," who, his father complained, had made him sound like a Yankee. Speech training was very frustrating, and Golladay gave it up entirely, he said, when his voice began to change. Years later, as a college student at Gallaudet, he tried again and was successful in recovering his speech. His voice is soft, his style of speaking somewhat bookish and a trifle old-fashioned.

After graduating from Gallaudet, he taught at the West Virginia School for a short time, then left "just out of restlessness. To see more of the world."

In addition to acquiring teaching credentials, Golladay had learned the printing trade and during the 1930s made his living as a journeyman typesetter. In 1941, he was a proprietor of his own printshop and publisher of a weekly newspaper in a small town in North Dakota. He tried to enlist in the Navy during the war. He understood that all the big ships had their own printing presses and volunteered to take over the job of publishing the daily papers on board. He also tried to join the Army, and says he was very disappointed when they wouldn't take him either. He sold the paper and went to teach at the American School in Hartford, and never worked as a printer again except during summer vacations.

Golladay stayed at the American School for twenty-seven years. He enjoys teaching and writing, has published numerous articles, a dictionary of idioms for the deaf in 1966, and many poems. He came to Rochester in 1969. I asked him about the courses he teaches. "World literature," Golladay replied. "Four genres. Short story, poetry, drama, and the novel. This semester, I will concentrate on plays. We will read *Antigone*, and several modern works. Arthur Miller's *The Crucible*. The students always like that."

"Do you use an interpreter?"

"Certainly. Otherwise, the hearing students get more involved in watching me perform than they are in literature."

"Are there more hearing students in your classes than deaf?"

"Many more," he replied. "And it's very good for the deaf students to be challenged by the integrated classes. I wish there were more of them. You should see how interested they are, and excited by the work. At Gallaudet, sometimes I think they get off too easy. At RIT they know they're here to get a B.S. degree and they feel challenged."

Golladay insisted that his deaf students are good readers, and like to read. "Only a quarter have real reading problems," he said, "and another quarter—maybe even a third—are really good readers."

Professor Robert Panara is also a native speaker of English. He is an extremely affable-looking man in his fifties, with a friendly smile. He looks like a New Yorker; he grew up in the Bronx. He was the first deaf professor in Rochester, and came in 1967 to get the program going "and persuade people like Loy Golladay to join us."

He lost his hearing at ten, after meningitis. It left him with tinnitus—something inside his auditory system is still vibrating. For forty years he has had a ringing in his ears (the condition is not uncommon among people who are adventitiously deaf). Panara had no help whatever during his childhood. "They didn't have Vocational Rehabilitation in those days. I just kept going to P.S. One-oh-three on the Bronx Parkway," he said, and shrugged. "Because I could read, I didn't have much trouble. Then I read my way through DeWitt Clinton High School. I had been out for a few months when I heard about Gallaudet, so I went there right away. I learned sign language in one year. After Gallaudet, I taught at the New York School for the Deaf in White Plains and commuted down to NYU to take graduate courses at night. I was a graduate student," he leaned across the table and smiled, "you won't believe it. Eighteen years altogether. After four years, I got my M.A. Then I went to Washington to teach at Gallaudet, and was supposed to be working on my Ph.D. at American University. I took an awful lot of courses," he said. "I really enjoyed being a graduate student. I just stayed in that category they used to call ABD: all but the dissertation. Then things started happening. The National Theatre of the Deaf was organizing, and I went to Waterford to work with them, and after that, I was asked to come here, to get NTID started.

"When I came here, I began making contacts among the hearing college students at Rochester Institute of Technology. I talked and gave demonstrations to thirty-five student organizations. Explained the problems of deaf students, tried to anticipate others. Tried to prepare them for the coming invasion of deaf teenagers. I told them about the interpreters who would be in their classes, that volunteers would be needed as notetakers, and so forth. One hundred and twenty-five hearing students volunteered for interpreter training, and from those we organized our future interpreter corps. Since then, we regularly get RIT students taking sign language and interpreting." Panara turned to the young man sitting beside me, the interpreter, and asked, "Maybe that's how you became an interpreter?"

"No," replied the interpreter. "I was working on a construction job in Rochester, and I met a deaf guy who was working there, too. He taught me a lot, then I came here and started taking courses."

"Isn't that wonderful?" said Panara. "Thank you." He turned back to me. "See, just being around deaf people makes youngsters like this interested in our language. We've never had any shortage of potential interpreters. They learn it quickly and with open minds.

"After the initial year the response to NTID was fan-tastic. It just grew, grew, grew—like Topsy," he said, smiling again.

I asked about ASL, and what its status was at NTID.

"We don't teach ASL as such," Panara said. "At the college level we really have to concentrate on English and have to use

English signs. We fought so hard to get total communication at all. Negotiating with the oralists was so difficult, and the only reason, I think, that they aren't still fighting it here is because we promised that the sign language we used would be based on English."

"But we all use ASL," said Golladay. "Every day. Some people say it's the native language of the deaf, and that's true. When I'm teaching, I often explain a scene in ASL, silently. Sometimes it's easier to convey a meaning in ASL, especially if the text is complicated or obscure. But, words—" he sighed. "When I became deaf, I still remember, I was hungry for words. It was like being under a bell jar. I don't know what I would have done if I hadn't been able to read. I listened to words on paper."

I asked him if he thought the experience was the same for his students, most of whom had been born deaf. "Maybe it's a little different," he answered. "Maybe they don't feel as starved as I did, but I honestly think they all value words. Very much."

We could have talked longer, but the interpreter announced that his scheduled time was over and he had an appointment elsewhere. He offered to send another in his place, but the two professors rose and said they didn't want to monopolize my time. "We are the old school, anyway," said Golladay, and urged me to see more of NTID. Panara almost apologized, saying he always talked too much. He showed me his name sign. It had his initial, P, and was based on the sign for talk: extended and exaggerated by four rhythmic beats, to armslength. "Everybody knows I'm a talker," he said cheerfully; then they left.

"The building was designed for manual communication," said my guide from the NTID Visitor's Bureau, a young, articulate black woman, whom I will call Donna James. "Notice the wide halls and open staircases. It was planned to give good visibility across open spaces and from floor to floor." Miss James was extremely thin, coolly stylish. She was also one of the few black people I had encountered in post-secondary deaf education. The elementary and high school on the Gallaudet campus had large numbers of black students (more than half), but at Gallaudet College there were very few. On inquiring, I had been assured that since all the black students lived in the District of Columbia, they preferred to go to NTID, to get away from home and have a new experience. "Are there many black students here?" I asked.

"Hardly any," Donna James replied. "I've wondered about that, too." She showed me a Vistaphone. "Stromberg Carlson direct cable." It was a small oval television screen set on a pedestal, with a TV camera built in. The Vistaphone can both send and receive images. Signers standing in front of it can have a conversation. "Or you can write out a message and hold it up in front of the screen and do it that way. It's an experimental model, we only have a few. All the offices have TTYs, and amplified telephones."

Miss James was obviously a novice signer. I noticed that in her exchanges with deaf people, her signs, though earnest, were hesitant, and she frequently had to ask for a correct sign. "I've only studied sign language for a few months," she said. "Just finished the course, and I'm really trying."

"Did you have to take the course to get the job?"

"On the contrary, I had to insist they let me take the course. I used to work at the front reception desk and it was ridiculous. People would come in and I couldn't communicate with them. I made them teach me. It's better now. I don't feel like I'm making such a fool of myself."

She brought me into one of NTID's famous cluster classrooms. "It was specially designed for manual communication," she said. The room is circular, new, and very modern. Two banks of raised desks, the second higher than the first, were arranged in a semicircle; a speaker standing at the bottom of this small amphitheater would be visible from all points in the room.

"The room has special soundproofed construction. There are six inches of soundproofing baffles behind the walls."

Since the students were deaf, the need to enclose them behind six inches of soundproofing escaped me. The thing that really bothered me about the room was that it had no windows.

"That's designed on purpose," said Ms. James, "to eliminate distractions. Deaf students don't need distractions. They need to concentrate." She seemed to be repeating something she had memorized. "They just don't need that," she went on, picking up the thread. "And, look." She walked to a wall switch. When she flicked it on, an extremely bright white light began to flash on and off, about twice a second (I had to shield my eyes), until she turned it off. "If a deaf student should fall asleep, this light will wake him up. The teacher doesn't have to interrupt the class. The light will wake him."

Against one wall was a large blackboard. Around the rest of the curving walls, the surface was covered with thin strips of blond wood set against a black surface, producing an effect of moving stripes. Donna James saw me looking at the wall. "That's one feature they goofed on," she said. "That's the only thing. It's quite difficult to read the student's signing against the background."

"The interpreter probably stands against the blackboard?"

"There are no interpreters at NTID, as a rule."

"No interpreters? I just talked with two professors who told me they had interpreters in all their classes."

"They teach in mainstreamed classrooms at RIT. Interpreters are only used in the degree programs at the Rochester Institute of Technology, in classes where there are both hearing and deaf students. College classes. Here at NTID, all the faculty do their own signing. Actually, they sign and speak at the same time. When I took my course, there were a few new faculty in it. It's up to the faculty to learn it or pick it up in the classroom. At NTID we use interpreters only for outside speakers, visitors, special events. And we train interpreters here. Many Rochester students take courses in sign language and interpreting. Hearing students, of course. Interpreters have to be hearing. Occasionally an interpreter might be assigned to a teacher here at NTID, under some special circumstance, but as a rule all instructors are responsible for signing their own lectures."

"How do they manage?"

"I think some of them have a real hard time. But they struggle through." James locked up the empty classroom. We walked down the hall and into a room from which we could hear the sound of piano music. It was a backstage area behind the auditorium. A young woman was seated at a piano, playing Chopin, with spirit. Fortissimo. "Is she deaf?" I asked.

"I think so," answered Ford. As we passed through the room, I noticed a hand-lettered sign taped to the piano: ACOUSTIC PIANO.

James Stangarone's title at NTID is Career Opportunities Specialist. He's an admissions officer. A native signer and an interpreter, he also supervises the hiring and training of interpreters for the Institute. Stangarone was almost an hour late for our appointment, which gave me a good opportunity to study the school's Official Bulletin. It was designed in a magazine format on thick expensive paper stock, with lots of photographs. Behind all the gloss, the high-technology fittings and the sesquipedalian titles, NTID proved a rather modest enterprise.

Entering students are expected to have an eighth-grade level of achievement or better, in reading, writing, and mathematics. "It is a college," explains the bulletin, "because it offers postsecondary education opportunities through the master's degree." "Opportunities" is the key word in the statement. It is possible for a small number of NTID students to go on to one of Rochester Institute of Technology's other colleges and receive a bachelor's or master's degree. NTID awards associate degrees (AAs) to only about 30 percent of its students. The rest, the majority, are in certificate or diploma programs that require anywhere from six months to three years of matriculation.

Since so many of its students have only an eighth-grade education, NTID's work is clear-cut: to teach, fairly quickly, all the things that the students weren't taught in their previous schools, and teach them a marketable skill as well. The theme, message, and mission of NTID is employment. Being competitive in a modern society, claims NTID, means having a high degree of technical competence. Or some degree of some sort of competence. According to the bulletin, NTID offers a certificate course in Office Practice and Procedures to prepare students for positions as general clerk, clerk typist, file clerk, billing clerk. It is approximately a one-year course. The duration of all courses is given approximately; additional time is often necessary for their completion.

A diploma course entitled Manufacturing Processes (approximately two years) qualifies holders of the diploma for these positions: assembler, machine tool operator, quality control, tool and die apprentice, mold-making apprentice, production machine operator. All factory jobs.

Many of the truly technical curricula seemed to be more serious, and most take several years to complete. They include optical finishing, photography, drafting, and of course, printing, which offers training in the newer cold-type processes.

NTID has a good record of placing students in jobs, and the bulletin is liberally adorned with chatty profiles of former students who are now employed. There is a photograph of a young woman sitting beside a large desk calculator. After completing her NTID course in business technologies, she found work in a Chicago bank as an accounting technician. The accompanying text describes the young woman exclusively in hearing terms: "There is the noise of traffic, the roar of the Loop overhead, the drone of people on their way to work discussing the day's events; and even though she can't hear all this activity, she's still caught up in the exciting vibrations of the city."

Turning to course descriptions, most of the math and science is at the high school level, with a sprinkling of elementary college courses. Under general education—all required courses—are only three areas of study: developmental education, English, and communication. The deaf students call developmental education "charm school." The courses concentrate on social and personal skills, and explain in highly conventional terms the human values of the hearing world and what will be expected of the deaf individual: "human relationships, conventions of the job-search process, co-worker relationships, relationships with the supervisor," and at the end of the sequence, a course that teaches "dependency reduction."

Six English courses are offered, four designed to familiarize the students with particular technical vocabularies (one is called English of Technology). I found myself hoping that the educational specialist who teaches it isn't the same person who wrote the description: "This course series covers the vocabulary and structural forms found in contemporary literature in the English language. Through this media English is taught to give students a full spectrum of the various components of modern English. The literature words covered vary over a span of three quarters."

I wondered what sort of reaction a deaf student might have to this paragraph—a deaf student with an eighth-grade reading level who was probably a little nervous about English to begin with.

Under the heading "Communication," I found that the largest number of courses offered in the institution were in the Audiology and Speech Pathology Department. There were twenty offerings in speech, oral training, speechreading, pronunciation, and "speech lab." (The TV documentary series NOVA, in its program on deafness, estimated that NTID students spend half their time in speech training.) There were also three courses in manual communication based on the simultaneous method of signing and speaking.

Prominently displayed in the bulletin was a half-page photograph of five people wearing large brown paper bags over their heads. They were all faculty members. Round eyeholes had been cut in the fronts of the bags. The text described this scene as having been part of a mini-convention run by NTID's Professional Development Office. It read: "The participants had paper bags covering their faces and each acted out emotions of fear, anger, frustration, and rage through body language. 'Teachers must work at being good communicators,' stated the leader of the demonstration."

I didn't know what to make of it. Everyone at NTID seemed to be going to a great deal of trouble to avoid learning sign language. Did they really think they could teach technical subjects with body language? I wasn't at all comfortable with the idea of teachers expressing fear, anger, frustration, or rage in an academic classroom, either. But I was completely nonplussed when I read the following declaration by the director of NTID, Dr. Robert Frisina: "When in the course of human events the challenge of deafness confronts NTID, it is necessary for the people in each of its departments and its divisions to declare their interdependence and build those programs which enable the departments to survive and NTID to flourish . . . we hold these truths to be self-evident. . . ."

James Stangarone arrived just then, apologetic for being late, and appearing very busy. He is a large man, muscular and hale, about forty. On his office wall is a photograph of him, dressed entirely in black, his hands raised, interpreting. A smaller figure near the edge of the picture, standing behind a lectern that bears the seal of the presidency, is Jimmy Carter. "That was the White House Conference on the Handicapped," Stangarone explained. "It was a great honor for me to interpret for the President."

Stangarone's parents are deaf, he has had long experience as an interpreter and a teacher. Before coming to NTID in 1968, he taught at the California School for the Deaf at Riverside. He hired and trained many of the early interpreters at NTID. He's been associated with the Registry of Interpreters for the Deaf since it was first proposed in 1964, and later became its president. Actual certifying began in 1972; by 1980 the Registry had 65 chapters, 3 in Canada, and 4,000 members, 2,500 of whom are certified.

I asked if sign language was taught to NTID students.

"Most students sign when they come here. About two-thirds. Last summer we had three hundred and fifteen students in the vestibule program (a summer preparatory program), two hundred and twenty-five knew sign language. The others were mostly from mainstreamed programs in regular public schools."

NTID, he said, accepted students whose hearing loss was greater than 70 dBs down in the better ear. "Sometimes a little less, sixty-five. Kids who would have a hard time in a hearing school. They're educationally deaf.

"We prefer that they have at least an eighth-grade education when they come, but they don't always. The engineers are different. We have about forty undergraduates right now over at RIT. Engineers and computer scientists usually come with quite high math scores.

"This is a practical educational institution with a fantastic record for placing graduates. We have to be. All the funding from HEW is tied to results. They wouldn't stand for it if we didn't get our students jobs. We train people for jobs that really exist. The prospects for higher education in this state are grim. Projections show that by the year 2000, half—fifty percent—of the colleges in New York State will be closed. One of the reasons is that they aren't teaching useful skills."

I asked if the interpreters at NTID were trained in ASL.

"That's not an issue," he answered. "We interpret into English as accurately as possible. By the time deaf students get to college and are taking courses at RIT, they know English and can read English signing as well as they can read ASL. They're bilingual.

"Sometimes in a courtroom or a doctor's office, with older or uneducated people, ASL might be called for, otherwise, no. All the young people know English signs."

The Alexander Graham Bell Association had been calling for the training of more oral interpreters, and I asked if the Registry had received many requests for oral interpreters.

He smiled. "No, no. Very few," he answered. "But we want to serve everybody. We take those requests seriously and do provide oral interpreters."

I asked him to comment on the large number of women in the field. "That's all over," he said. "Now that interpreting is getting to be a profession and interpreters are earning a decent living, more men are entering the field. The days of the part-time housewife interpreter are pretty much gone."

Before leaving NTID that afternoon, I looked in at the Audiology Department, and Nick Orlando, head speech pathologist, showed me around. He took me into a small room used for speech training. There were gleaming microphones and beautiful headsets. "Are the rooms looped?"

He shook his head. "Hard wire. None of the rooms are looped."

"What wire?"

"Hard wire," he said again. He reached across the desk and picked up the wire, very hard indeed, and black, that led from the microphone on the teacher's desk to the earphones worn by the deaf students. "Better transmission than radio. Clearer," he said. "Louder." He walked me into the speech lab. Two banks of TV monitors, one atop the other, covered the walls. Each had a set of earphones and a library of videotapes on a variety of subjects: conversational exchanges, technical terms, and so on. Orlando called my attention to a series used in a course called *Pronunciation:* Webster's Diacritical Markings—dī·ə·krit·i·kəl märk·iŋz. They were teaching this additional and more complicated sound-based notation system to the deaf students at NTID, he explained, and were planning to package the method and sell it to elementary and high school programs for deaf children in other parts of the country. "It will help standardize pronunciation among the deaf. We have fifteen Ph.D.s working here in the Audiology Department."

"What do they do?"

"Oh," he said, "research."

"Like what?"

"You know what research is. Evaluating things. Seeing how the programs work. If red captions are better than green ones. Things like that."

"You publish the results?"

"I think so."

"Good, I'd love to see it. Do you have something I can take with me?"

"Ask at the Visitor's Bureau. A lot of it is the *NTID Focus.*"

NTID Focus is a slick, in-house magazine. It looks as if it's published by the same people who put out the bulletin. Orlando walked me down to the lobby. He was interested in sign language, he said, and often wished that he had more opportunity to learn it well and use it. "The only ones here who really get to know it well are the faculty who live right in Rochester and see a lot of the students. Invite them over for dinner. That's the way to learn," he advised, and said goodbye.

Professors Golladay and Panara had promised to send me information about themselves, and there was a large envelope waiting for me at the front desk. It contained a lot of useful material, articles, course descriptions—and a small sheaf of poems. All were well-conceived, intricate sonnets; two were about interpreters. One had been written by Panara, and the rest by Golladay—five in all. I was impressed by them, and moved. After a day touring NTID, I felt that there was a great discrepancy between the stated aims and the actual accomplishments of the institution, a gap that was filled by indifference and jargon. It was very pleasant to end the day on a friendly, cultural note.

IV

While visiting California, I heard a story about a woman who had been deaf most of her life. She was raised as a deaf person, went to a deaf school, married a deaf man; when she was past forty, a doctor looked in her ears and announced that she had a kind of conduction deafness that could probably be corrected by surgery. "She had the operation," my young deaf informant told me, "and became a hearing person. Her whole life changed. She divorced her husband, lost her old deaf friends. I think it was a terrible experience for her. She became an interpreter, and of course, she's the best interpreter there ever was. She *knows* what deaf people want. I think she lives in Rochester. Last I heard, she was losing her hearing again and getting her old friends back."

My informant couldn't remember the woman's name, but the story sounded interesting, and I wondered if I could locate her. I had forgotten how small the deaf community is; the first person I asked knew all the details, and gave me a phone number. The woman I was looking for was Alice Beardsley. She answered the phone herself at her office at NTID, where she works training interpreters. We made an appointment for lunch.

Mrs. Beardsley is a striking woman of fifty-eight with a pale, delicate face, and white hair that seemed almost transparent. She was dressed all in white. The only color about her was a bright scarf at her throat and her clear, green eyes. She seemed fragile, almost fey, but displayed no reticence whatever in expressing the resentment she felt toward the world around her for most of her life—and the people in it.

She was born Alice Benedict, in Corning, New York, on a farm. April 19, 1922. Her father died when she was two. "In the springtime when I was five, I had measles and scarlet fever. That's probably what made me deaf, but when I recovered, nobody noticed it. They thought I was still getting over the diseases and was naturally frail. When I went to grammar school, they kept me in the first grade for three years. They thought I was retarded. The summer after my third year in first grade, a man came to cut the alfalfa, a farmer from Savona. He told my mother, 'I don't think she can hear.' He said he had grandsons who were deaf, and that they were going to a special school in Rochester. My mother and I went up to Savona. Two teachers from the school came to the farm to see me, and confirmed that I was deaf.

"My mother brought me to the school, the Rochester School for the Deaf, that year. I was eight—1930. I remember what I was wearing. White sandals and a pinafore. She didn't bring any other clothes for me, she just left me. I never saw her again. She died on Christmas Day. They didn't come for me in time. I went home for the funeral, and when I went back to school I became a ward of the state.

"I never left the school. At vacations, I had no place to go. I lived there and went to the superintendent's house for my meals, and for Thanksgiving and Christmas. The superintendent and his wife took a special interest in me. I was a good student, learned speech well, and had good manners. They were big on etiquette, and taught me how to have tea." She laughed. "I was their pretty little lady; a pretty little green-eyed blonde and a terrific student. The superintendent often praised me, but I never felt much affection for him. He looked like Hitler.

"It was a good education I had. We used the Rochester Method of course, all fingerspelling, speech, and lipreading. We had our home signs, though. When we got caught, the roof fell in. Especially on me. They'd say, 'You! Alice Benedict, of all people. We expected it of the others, but not you.'

"I was at the school for eleven years. It was my home. We had many happy times in the girl's dorm. I loved all the girls I grew up with at the school. When we graduated, I went with the other girls—eight of us—and we all got jobs in a factory in Rochester. I was the only one still living at school. When I told them I was going to work in a factory, they wouldn't stand for it. I was much too good to work in a factory. I had really wanted to go to college, but the superintendent wouldn't stand for my going to Gallaudet either. He was having a big feud with the president of Gallaudet at the time. I think they hated each other, and not many Rochester students went to Gallaudet. The super persuaded me that I was already educated beyond anything I could get at Gallaudet.

"When I graduated, I had a New York State Regents diploma; only two of the twenty-three graduates in my class had made the Regents. The super absolutely insisted that I had already taken all the courses that Gallaudet offered, and I could get a degree from Gallaudet by spending only one year there, and it wasn't worth it. I still wanted to go, and I was very unhappy about being separated from my friends who got swell jobs in the factory. I stayed at the school as a supervisor of the older girls. There was only one deaf teacher at the school, a math teacher, and there were a couple of deaf supervisors in the dorms. The other teachers were hearing and lived off campus. They were mostly maiden ladies, and sometimes spent forty years teaching. Devoted their whole lives to the school.

"I was nineteen when I left to get married. They arranged the whole thing. I didn't want to get married. I didn't know anything about the opposite sex; never had been out with a boy. The man they picked I didn't know very well. They kept pushing me and arranging things. He was well off, had a lot of money. He was older than me and deaf, too. That's the only thing we had in common. I was married for thirty years and had two children, two girls. They were both wonderful, and I'm still very close to both of them.

"I learned ASL after I was married, in the late 1940s. The first time I saw it, I said to myself, I've got to learn this wonderful language. A deaf woman in Rochester taught me. I learned very quickly. I had lots of deaf friends, women at the deaf club and at the church.

"I really started having trouble with him—Beardsley, my

husband—in the sixties, when the girls were in high school and wanting to go to college. No money for their education. So I went to work, at the age of forty-one. Wish I'd done it sooner. I became the manager of a dry-cleaning store. Only a couple of people worked there. I was at the counter, wore hearing aids in both ears. It was very difficult. I had been a good lipreader—I could read on the sides. Between that, and the hearing aids, I managed. Everyone was nice and patient. It was nothing keeping track of the clothes. Not much was required, if you think about it. They wanted their clothes on Wednesday, or on Tuesday. My daughter enrolled in a nursing school in Auburn. She's a nurse now, in California. The other one is business manager for the Red Cross in Rochester.

"The following year, 1964, I had a terrible ear infection and went to a doctor in Rochester. I guess it was the first time I ever had an examination. He told me about an operation he had just read about, and he said he'd do it for me if I wanted. It's called tympanoplasty."

Tympanoplasty is one of those miracles of modern surgery that ear surgeons now consider rather routine. The procedure was known in the nineteenth century, but because of the high risk of infection was performed only in life-threatening situations. With the availability of antibiotics, and the development of high-quality surgical microscopes, it has become a cure for conduction deafness, which occurs in the middle ear. The restoration of normal or near-normal hearing by surgery is always surgery to the middle ear. Sensory-neural deafness results from damage to or malformation of the inner ear, the cochlea, and is irreversible. A surgical procedure has recently been developed to implant platinum wires in the human cochlea, but that operation remains experimental.

The middle ear is a small, enclosed cavity. Sound enters it through the tympanic membrane: the eardrum. When pressure from incoming sound waves reaches the tympanic membrane, it vibrates. Inside the cavity there is a chain of three very small bones (ossicles), called the malleus (hammer), the incus (anvil), and the stapes (stirrup), which are set in motion by pressure transmitted by the tympanic membrane. These bones, connected by tendons and muscle, act as transformers of the sound waves and amplify the pressure (about twenty times) while conducting it from the large surface of the eardrum, through the middle ear, and to a second smaller membrane, the oval window, leading to the cochlea.

Any number of things can go wrong in the middle ear to disrupt the pressure needed to maintain successful conduction. The tympanic membrane might be punctured or torn. The bones might be diseased, injured, dislodged, or missing altogether. Often, the three ossicles become rigid, fail to move. Through tympanoplasty, the eardrum can be repaired by grafts, or a substitute made. Using surgical instruments like watchmaker's tools, the bones can be removed, made mobile, or even replaced.

"My doctor," said Alice Beardsley, "took a small piece of bone from my skull and fashioned tiny new bones for my middle ear. The operation was a success. The first thing I ever heard was the sound of myself swallowing water.

"I remember waking up in my hospital room. I was very thirsty. There was another woman in the next bed, sleeping. I took some water from my bedside table and heard myself swallowing. It was so loud, it frightened me. It was so loud I was sure I was bothering the other woman. She turned over and said something to me, and she was shouting. I was sure I had woken her up. When my daughter came to see me, she said, 'Why are you whispering?' and I said, 'Why are you hollering?'

"I was surrounded. Noise all over the place. Everything was a blur. I only had hearing in one ear, my right ear, and never could tell where any sounds were coming from. An airplane could be anywhere. In my kitchen, if I was standing near the refrigerator when it went on, I'd jump out of my skin. I was on tranquilizers for nine months. It was traumatic. The noise, the cars.

"One morning I heard an awful racket. There were a bunch of starlings on my lawn, and they sounded terrible. Is this the birds I've read about all my life, singing sweetly? It wasn't sweet at all. It was a terrible squawking. I just wanted to be by myself and be quiet. I was getting better, though. I realized that I had to learn to listen. Learn not to pay attention to the unimportant things. If a fan went on, I just had to force myself not to pay attention, and learn to listen, especially for voices; to get used to the noise and concentrate on what I wanted to hear.

"I couldn't go back to my old job; the dry-cleaning machines were just too much for me. I still had to take tranquilizers. I went to a family camp on Seneca Lake to be by myself. To pray. And while I was alone, I got close to God. After that, I began to feel better. It took almost a year, and it took a lot of meditation, too.

"Gradually, I got used to hearing. In 1965, I got a job as a sales manager for a gift-wrapping company, and I also became an interpreter. I was the first real interpreter in Rochester and got lots of calls. There was much work. Doctors and lawyers who needed an interpreter called me. The word got around fast, and it seemed that every deaf person in Rochester suddenly realized how useful it was to have an interpreter on call. Sometimes I felt like I was their slave. That year, I was elected president of the Empire State Association of the Deaf, and was president till 1972. I was vice-chairperson of Governor Rockefeller's commission to study problems of the deaf for nine years. No pay," she said. "Except for the doctors and lawyers, I almost never got paid."

In addition to feeling exploited, Alice realized that the deaf community's reaction to her change of status was one of increasing wariness, and possibly distrust. They counted on her to act as go-between. They relied on her to explain their problems to the hearing world, and they expected her to reveal to them all the secrets of the hearing. "I didn't know any hearing people," Alice Beardsley said. "Now that I could hear, they were more of a mystery to me than ever. Even as I got to know them, over the years, I never figured out any secrets. Nothing deaf people didn't know already.

"In the late sixties, NTID was going up, and needed interpreters. I applied, but was not accepted. In 1968, I applied again, and they hired me part-time. In May 1969, they put me on full-time. When the Registry began certifying interpreters, I was one of the first to get a Comprehensive Skills certificate. I had some perfect scores—four one-hundreds. My low was ninety-seven. These scores still stand today," she said.

Hearing interpreters have criticized Alice for including too much chit-chat in her interpretations, especially in the classrooms. "I interpret everything," she said. "Jokes from the back of the room and wisecracks from the hearing students and the professor. Deaf students hardly ever get any of the humor in their classrooms, but I try to keep it all in my interpretations. They all say they appreciate it."

Her two daughters had both left home, and her own growing independence created a more serious alienation between Alice and her husband. They saw less and less of each other and were finally separated in 1974.

In August of 1975, Mrs. Beardsley decided that since the operation on her right ear had been so successful, she would have it performed on her left ear, too. The same doctor, the same procedure, but completely disastrous results. She lost the little residual hearing she had in that ear, and suffered damage to the inner ear which destroyed her sense of balance. "I was completely shattered. I couldn't get out of bed. I had to cling to a wall to walk across the room, and was constantly dizzy. All winter long. Psychologically, it was horrible. I went on tranquilizers again. Toward the end of winter I was in a panic. I couldn't get around, couldn't interpret. I was worried about supporting myself ever again. Contract time was coming up and I was deathly afraid they wouldn't renew me. I was on the verge of suicide.

"I had to go for a third operation. The doctor removed my semicircular canal, which restored the balance. NTID gave me another contract, and I went back to work. My hearing wasn't as good as it had been right after the first operation.

"Then," said Alice Beardsley, with the sly look of an unlikely survivor, "you're not going to believe this: In February 1977, I had a heart attack. I died," she said. "I was actually dead, and I saw God. They brought me back to life in the intensivecare unit. I was *there*," she said, "and I came back. My minister was with me in the hospital and he understood what had happened."

The last time I saw Alice Beardsley was during the summer of 1979 at NTID. She doesn't hear well enough to interpret any more, but does what is called reverse interpreting—from signs into speech. She still trains interpreters, though, and teaches ASL. Her good ear has been fading steadily; she can hear only a little from it, and nothing from the other. Being a hearing person for a decade did not make her happy, but it certainly changed her life. She found hearing people somewhat more open, she said, less timid and suspicious than the deaf. The attitude of hearing people toward the deaf, however, she considers extremely callous and negative, and she feels she made no contribution at all toward increased understanding.

She has found great comfort in the expression of her religious feeling, and in the relationships she has formed with her minister, his family, and other members of the congregation, hearing and deaf. She is a lay reader at her Episcopal church, and deliverer of the chalice, she told me. She also conducts prayer meetings and services informally for students at NTID, some of them with strong mystical overtones.

She has found great satisfaction in her work. "I was the black sheep at the Rochester School because I became a signer—and a professional signer at that—but right now," she said, very pleased, "four teachers from the Rochester School for the Deaf are learning signs here at NTID. Next fall, I plan to be teaching ASL at the school on Saturday mornings."

She seemed to me a unique, fathomless person with an impressive talent for survival. A paradoxical person, both earthy and ethereal, hearing and deaf—but often neither. She is intelligent, resourceful, and serene on the surface. She says she is happier now. Her bitterness is keen, and the pain vividly remembered. "Everybody knows me," she said. Everybody does know her, everybody knows her story, and everybody respects her.

Last time I saw her, we found ourselves laughing at a very old deaf joke. *Question:* What is the greatest problem facing deaf people today? *Answer:* Hearing people. We were walking down a hallway, Alice laughing and shaking her head. "Oh, yes," she said, "that *is* the biggest problem. Hearing people." She sighed. "And deaf people."

Apeing Sign Language

Have you seen at the King's Garden, in a glass cage, an
orangutang who has the air of a St. John preaching in
the wilderness? ... Cardinal de Polignac said to him
one day, Speak, and I'll baptize you.—*The Dream of
d'Alembert*, Diderot (circa 1769)

I

In the intellectual excitement that accompanied the new linguistics of the 1960s, a large diversion appeared in the form of a small
female anthropoid ape, the chimpanzee Washoe. Her teachers
and sponsors (sometimes called her foster parents) were
R. Allen Gardner and Beatrice Gardner, two little-known psychologists working at the University of Nevada in Reno. The
Gardners claimed that Washoe was successfully learning American Sign Language. The project began in 1966; the first results
were published in 1969, and it took a full decade to work through
the linguistic claims made for the animal and for the other apes
(some were gorillas) that followed Washoe through a highly
publicized career in sign language schooling.

The Gardners were not interested in linguistic theories, they
said, and claimed to espouse no particular theory of language.
They rejected with special vehemence, however, the suggestion
that language was an innate faculty of the human species. The
Gardners believed that language was a form of learned behavior,

not unlike any other kind of behavior; that it was acquired through imitation, through observation, and when nourished by positive rewards. In their demonstration experiment with Washoe, they sought to prove this view by teaching language to their nonhuman primate in exactly the way they supposed human children learned language. The infant chimpanzee was brought to Reno and domiciled in a well-appointed house trailer in the Gardners' backyard, which also had a spacious playground, exercise equipment, and toys.

Attempts to teach apes language are exact inversions of the deprivation experiments described earlier. In the ancient history of Herodotus, and in the modern story of the deaf children that is related to it, all the subjects lived in an impoverished environment, deprived of normal language input and left to their own devices. In contrast, Washoe was placed in a linguistically enriched milieu filled with the artifacts of human childhood, inhabited by numerous human companions, and saturated with human language. The only thing she was deprived of was contact with her own species. Her caretakers signed to her, more or less continuously, during all her waking hours.

Washoe was dressed in children's clothes, played with, given toys, taken on frequent outings, and fed a human diet (rich in candy and Coke)—all accompanied by a constant, running signed commentary. Each carefully selected person, object, food, or activity that formed part of the daily round was identified with a sign in the hope that Washoe would associate the sign with the thing and would imitate her companions. Although Washoe's environment contained far more linguistic input and stimulation than any human child's, the chimpanzee showed no inclination to imitate any of the signs.

"It was not until the sixteenth month of the project that we achieved any degree of control over Washoe's imitation of gestures," wrote Allen and Beatrice Gardner in 1969. "Eventually we got to a point where she would imitate a simple gesture, such as pulling at her ears . . . first we make the gesture, then she imitates. . . . Up to this writing, however, imitation of this sort has not been an important method for introducing new signs into Washoe's vocabulary."

They rewarded Washoe for any gesture, for any close approximation of a gesture, for any purposeful or random movement of the hands. Washoe used a begging gesture familiar to all primates: the extending of an open palm. It occurred naturally and required no instruction. It was reported as the first sign acquired by Washoe and translated as *come/gimme*.

The Gardners then began a program of formal instruction using a number of conditioning techniques. In the presence of an object (the stimulus), they moved the animal's arms and molded its hands into the proper sign shape, held them in that shape, then administered a reward. It is a standard method in all animal training. With a great deal of drill, Washoe was able to make the sign (or nearly), earned rewards and much approval. Eventually, she was able to make the signs alone, without molding, merely by being presented with the stimulus.

Neither of the Gardners had been trained to work with non-human primates. Allen Gardner had worked mainly within a rather narrow area of experimental psychology called probability learning. Beatrice Gardner had been an ethologist; her best-known work was on the hunting habits of the jumping spider. The Gardners were not linguists, they were not ASL signers, nor did they appear to be familiar with the growing field of child language acquisition. "Behavior is lawful," they declared, and proceeded from the assumption that the same fundamental laws applied for all kinds of human and animal behavior: hunting in the spider, language in the child.

Chimpanzees, the Gardners argued, have never been observed to use language because they have never enjoyed a human language environment; nobody ever taught them. "Only the devout Chomskyan nativist would expect language to unfold normally in human children who were kept in a cage," they wrote indignantly. The widely held observation that no great similarity exists between animal communication systems and human languages was dismissed as a dwelling upon mere "surface dissimilarities."

It wouldn't make any kind of biological sense if apes had the ability to use language but never used it. Nothing evolves if organisms fail to use their capacities. To quote an analogy from Chomsky, it would be "similar to the discovery, on some unexplored island, of a species of bird that had never thought to fly until instructed to do so through human intervention." The biological issues implied by the Gardners' work were never seriously addressed, but only stated in vague terms of similarities and continuities. With each sign that Washoe learned, however, she was considered to be bridging the gap between ape and man.

It was an heroic effort. The Gardners, their students, and their research assistants expended enormous amounts of time, energy, and ingenuity on the project. "Within fifty-one months of training, Washoe . . . had acquired 132 signs." Washoe was then five years old; it had taken her more than four years to learn 132 signs. That averages out to be about thirty signs a year. Harder than teaching the signs was getting the ape to use them. In addition to drilling and prompting, the Gardners and their staff spent a lot of time in what they called "eliciting" signs: setting up the appropriate context and producing necessary objects as conversation pieces. Cats were procured, and spoons, and automobiles; hats, shoes, and dogs (or pictures of dogs), in the hope that Washoe would make the appropriate signs for these things. If she failed to produce the sign spontaneously, they requested it directly.

In order to keep the signs on Washoe's list current, the researchers rotated all signs, and each day designated one the Sign of the Day. They went about eliciting this sign vigorously, relentlessly, contriving to bring the targeted object to Washoe's attention. (It reminded me of a passage in *Gulliver's Travels* about the people who had given up talking and instead carried around with them all the objects they wished to discuss. Simple, ordinary people carried small sacks, but old and learned ones hefted huge, heavy bundles wherever they went.) Actually, signs for objects were fairly easy to elicit. Other signs required more elaborate measures. In order to elicit the sign for *hurt*, they showed Washoe their cuts and bruises. The sign *spin* was elicited by having people whirl around the room "as in dancing." It must have taken a lot out of them.

Adding to the problems of tutoring an ape in sign language was the fact that people on the project were not fluent in sign language. The teachers had to learn the signs before teaching them to the ape. Often the project directors themselves were uncertain about how a particular sign should be made. By the time it was taught to the chimp, "It lost something in translation," said a deaf friend ruefully.

Comprehension posed a different kind of problem. Though ruthless about eliciting signs, the Gardners were quite benign in their testing procedures. When Washoe was tested on *wh* questions, she was scored as correct if her answer came from the correct category. "For example, when someone asked Washoe, *Who that?* while indicating Roger Fouts . . . incorrect name signs such as *Susan* and *Greg* were [also scored as] correct. . . ." In none of the published material is it ever established how much Washoe did understand; there is only the experimenters' judgment that comprehension had been demonstrated by the "appropriateness" of the chimp's responses.

In 1970, when Washoe was five years old and had spent more than four years in Reno, she was sent to a primate facility in Norman, Oklahoma, to live out the rest of her life—possibly another thirty or thirty-five years. Accompanying Washoe was Roger Fouts, her long-time trainer and former graduate student of the Gardners, who had earned a Ph.D. for his work on the project. Their host was William Lemmon, a clinical psychologist on the faculty of the University of Oklahoma who kept a rather informal collection of animals—cows and pigs as well as apes—in a place that is generally described as a sort of farm.

When Washoe took up residence in Norman, the public got its first look at her. During the four years in Reno only a small number of persons had actually seen the ape. The Gardners and their students had worked in virtual seclusion, and publications about Washoe's progress were few. The best-known record of that progress was a film. As a scientific document a film is not entirely satisfactory, since it is often not clear how individual scenes were prepared, nor to what extent, especially in this case, the subject may have been rehearsed. The Gardners, in short, had worked in secret, keeping their raw data to themselves, and had released only carefully selected material.

Even the most enthusiastic journalists were denied permission to visit the site of Project Washoe. Emily Hahn, a supremely sympathetic journalist, former owner of chimpanzees and resident of Africa, who had already declared herself "on the side of the apes," was consistently denied the meeting with Washoe that she had long and earnestly sought. When Washoe arrived in Oklahoma, Emily Hahn hurried there forthwith, and, rather disappointed, found Washoe of enormous size, vastly overweight, frantic for candy and all the other sweets that had been her rewards during training. The ape was placed on a diet by Dr. Lemmon, who, not averse to anthropomorphizing, referred to Washoe as "the girl," and offered the opinion that Washoe was "the greediest chimp I've ever known. All she thinks about is her stomach."

Roger Fouts remained in Norman and began teaching sign language to all the chimps considered young enough to learn. Dr. Lemmon's farm has become the Institute for Primate Studies, known as one of the centers for providing sign language instruction to apes. Despite the upgrading that the Lemmon establishment has undergone, those engaged in the various chimp projects display a certain amount of species confusion. One chimp, Lucy, adopted by Dr. Lemmon's secretary, eats at table, feeds guests (whether they want to be fed or not), sleeps in the same bedroom with her foster parents, and is said to mix drinks charmingly. Another chimp, Ali, was baptized in a proper ceremony by a "trendy" priest. The baptism was reported by Emily Hahn (and was said not to be the first on record). "He's a Catholic now," said the ape's foster mother; "why shouldn't my baby join the church? Why hasn't he a right to be saved, like anybody else?" Ali's domestic arrangement did not endure, however, and he was returned to Dr. Lemmon's farm in 1974, where he fell into a profound depression and pulled out large quantities of his hair. To this day, I'm told, he remains conspicuously bald in spots. Although he has been a star pupil on the sign language project and is said to know a great deal of English as well (one writer declared that English was Ali's second language), he has not told anyone about his experiences.

After leaving Reno, Washoe's vocabulary did not expand, nor did she acquire conversationalists among her own species. Although other chimpanzees at Norman have been receiving instruction for a number of years, accounts of chimp-to-chimp communication remain anecdotal. Neither has Washoe had much reproductive success; two pregnancies have failed to produce viable offspring. Her trainers are very disappointed, and express deep emotional stress. What they want from Washoe now seems very much like grandchildren. In the absence of natural progeny, Washoe has been provided with a chimpanzee foster child, and press releases promise signed exchanges between the pair. In the last photograph I saw of Washoe, she and the infant were sitting on a shelf in a very bare iron cage.

It is difficult to imagine how a second-generation linguistic ape would go about learning language. According to the Gardners, no creature learns language in a cage; and from Washoe's own history it is clear that apes do not learn language by imitation or example. In order to be successful, Washoe and her infant would have to be housed in an enriched human environment with many objects suitable for display as stimuli during language instruction. Washoe would have to be an accomplished behaviorist, skilled at shaping and molding the infant's hands into the desired sign, and at administering rewards for correct responses. I wondered how she would go about eliciting signs.

II

Almost all we know of wild chimpanzees we have learned since 1960 through the efforts of Jane Goodall, the solitary young ethologist of great physical courage who, in addition to her scientific commitment, has expressed boundless affection for wild chimpanzees and great pleasure in their company.

Dr. Goodall observed wild chimpanzees using a number of hand gestures, probably for communicative purposes. There are particular hand movements used for greeting, and for making threats. There are also begging gestures (the hand outstretched), and these most social of all apes use their hands to make contact with each other to indicate various emotional and physical states. A cool gestural language like ASL seems particularly inappropriate for chimpanzees because they are foremost a raucous bunch of stompers and screamers. They are quick to become excited, feel frustrated easily, and angry. Their cries, hoots, barks, and screams, accompanied by stamping, drumming, and bashing, are described by Goodall as only slightly less deafening than the trumpeting of elephants. In the wild, they spend six or seven hours a day feeding and the rest of the daylight hours playing, ranging far and freely over their jungle territory, mostly looking for food. At sundown they build clean, commodious nests from leaves (with varying degrees of competence), and spend their nights aloft. In the jungle, they remain silent in their trees, avoiding the attention of nocturnal predators. In captivity, they frequently scream all night.

Chimpanzees fear and avoid human beings, as they do all

larger mammals. They seem not to realize the advantage of their superior strength and prefer to deal with smaller species. They readily hunt, kill, and eat monkeys, baboons, and anything else they can corner.

Goodall spent more than a year, alone, following a band of chimps around the Gombe Stream Reserve in Tanzania. Eventually, they came into her camp and ate from her hand, a situation she later regretted. In removing the chimpanzees' reluctance to mingle with humans, she feels she has jeopardized the safety of the scientists who will follow her, as well as the autonomy of the chimp colony. Although she has expressed complete confidence in the chimpanzees as far as her personal safety is concerned, when she returned to Africa with her own small son, she kept the child locked in a cage, safe from the appetites and whims of the apes.

Physical similarities between apes and humans were recognized by the ancients, but it wasn't until the seventeenth century, when the first anthropoid apes arrived in Europe, that the idea of gradations between monkeys and men was first articulated. A biologically missing link was not proposed until Darwinian evolution became a dominant intellectual force. Thomas Huxley, in his book *Man's Place in Nature* (1863), offered the opinion that the higher apes were more closely related to man than they were to other apes. This interesting remark has been turning up in a large number of articles about chimpanzee research— circa 1970—and is presented as a biological fact. Unfortunately, it is without meaning. The biochemistry of the human body is only beginning to be known. When and if the genes are fully understood, the opinion will still be meaningless, because similarity will depend on which features are being compared.

Over the centuries, the gap between ape and human has widened and narrowed in odd and erratic cycles. As substitute man and literary metaphor, the ape has symbolized the human being in a degraded, primitive, or diminished form. When men were considered fallen angels, apes were considered fallen men: the formerly human, sinful and punished, deprived of speech, cast out. Demons. In modern writing, the ape is a symbol of the primitive nonwhite, non-European races who provided the Victorians with a buffer against the anxieties aroused by evolution. (Look how far *we* have come, they said to themselves.) To the ape were attributed all the uncivilized, un-Christian, criminal urges known to man: he was a brute, thief, liar, murderer, rapist. Offsetting the ape's great strength, cunning, and prowess was its manifest lack of intelligence. In their tremendously entertaining book *Men and Apes*, Ramona and Desmond Morris have made the following observation:

> In effect, Darwin set off two trends in the present context. One was to consider the behavior of living animals, especially monkeys and apes, as worthy of detailed scientific study. . . . The other development, which accompanied it, was the 'uplifting' of our poor relatives to a level that, while keeping them in a suitably inferior status, nevertheless raised them to a place that did not disgrace their richer, human cousins.

And this is how we find them now: more deprived than debased; socially rather than morally inferior; linguistically handicapped; in need of uplifting. The twentieth-century ape seems less like a demon or a brute, more like a mentally deficient human being.

In addition to the Gardners' project with Washoe, several other apes have received "linguistic" training. David Premack, at the University of Pennsylvania, taught his chimpanzee, Sarah, to answer questions and solve problems by using a set of arbitrarily shaped and colored plastic chips. His wife, Ann J. Premack, wrote a book describing the experiments and claimed that the system was analogous to reading; the title of the book is *Why*

Chimps Can Read. Both Premacks have urged that the symbol system used with Sarah be adapted for retarded children.

Francine Patterson, while a graduate student at Stanford, procured an infant gorilla named Koko from the San Francisco zoo and made headlines by claiming that the animal had not only learned ASL but could use the language with extraordinary sophistication. According to Patterson, the ape enjoyed composing English rhymes, and displayed a talent for punning—all in ASL.

III

During the spring of 1979 I realized that I had been meeting a number of people, hearing people, who were very excited about ASL—not because 500,000 deaf Americans use it every day but because they believed it might be taught to apes.

I had seen the Gardners' classroom film, *Teaching Sign Language to the Chimpanzee, Washoe,* which was oddly soporific, and had watched the NOVA film *The First Signs of Washoe,* as well, but thought I should look at them again. Both films were in the library of Gallaudet College.

Everybody is always nice at the Gallaudet Library. The deaf students who worked at the desk were helpful, courteous, and good-natured about my signing. I leafed through the catalogue; it had to be the most esoteric film collection anywhere. Among the N's, I noticed *Newton's Three Laws* in ASL (no sound, no captions) and *Nixon's Resignation Speech* (captioned). The films are all on TV cassettes for use in monitors arranged around an open room. The dozen or so monitors are frequently all in use, but as this is a deaf community, the sound is usually off. The room was quiet. When I turned up the sound on my film, it didn't appear to disturb anyone.

A student who worked at the desk passed behind my chair several times, stopping to watch Washoe and to heckle me. She tapped me and pointed to the screen. "What's that sign supposed to be?" I stopped the tape, ran it back, then forward. *"See?"*

She laughed silently. "That sign means . . ." she finger-spelled, *"b-l-i-n-d."*

Later, she was tapping me again, telling me that my signs were better than the chimp's. Though she was smiling, there was umbrage in her remarks, on her face, and a belligerent stiffness through the shoulders. "I'm only doing research," I told her.

When I returned the films several hours later, there was a message for me at the desk, and this exchange in the library eventually led to my meeting a deaf man who had spent several months working with the Gardners' chimpanzees in Reno.

He came with an interpreter and was very serious. It was understood that he was critical of the research but seemed nervous about criticizing the Gardners, whom he characterized as important hearing people. We agreed that I would not use his name.

"I never met Washoe. She had left years before I got there. We worked with a group of chimps. They were different ages and had all come when they were just a few weeks old. The Gardners had moved everything out of Reno and away from the university and bought a big, old dude ranch. They have lots of money and get lots of grants. *National Geographic* gives them money. You know who they are?" He opened a manila envelope and took out a copy of the *National Geographic Magazine* with Koko the gorilla on the cover. Opening to the masthead, he pointed to a name: Melville Bell Grosvenor, Editor Emeritus. "Alexander Graham Bell's grandson," he said; then pointed to another name, Gilbert M. Grosvenor, Editor. "I think he is Alexander Graham Bell's great-grandson. Oralists," he said. "They have given grants to people who want to teach sign language to chimpanzees or gorillas." He offered me the magazine.

"Tell me what you did in Reno."

"I wasn't there long. There was a very high turnover among the deaf," he said. "The Gardners wouldn't listen to anything the deaf people told them about ASL. They thought we didn't know anything about it and were just trying to make trouble.

"There were three shifts a day. I'd go in, wake up the chimp, change the diapers, and put clothes on. Sit him in a chair and warm up milk. Just like for children. I put a little bit of milk in the cup and waited for the sign *drink*. Thumb in mouth. I made the *drink* sign. Waited. When he made it, I'd put a few drops in the cup, and waited for the sign again." He folded his hands and sat back, waiting. "By this time the chimp was screaming." He smiled. "Even I could hear it. I wasn't supposed to give any food until he made the *eat* sign. The little ones couldn't close their hands, couldn't make the sign right. They always made a lot of mistakes and were never really right continuously.

"I took the chimp for toilet training every twenty minutes. Kept chart. They wanted to know, in the potty or out. You had to check it off. In or out. They kept all kinds of records. The most important was the logbook of signs. Every time the chimp made a sign, we were supposed to write it down in the log." He laughed. "They were always complaining because my log didn't show enough signs. All the hearing people turned in logs with long lists of signs. They always saw more signs than I did. The Gardners were disappointed in me. They thought I was too stupid to recognize a sign when I saw one.

"I watched really carefully. The chimp's hands are moving constantly. Maybe I missed something, but I don't think so. I just wasn't seeing any signs. The hearing people were logging every movement the chimp made as a sign. Every time the chimp put his finger in his mouth, they'd say, 'Oh, he's making the sign for *drink*,' and they'd give him some milk. For part of the day, I was supposed to just sign to the chimp about things he knew, things around the place that he knew the signs for. I signed my head off. That's what I was being paid to do; but mostly the chimp didn't seem to notice.

"There were special times during the day for teaching. Mold the chimp's hands, and hold them. Very tight at first, then not so tight, with less pressure, until the chimp held them in the right place by himself. It took a long time. The chimp never paid attention. His eyes would be wandering all over the place. I never saw anything like it. I felt ridiculous. Deaf people can't talk to someone who isn't looking at them. Can hearing people talk to anyone who isn't paying attention, who has their fingers in their ears? I'd try to get his attention. Grab his chin and made him look at me. They never paid attention to anything except the food. Or the tickling. Tickling was one of the rewards. It bothered me. You'd tickle them on the neck, or on the stomach. I felt really sorry for them, sometimes it seemed they would laugh themselves to death.

"They always held up their arms so you could tickle them under the armpits. Like this. They hold up their arms—long, long arms—over their heads. Sometimes their hands would touch. They'd keep their arms up until they were tickled, then they'd lower them, to stop the tickling. They caught on quick that when they held up their arms, they would be tickled. O.K., a few days later, I look in the log and see the sign *more: arms held over head, fingers touching.*" He shook his head. "The *more* sign in ASL is not made over the head but in front of the body, and the hands are not just flopping, they have a definite shape. But everybody had seen the chimp do this and it was recorded as a sign. If I said, 'That's not the correct sign,' they said it didn't make any difference, it was still recorded.

"When the chimp scratched itself, they'd record it as the sign for *scratch.* Once one of the chimps escaped. Ran right out of the yard, and when they finally got it back, I said, 'Why don't you put it in the log that the chimp was making the sign for *escape?*' They didn't think it was funny.

"The deaf people on the project were second-class citizens," he said. "The hearing people were graduate students. Wrote articles, got degrees. We weren't part of that, we just worked there.

"Another thing that bothered me was that they always called it Ameslan. In all their articles, Ameslan. I told them, deaf people always call it ASL. They told me I was wrong." He laughed.

"Chimpanzees have their own gestures from the wild. Natural gestures. They touch each other, sometimes with the back of their hands. I would never call that a sign. It's sort of a submissive gesture, that's all. They stick out their hands for things. It's reaching, it's not a sign. It's like a dog that comes up to you and lets you know he wants something. You know what the dog means, but he isn't talking. The chimps hold out their hands. They do it all the time, without being taught. They want something, they reach. Those things the people in Reno called signs. Sometimes they'd say, 'Oh, amazing, look at that, it's exactly like the ASL sign for *give*!' It wasn't.

"Their hands were queer. Different. They could curl their fingers all the way around. If they grabbed your hair, it really hurt, and you couldn't get free. Some of their signs were pretty good. A little like ASL signs," he said. "Once they learned, they wouldn't use it quite right. They couldn't seem to memorize the signs. It was all very messy, and the sign order was completely wrong. They'd learn three or four signs and sign all of them all the time in no order. *Cup me can't gimme can't can't gimme.* Like that, until they got their reward.

"Do you know what they want?" he asked me suddenly. "The Gardners. They want a deaf family to adopt a baby chimpanzee. In their house. And raise it like their own child. Crazy?" he asked. "Don't deaf people have it hard enough?"

Before he left, he asked me if I knew Laura Petitto. "She worked with a chimp," he said. "Longer than I did. She is hearing. Works in the linguistics lab. Go talk to her. Very smart person," he said. "A good signer." He thought that over for a minute. It's a high compliment to call a hearing person a good signer, and I thought he'd qualify his statement, but he let it stand.

IV

I had acquired a mountain of paper. For almost three years people had been giving and sending me, more or less continuously, vast quantities of published and unpublished matter: reprints, preprints, and offprints, many of which I carried with me in the hope of reading and understanding soon. Among the accumulation, I remembered noticing the name Laura Petitto, and immediately after my conversation with the deaf research assistant, I found two articles—one signed Petitto and Seidenberg, and the other, Seidenberg and Petitto—both about linguistic apes.

Laura Petitto, it turned out, had raised a chimpanzee in New York City. In full view of the world, as it were. The director of the project, Professor Herbert Terrace of Columbia University, had published every scrap of data that was generated by the four-year project, and had drawn completely negative conclusions. Although Terrace's results were essentially the same as those of the Gardners and Francine Patterson, he had concluded that the ape's capacity for language had not been demonstrated.

The publication of negative data in scientific journals, and the publication of Terrace's popular book *Nim*, gave the ape language controversy a new dimension. Serious doubts were raised about all the previous claims made for the language-trained apes (whose trainers reacted with great personal affront); scholars from several marginal areas were goaded into taking sides; and the whole thing erupted in an extremely uncouth shouting match at the New York Academy of Sciences in 1980 that was reported in all the newspapers. At stake (or so it seemed) were questions about the nature of language, about philosophy, and the meaning of meaning; about animal mind, and human nature. At another level, the issue seemed to be: My ape is better than your ape.

When I asked about Laura Petitto at the linguistics lab, I was told, "Of course, you should meet Laura." She was working at Gallaudet temporarily, on a particular ASL project, and was "between graduate schools." William Stokoe walked me to her office, a communal office with many desks. Laura Petitto, who is small and dark, was engaged in a signed conversation with one of the other occupants. When she finished, she turned to us a young, animated face that looked right out of the High Renaissance. I complimented her on the articles, and we talked about them for a short time. She certainly was, as I had been told, a very smart person (the kind that professionals in the IQ business call high g). "Mark's here, too," she said. "Mark Seidenberg, my collaborator. He's talking to some people in the Psych Department right now, but he'll be back. He's only here for the day." We agreed that the three of us would meet for lunch.

Laura Petitto was twenty-four years old. Mark Seidenberg was twenty-five, smart, aggressive, and articulate. There was so much g around at lunch that I found it a little intimidating. Sitting in a Gallaudet coffeehouse, the two of them laid out the whole theoretical argument for me in perfectly lucid terms in about forty-five minutes. Then they were off. They had some work to finish before Seidenberg left to return to New York, and it wasn't until later that I could talk to Petitto about her role in raising the chimp.

Herbert Terrace, professor of psychology at Columbia, had been the director of the project. I knew him; had met him ten years earlier, and when I heard about the project, it didn't match my recollection. I remembered him as a rather quiet, fastidious young man, a bachelor, an urban sort of person. He was a former student of B. F. Skinner's at Harvard, and a thorough behaviorist, and I recalled his talking about racks and relays and pigeons. I couldn't imagine this softspoken, well-groomed young man mixing it up with an unkempt, super-active wild ape. (It's a hard thing to imagine about anyone.)

Terrace, I learned, had plenty of preparation. He had been thinking about repeating the Gardners' experiment for several years. He had actually visited Washoe in Reno, had researched the subject extensively, had made contact with the Institute for Primate Studies in Oklahoma, and had already had the experience of keeping a chimpanzee in New York. In 1968, he had brought one of William Lemmon's chimps to the city and kept it for fourteen months of "socialization."

Working with Terrace from the beginning was Professor Thomas Bever, professor of psychology and linguistics at Columbia, and former student of Noam Chomsky. Bever's presence on the project made it the only language project involving apes that actually included a linguist (Mark Seidenberg was Bever's graduate student). With both the Skinnerian (behaviorist) and the Chomskyan (innatist) points of view represented, Terrace and Bever wanted only to replicate the Gardners' experiment. They had no quarrel with the Gardners, and no reason to think they would get different results. In stating their aims, they did specify—as the Gardners had not—that they were interested in learning whether a chimpanzee could create a sentence; that is, could the animal use language in new and creative ways, as humans use language? Otherwise, the only difference they saw was that they would be working with a male rather than a female ape.

When the chimpanzees arrived in New York, they named him, whimsically, Nim Chimpsky, after the famous linguist. I had the impression that they were a little sorry afterward. "Why didn't you call him B. F. Chimper?" I asked. "We never thought of it" was the answer. Everybody called him Nim.

Laura Petitto had joined the project early, as a volunteer, and had become one of Nim's teachers. It wasn't until Petitto took over that the research was really under control. In his book, Terrace acknowledges her central role repeatedly, expressing extravagant, almost pathetic gratitude, and the book is dedicated to her. She was nineteen years old when she first joined the project.

"I met Nim in December of 1973," Laura Petitto said. "He was only a few weeks old. He came right to me, and everybody thought that was a good sign. I didn't think he was cute, and I didn't trust him, but I felt in awe of him. He seemed so close—it was like seeing an evolutionary link. It was like touching prehistoric man. I thought I could cross over the phyla into his mind." She laughed. "I was nineteen years old, what did I know? But it was a powerful feeling; I was fascinated.

"The idea that one chimp can be placed in our environment and develop a concept of self in the human sense is *false,*" she said. "Chimpanzees are wild animals, very hard to work with. They are manipulative; always waiting for you to let your guard down, to trick you; always looking for a door that you accidentally left open. It was exhausting. He was wired differently, wired to fight for dominance. I dominated him on his own terms and that's what worked. I didn't let him get away with a thing. I hooted at him, barked at him, swatted him. All of us did. I was much better at being a chimpanzee than he ever was at being human."

When Petitto began working with Nim, she was an undergraduate, majoring in physiological psychology. Her main interest was primates; she had worked on a baboon project in New Jersey the previous year. All through 1974 she continued working with Nim. In the fall, as she entered her senior year, she was planning to apply to a graduate program at Rutgers in psychobiology. Meanwhile, she had been taking courses in ASL at the Deafness Center at NYU.

"Many people came to the project claiming to know ASL, but only a few did. Some knew a little signed English, or how to make isolated signs. I took a course, then I took a more advanced course.

"At first I just went to take care of Nim, very informally, not much more than babysitting. I played with him, signed to him, and tried to teach him some signs. I took it all very seriously. Before officially becoming a teacher, I watched Nim for a long time. There was an observation room attached to his classroom at Columbia. I sat there for weeks, watching the other teachers working with him; studying him. By the time I went into the classroom and took any real responsibility for him, I knew him pretty well.

"In the spring of 1975 I more or less took over. I was still planning to go to graduate school at Rutgers in the fall, but somehow Herb Terrace talked me out of it. I'm not sure how, but he persuaded me to stay on the project, and I can't say I'm sorry. Then, he surprised everybody by finding an extraordinary place for all of us to live. He talked Columbia into letting us use an empty house in Riverdale that they were just paying taxes on. Me and Nim, and two other people, Walter Benesch and Amy Schachter, moved into a mansion. The Delafield Estate. It had twenty-seven rooms, ten bathrooms, thirteen and a half acres overlooking the Hudson. It had been left to Columbia with a botanical collection, and had never been used. It was for sale, and I think it's still for sale. A big, beautiful white elephant of a house. There was a pond in the garden, weeping willows, rare ferns, wild bamboo, and a vegetable garden. I felt like Heidi," she said. "I'd go tripping out of the house and come back with a skirt full of vegetables. There was corn, peppers, French beans, Jerusalem artichokes. A caretaker came and tended the grounds. Nice old man. He thought we were crazy.

"Amy lived on the top floor. Walter and Amy both had full-time jobs. They took Nim for two evenings a week and one day each on weekends. Amy worked in primates at the Bronx Zoo. She was on a pilot project, putting people in touch with gorillas, or something. She worked with Joe Willy, one of the zoo's animals who had been rejected by his mother. Amy went right into his cage. An interesting person.

"Nim had a room on the top floor. The house was effectively split in half; the family wing and the servants' quarters were completely separate, which was convenient for us. We closed off most of the big rooms—like the ballroom and the solarium—and lived in the servants' part of the first floor. We made a classroom for Nim out of the coalboy's room behind the kitchen. The only room we used in the family wing downstairs was the dining room. I had the windows padded and the chandeliers removed, and made a playroom for Nim. A carpenter came and built a giant T structure with a tire and a rope. I took him to Columbia five days a week . . ."

"How?" I interrupted. My ability to visualize this colorful scene and write it down was lagging behind Laura's rapid account.

"I drove him," she answered. "In my car." She made the sign for *drive*. She often signed as she talked. "Down the West Side Highway, across 125th Street. Then I parked and we walked to Schermerhorn. Nim's classroom was completely carpeted. He had three working sessions a day. We gave him sign language instruction, trained him, tested him, photographed and videotaped him. Cameras were set up in the observation room. Also, Nim was introduced to new volunteer teachers in the classroom. Before we let them join the project, they all had to be interviewed by Nim."

"What determined whether volunteers were accepted?"

"If they lasted for five minutes without being dismembered, we'd give them a try. If not, they were rejected," she said with a wave of her hand. "There must have been fifty people on the project most of the time. Teachers, data analysts, people who trained teachers, sign language consultants, go-fers—with fifteen or twenty being the core who actually took turns being on with Nim. It's hard to describe what it was like being ON with Nim," she said. "We had a room where the teachers could go and lie down afterward. It was exhausting. We were always fighting for his attention, constantly fighting for dominance.

"Close to a hundred volunteers worked on the project over the entire four years, and I doubt that more than five or six outside the regular staff had a real relationship with him. But it's not easy having a relationship with a wild animal.

"After moving to Delafield and getting into the swing of commuting to Columbia every day, the research began to go very well, and Nim's progress speeded up. Learning the signs didn't mean a thing to him. He hated it. He hated the whole thing, but he knew I wanted him to do it. He knew it was important to me, and he used it to manipulate me. I mean," she said, "he used the whole signing situation as a tool. The actual signs he didn't need. For his purposes, he had plenty of other means. He lied to me all the time. But not in sign.

"Teaching signs went very slowly, especially at first. Patience and practice. Lots of drilling. We used exactly the same methods that the Gardners had used with Washoe. Molding and shaping his hands. He'd drop his hands; just let them go limp. I'd pick them up and shape them again. He'd drop them. I'd shape them. I'd act cool and irritated if he continued being uncooperative, and sign, *Behave. It's time to work.* If he held the shape, I'd be encouraging, warm, affectionate. It worked both ways, these situations. If he wasn't in the mood to cooperate, if we had a fight at breakfast or in the car, he'd spend all his time acting wounded, or pretending he had no idea what I wanted of him. Sometimes he'd seem so-o-o weary, full of ennui, and as soon as I blinked, he'd try to take off and go harass the secretaries—they couldn't stand the sight of him. With reason," she added. "Whenever he was acting particularly angelic, or tranquil, or tired, I was always on my guard. If I could get these things straightened out, we'd get back to teaching signs."

"Did he learn any signs without molding?" I asked.

"By imitation, you mean," she said. "There were one or two signs. Not many more than that. Generally, he didn't imitate the signs, they all had to be molded."

I had often wondered why the apes didn't imitate their teachers. Apes have a reputation for imitating all sorts of human behavior. There is even an English word for it: to ape. When I asked Laura Petitto, she said: "I think the definition of the verb 'to ape' means imitating in the sense of making a poor copy devoid of intent; going through the motions without purpose or meaning. And that's just what Nim did. He loved to stand at the sink and do the dishes. People would come in and say, 'Oh, look, he's imitating you doing the dishes,' but he wasn't. He was just rolling the plates around in the sink and slopping in the dishwater. It was some sort of hilarious ape ritual, but it didn't have anything to do with washing up after supper. It wasn't the kind of imitation that only an expert can tell from the original. It was the other kind. Apeing. He obviously enjoyed himself. It was a great treat, being part of the things we were doing and being with us. It was one of his rewards," she said. "Better than food.

"We didn't like to give food rewards except when it was mealtime. We praised him, or tickled him, or played with him. The worst thing we could do was to ignore him. The worst punishment I could inflict was to just walk away and leave him. He was a glutton, of course, and food always interested him. He rarely turned down anything to eat. Meals were great events," she said with a grimace. "Happenings.

"All through '75 and '76 the project went just great, considering we were working with a chimpanzee. It even had a kind of glamour. He knew what we wanted, and got to be pretty good-natured about doing it. If he didn't know a sign, sometimes he'd give me his hands. Just bring them over and hold them up for me to shape. His attitude was, It's your game, let's get it over with. He didn't have much choice, I suppose. He was very intelligent, very quick, and learned to do just a large number of things that we demanded of him."

"When did you get the idea that it wasn't language?"

"It crept up on us. We had all learned a lot of linguistics. Herb was reading linguistics and doing the linguistic analyses. I was reading the linguistics of ASL, and going down to the Deafness Center. The conversations I was having with deaf signers had nothing in common with what was happening with Nim.

"In a sense, it was a great advantage being in a place like Columbia with so many people wandering in and out. You can't imagine the number of intellectual busybodies there are at Columbia. People like Mark Seidenberg, asking obnoxious questions. Making suggestions, looking at data. There may have been drawbacks about being in a big city, but there were many advantages. A great variety of people and skills and resources, and that atmosphere of academic openness and competition. We weren't just talking to each other.

"In August of 1976 we got a lot of things together for a site visit from a granting agency. We went over data, wrote reports, selected films. Did things that people in research tend to put off doing. We got more tightly organized, and did some preliminary summing up. I spent a lot of that time looking at films, carefully, and many of them I watched with Dick Sanders, who had been on the project for a long time. Dick is a psycholinguist, and was doing a discourse analysis of Nim's conversations for a dissertation. Sounds odd, analyzing the discourse of a chimpanzee, but that's what linguists call it. As we watched the tapes, we began asking each other, Is anything really happening? It just didn't seem like this animal was talking to us. If he was saying something, why weren't we getting it? Our results were the same as the Gardners'; why didn't it seem like language?"

"Did the other teachers feel the same way?"

"Some did," she answered. "It was never the sort of question that was debated, or anything like that. We had a big morale problem. Most of the people working with Nim weren't getting paid. They wanted to teach sign language to a chimpanzee. If anyone said that it might not be language, everybody would get terribly depressed and apathetic. But, quite a few of us were telling Herb, Nim may not be doing what we think. We had totally believed everything about Washoe; then we began to wonder. It was a while before I had time to go over the Gardners' data carefully. When I did, I was surprised how little there was, and how questionable all their conclusions seemed. There was not much information, not much published, and the raw data was never released. Most of their claims, I thought, were based on serious overinterpretations. I did a frame by frame analysis of the films. Very tedious and time-consuming. A fifteen-minute segment can take weeks.

"I looked to see who had initiated the conversations: it was usually one of the teachers, not Washoe. The context in which the signing was going on was not clear. There was lots of cueing. Very restricted number of handshapes, too, glossed differently at different places in the film. Washoe got food rewards all throughout the film, and during some of the testing. I'm not saying that giving food negates any of the research, but it ought to be made clear what part of the training did and did not include food rewards. In one scene, Washoe is supposed to be seeing herself for the first time in a mirror. She's led out and looks really quite interested in the mirror, which is propped up on the grass. The mirror gets knocked down, and there's a whole pile of candy behind it."

Some of the negative conclusions about Nim's signing fall into the area of sociolinguistics and concern the "rules" that all of us follow in conducting conversations, rules like when to talk and when to listen. Nim's signing didn't observe these rules. He typically interrupted his teacher's signing by beginning to sign himself. In one to one conversations with adults, human children rarely interrupt, and usually wait for their turn. (Children often interrupt other people's conversations, but not conversations in which they are taking part.) I asked Laura how these observations were made.

"That's Dick Sanders' work. That came out of the discourse analysis. He's very well trained in psycholinguistics, and familiar with the developmental literature in children. He concluded that Nim showed very little sense about what was going on. Actually," she said, "turn-taking is even more constrained in ASL than it is in spoken language. It's just about impossible to have a conversation in ASL if two people are signing at the same time."

When the data about turn-taking was published, owners of the other signing apes responded that *their* apes had no such problems, and implied that Nim was merely a spoiled brat of a chimp, and what could you expect from those permissive people in New York who didn't know the first thing about providing a wholesome, disciplined home life for a growing primate?

During her two years on Project Nim, Laura Petitto's interests turned to the more humanistic side of science. Her enthusiasm for apes and psychobiology declined at approximately the same rate that her enthusiasm for ASL and psycholinguistics increased. In the fall of 1976 she went to San Diego to work at the Salk Institute. "Ursula put me in an office with three deaf, native ASL signers. That was it. I really began to understand ASL, the true language. Carlene Pedersen and Ella Lenz, both very intelligent and saintly deaf linguists, taught me, and I'll always be grateful to them. I'm a pretty good ASL signer now. Oh, nobody would ever mistake me for a deaf person—I'm not *that* good. Every once in a while, though, someone asks me if one of my parents is deaf. That's a compliment."

"When you went to California, did you think Nim had language?"

"No. But Herb still did. It wasn't until after Nim left that he finished the statistical analyses and confronted the data. Of course, nobody knew for sure until then. But, you know, the data speak. Herb was surprised, but not terribly resistant. There were so many things. Nim's combinations weren't sentences, just strung-out repetitions. There was no syntax, no real exchange of information going on . . . It wasn't just one thing, there were many, many ways that it wasn't human language. The data didn't show all the ways, either."

With Laura Petitto's departure, Project Nim wound down, and Terrace decided to terminate it altogether within the year. In his book, *Nim*, he describes his sadness at returning the chimp to the Institute for Primate Studies in Oklahoma, sentencing him to a life of chimp-chow, cages, and ape companions. He was feeling so sentimental about the animal, and so solicitous about Nim's mental and physical condition on the long trip, that he chartered an airplane and escorted the sedated ape to his ultimate home. In an aside, Terrace comments that the hardest part of the move was his inability to communicate with Nim; there was no way to talk to the animal or explain what was happening. Nim's 125-sign vocabulary was useful for bananas, oranges, and tickling, but useless in a real-life situation.

In 1979, Laura Petitto began dividing her time between the

Salk Institute and Harvard University, where she became a doctoral candidate in a graduate program on language and cognition. Final results of the Nim project were completed and published in 1979 and 1980. When the major article about the project appeared in *Science* (the authors were Terrace, Petitto, Sanders, and Bever), indignant replies were written by Gardner and Gardner, Patterson, and others—and replies to those replies continued for several years. Generally, however, Petitto likes to think the project is behind her. She teaches the linguistics of ASL and continues her research on the acquisition of ASL by deaf children. (She received a MacArthur award in 1983.) Like all lively and committed graduate students, she is busy, but during a lull in her active schedule she met me at Columbia to show me some data. We turned our backs on a beautiful spring day, descended into the subbasement of Schermerhorn Hall, and watched videotapes of Nim.

Laura Petitto may never have thought he was cute, but I thought he was cute. He certainly was animated. The camera revealed little chimp hand marks all over the classroom walls and even on the nine-foot-high ceilings.

On one of the tapes, a meal was in progress. Nim was gesturing eagerly. "Situations with food are not indicative," Laura said. "If you have food, you have him. Look at that!" she commanded, pointing to the screen in disgust. "He's signing *drink* when it should be *eat*. Four years and he still hasn't got *eat* and *drink* straight. Four years!"

"You don't count it correct if it's in the same category?"

"Absolutely not!"

When I asked how Nim took to language training, and if she thought he enjoyed any of it, Laura invited me to observe the chimp's general demeanor on the screen. "Look at him," she said. "See for yourself. He hated it. He only did it because he had to. He did it for us. Otherwise we'd be mad. Look at these tapes, any of them." I picked one out at random and she put it on the machine. "What do you think?" she asked. Nim, in a typical sequence, was doing a little clowning, a little maneuvering, a little aimless staring around the room, and was taking instruction—from Laura herself—sluggishly. "He couldn't care less," she said.

In addition to Nim's perceptible lack of caring, he also showed only meager talents for signing. As my deaf informant had said, chimpanzees can't seem to make the signs correctly; their hands are not the right shape. Laura also told me that Nim could only make the contact signs—signs that involved the hands touching each other, or touching some other part of the body. He never mastered signs that had to be made in free space in front of the body. These latter signs are representations in space, very abstract, and constitute a large and important class of signs in ASL. Nim's contact signs, Petitto said, were far more "concrete." Generally, the chimp's signs were not standard ASL signs, nor were they very similar to the baby signs often used by very young deaf children during the first stages of language. They seemed to be ape signs, in a category by themselves.

On the tape we were watching, Nim wore a pair of children's striped overalls that said "Oshkosh" on the bib, and Laura was sitting on the floor beside him wearing jeans. They were both drinking from small cups. It didn't look like a subject and an experimenter in a scientific research project; it looked like a children's tea party. I asked Laura how old she had been when the tape was made. "Maybe twenty-two," she said. "Nim was three. Weighed fifty pounds, he could have killed me. He only bit me once." She showed me a scar on her forearm. "It was on my last day with the project. He knew something was going on."

"How did he know?"

"He knew. How does the cat know you're going away for the weekend, and hides so you can't lock him in the kitchen?"

"Were you ever afraid of him?"

She shook her head. "He just drove me crazy. I always managed to control and dominate. One animal versus another. Control was complicated," she said, seriously. "And sometimes quite subtle."

"Do you still think about the project, the experience?"

"It haunts me," she answered. "I think about it all the time. All sorts of questions remain, questions I never thought to ask while the project was going on. It also haunts me in the actual sense, too. Sometimes I dream I'm trying to teach sign language to a chimpanzee.

"I think the truly fascinating things about the chimp's social and emotional behavior have not been studied. Nim had, I'm sure, an intact communicative system *above* the system we gave him, and we never tapped into it. We only scratched the surface.

"Nim didn't do anything with the signs. He only used them for requesting things—and even that is too anthropomorphic a description—he never used them in the deeper human sense of making a request. It was an entirely different sort of transaction. It was pragmatic, social, emotional. Nim could never quite understand he was communicating. He never used the signs as a cognitive tool, and I do not believe that he used them to think with. He was never able to make certain connections; we imposed those connections of meaning and communication. He had his own powerful, deeply wired communicative devices. What we added was insignificant. It didn't really add a thing. It was superfluous.

"He was a fascinating animal, but he never left that domain. He was always a blink away from being a wild animal. He never was a rational being."

The willingness of the scientific (as well as the nonscientific) community to accept the claims for ape language was quite remarkable. Very quickly, the news that Apes Have Language appeared in textbooks in the fields of psychology, anthropology, zoology, ethology, psycholinguistics, and philosophy, and was the subject of countless popular books, news stories, and magazine articles. Koko appeared not only in *National Geographic* but in *Penthouse.* Most scientists were unwilling to get into controversies about "what is language?"—a point of violent disagreement among linguists.

From an outsider's point of view, the language of the deaf had always been described as a kind of simple pantomime, a primitive and easy system; it might well have been within the ability of a higher nonhuman primate. If the apes had been receiving instruction in, say, German, it would have been clear from the beginning that they weren't learning German or anything like it. But because very little was known about ASL among hearing scholars, few came forward to say that this was not ASL or anything like it—except the deaf, who were accused of putting on airs when they raised objections. It did not escape the notice of deaf observers that when *they* used ASL, they were told it wasn't a language; but if chimps could learn it, then it was.

The first generation of linguistic apes concluded their training in the 1970s. After Project Washoe, the Gardners acquired four young chimpanzees. One is already at the primate facility in Oklahoma; one got cancer, and was sent to a cancer research laboratory. The other two are practicing "transmission": the passing on of signs from one generation of ape to another. Roger Fouts left Oklahoma and took Washoe with him to Western Washington. Some of Lemmon's animals have been reintroduced into the wild in Africa. Koko was asked to leave Stanford. At least two lawsuits concerning these animals are pending, one involving the loss of a human finger. They all grew up to be apes, after all. I doubt that there are any plans or funds for new language experiments; it's over.

When we look at the numbers, it's interesting that the "vocabulary" sizes of the apes were all within a certain range. Washoe learned 132 signs; Nim had 125. Roger Fouts' chimps are usually credited with 40 to 90 signs. Accounts of Koko in popular magazines mention 400 signs, but in scientific journals, in her doctoral thesis, and in arguments with other scientists, Patterson claims only 100 signs for the gorilla. David Premack's Sarah, who did not learn signs but used plastic tokens, used 130 of them; and Lana, a chimpanzee on a different kind of project that used a computer, is said to have command of 75 items. The average number, then, hovers around 100, and this may represent as large a "vocabulary" of responses as an ape can be trained to execute or manipulate.

Investigations of the vocal-tract limitations of nonhuman primates in 1968 and 1969 by Philip Lieberman established fairly conclusively that apes are physically incapable of producing human speech. A look at the anatomy and evolution of the hand in apes suggests that apes have manual limitations as well, which make them physically incapable of producing human sign language.

The ape's hands are specialized for brachiating: swinging through the trees from branch to branch. They are also used for quadripedal locomotion: knuckle-walking along the ground. The palm of an ape is elongated, the fingers extremely long, narrow, and powerful for use in a hook grip. The thumbs are short, restricted in mobility, and lacking in the complete and perfect opposition that characterizes the human thumb and fingers. There is no way that chimpanzees or other apes can execute the handshapes and movements of American Sign Language—movements that are as precise and necessary for signing as control of the larynx is for producing speech. According to John Napier, British author, surgeon, and authority on the primate hand:

> One cannot emphasize enough the importance of finger thumb opposition for the emergence of man from a relatively undistinguished primate background. Through natural selection, it promoted the adoption of the upright posture and bipedal walking, tool using and tool making, which in turn led to enlargement of the brain through a positive feedback mechanism. In this sense it was probably the single most crucial adaptation in man's evolutionary history.

I am inclined to think that apes cannot master ASL for the same reasons that they cannot master any human language, and that those reasons are not found only in the workings of the larynx or the opposability of the thumb, but also, and more fundamentally, in the nature and biological history of the species. Apes are not incomplete human beings that have somehow been left unfinished by evolution. There is nothing in evolutionary theory to indicate that we have descended from anthropoid apes (chimpanzees, orangutangs, gorillas); rather, everything argues against it. From a common ancestor, apes and humans followed two different and distinct paths of evolutionary development for many millions of years. There is no reason to believe that the human hand evolved from the brachiating hand of the ape, or that human language evolved from ape vocalizations.

In his new book, *Hands*, Dr. Napier supports the most widely held view that the splitting of the African apes and human stocks took place before the specialized brachiating characteristics of the ape hand evolved. As selection for arboreal life adapted the ape hand for the trees, so the human hand was selected for tool using and toolmaking: "The distinction between tool using and tool making is of critical importance. One might say that any primate can *use* a tool (in the widest sense of the word) but only a human can make one. . . . The difference between using and making is largely an affair of the central nervous system and involves a qualitative shift in cerebral activity from percept to concept." Abstract thinking. Human toolmaking skills were probably "lost and rediscovered many times over, perhaps only becoming permanent with the evolution of speech and language."

All the ape researchers admit that their pupils were unable to make standard ASL signs. There are comments throughout the published work that instruction was limited to the signs the apes were able to form, and there are many descriptions of signs that were modified to the ape's manual abilities. Even with the modifications, the ape signs were described, in print, as being very close to ASL. Only the films showed what the signs actually looked like. Laura Petitto had noted a restricted number of forms (handshapes and movements) in Nim's signing—far fewer than in ASL—and saw similar restricted forms in the films of Washoe and Koko. The discrepancy between ape signs and ASL bothered most researchers very little, unless they happened to be deaf.

Wide acceptance of the claims made by the Gardners, Fouts, and Patterson was based on misconceptions about ASL, especially their own misconceptions. It depended on the false assumption that there are no correct forms in ASL, and that almost any hand movement might be designated a sign. Independent of the liberties that were taken with ASL, the ape projects were based on a mindless and mechanically behaviorist notion of human language learning. Human children do not have to be presented with a carefully arranged set of stimuli in the environment in order to learn language. Deaf children do not need their hands shaped or molded; they do not need to be conditioned or rewarded. They learn without rewards, and despite punishment. Neither words nor signs must be targeted, elicited, or drilled to assure their place in the human child's language.

With the failure of the apes to learn ASL, one of the most spirited and fascinating arguments of our time seems to have ended. It was a passionate effort, full of energy and conviction. The risks were extremely high; the cost in money, time, academic careers, emotional and intellectual drudgery, was—well, it was gargantuan. I can't help admiring them all for trying. But I can't help hoping that future generations of psychologists will choose not to go through it all again.

A Way of Life

I

The history of the deaf has not only been written, it has been set in type, printed, circulated, and preserved. Typesetting has been the historic trade of the deaf for more than a century, and today, large numbers of deaf men continue to earn their livelihood as printers. Frederick Schreiber, the first executive secretary of the National Association of the Deaf (NAD), quit his job as a linotype operator in a government printing office in 1966 to take the position. Schools for the deaf trained students on handpresses, and with the invention of the linotype in the 1880s, the vocational departments of many state schools—far in advance of hearing schools—began training skilled operators who went into the marketplace with a decided competitive edge. By the turn of the century thirty state schools were publishing weekly newspapers, and three schools boasted dailies. These facts alone raise serious questions about the illiteracy generally attributed to members of the deaf community.

There have been hundreds of newspapers and periodicals in the deaf community; many were (and are) models of printing craftsmanship, meticulously designed, written, and edited. Today, NAD is publisher and bookseller. Its magazine *The Deaf American* (formerly *The Silent Worker*) is mailed to all members of the organization (about 20,000), and to an additional 8,000 non-member subscribers. NAD's monthly newspaper in tabloid format, *The Broadcaster*, has a national circulation of 58,000, the NAD book catalogue lists 300 titles.

The printed word is inseparable from the most active and vital concerns of the deaf. In their quest for information, experience, and entertainment, they have been trying to caption films for their own use since the 1940s. Foreign films have always drawn deaf audiences because of the subtitles. In the late 1960s the Bureau for the Handicapped began making captioned films available to deaf organizations in modest quantities. Every deaf community has a club, and every club owns a movie projector. One of the principal activities of the state associations is acquiring and circulating captioned films among the clubs (deaf audiences didn't see *Gone With the Wind*, captioned, until 1970).

Captioning came to television in 1971, when WGBH, the public television station in Boston, captioned one episode of Julia Child's *The French Chef*. Since then, the pioneering Caption Center at WGBH has added print to thousands of hours of TV time, and in the process worked out most of the problems involved in presenting information in clear written English for the deaf. (Even persons with less serious impairments sometimes have difficulty with electronic sound and prefer captioned TV.) WGBH began captioning and rebroadcasting the World News Tonight, ABC's major newscast of the day, in December of 1973. By 1981 almost two hundred public television stations across the country carried the program, and the Nielsen survey estimated an audience of 3 million. I have been with deaf people who stopped whatever they were doing to watch it. The yearning for news has been particularly strong among the deaf. Cut off from radio and TV news coverage, they have always had to wait for tomorrow's newspapers to find out exactly what happened— the status of deaf printers was enhanced by their speedy access to the news. The Caption Center uses a concise, readable style designed for a sixth-grade reading comprehension. According to Nina Saltus, director of the Center, that is just about the same reading level at which most newspapers in America are printed.

Donald Torr, who runs the educational technologies office at Gallaudet, said there was no television on campus when he arrived in 1969. He worked through legal channels and with copyright lawyers to get permission to caption films at the college. During that period, the institution installed a closed-circuit televison system. When I visited Dr. Torr in his office, he flipped on a TV set beside his desk. A captioned film appeared on the screen with three lines of type rolling at a very brisk pace. "I insist on using verbatim captions," said Torr. "Always have. I've never had a complaint from a student that the captions are too hard. The only thing they complain about is that I don't supply them with enough movies." He smiled.

TeleCaption adapters necessary for receiving closed-captioned programs are sold through the Sears catalogue, and Sears reported sales of more than $11 million during the first eighteen months that the decoders were on the market. In 1981, forty hours a week of closed-captioned programming became available. During hours when no captioned shows are being broadcast, owners of adapters can turn to special channels that transmit readouts of news bulletins, weather reports, and sports results. Meanwhile, the Caption Center at WGBH has expanded its open-captioned programs for deaf viewers who do not own adapters and who might prefer non-commercial television. It is hard to reconcile all this captioning with the educator's belief that the deaf don't read. I'm inclined to think that many deaf people teach themselves to read in situations outside the deaf educational system.

The TTY is another example of deaf literacy. Using any of the telecommunications devices for the deaf requires both the ability to read and familiarity with a typewriter keyboard. In a beautiful and absorbing book recently published by the NAD to celebrate its centennial, *Deaf Heritage, A Narrative History of Deaf America*, Jack Gannon says: "By the 1970s, it is doubtful if any other minority group had as many members with typing skills." The Gallaudet College admissions data include the fact that about half of their freshmen arrive with typing skills of 40 words per minute or better. And many own their own typewriters.

It is an interesting kind of English that comes over the TTYs. Some of it reads like stream-of-consciousness; some like wire service news. It is not without warmth, and sometimes whimsy. It uses a full set of conventions, abbreviations, and symbols. I tend to write out a message before making a call, and am amazed to watch deaf friends sitting at their TTY keyboards typing with unhesitating enthusiasm, and reading the return messages with equal ease.

Deaf schoolchildren consistently demonstrate a superior knowledge of English spelling. Data going back to 1926 show that deaf children make half as many spelling errors as hearing children matched for reading ability and IQ. A 1948 study found that deaf children spelled even difficult words better than hearing children; the investigator dismissed the proficiency as a "concrete skill" probably learned through rote memory. A 1976 study that included six-year-olds found that even these youngest children "manifested clearly precocious performances." The six-year-olds mastered the first- and second-grade word list; scored 75 percent correct on the third- and fourth-grade words; and were 20 percent correct on fifth- and sixth-grade words. The study was conducted with a group of children who were, in the authors' description, a "garden variety" of deaf children enrolled in the state school in Florida. They were not selected for academic achievement, and the sample included children with multiple handicaps.

English—printed, spelled, written, and fingerspelled—is clearly a form of language in which deaf persons of all ages demonstrate both interest and competence. Refusal to take advantage of written English is yet another monumental failure of deaf education. Books have always been in short supply in schools for the deaf; reading and writing was considered a minor skill, trivial compared with speech. Oralism effectively deprived deaf children of two languages, signed ASL and written English.

One of the most important works in recent linguistic theory is Eric Lenneberg's *Biological Foundations of Language* (1967). Lenneberg was the first language psychologist to study deaf children seriously, both in their homes during infancy and in educational settings. He was not interested in ASL, and accepted without comment the social reasons for its rejection. However, he considered written English an essential form of language for the deaf, and found the "oralist attitude" harmful to the acquisition of language:

> Although words and sentences are written on the blackboard and the child also learns to write, the emphasis is usually on the production of sounds and lipreading. If communication between pupil and teacher fails, the child is often not allowed either to gesture or to make use of his newly acquired writing skills. . . . Many schools also instruct parents not to take recourse to writing for communication in the home for the same reason, and we have had many a teacher of the deaf tell us that it is not desirable for deaf children to make reading for fun a hobby while they are still in school. . . .
>
> I am inclined to believe that the failures in proficiency [are] not due to inherent learning incapacities of the deaf. . . . It is my impression that their language difficulties (in writing) are due to an acute input deficiency—they have just not been given enough examples (raw data to foster their own language synthesis) during the critical early years. This impression is corroborated by those deaf adults who write good grammar because they are invariably avid readers and have been so for many years. The argument that early acquaintance with and recourse to reading and writing is detrimental to these children's skills in oral communication lacks evidence. In fact, we

might assume that if these children had better knowledge of language, both of these other skills might be facilitated considerably.

Lenneberg goes on to say that instead of receiving a large sample of English sentences, as hearing children do, deaf children receive lectures on grammar:

> In his first year of language instruction, [the deaf child] is told that he must speak in *sentences* and that a proper sentence is made up of *nouns* and *verbs*, that nouns must have *articles*, and so on. These theoretical terms are written on the blackboard and also appear in some of the books that are used in the lower grades. Thus we have a situation in which the children are on the one hand quantitatively deprived of a large body of examples, and on the other are immediately given a meta-language, a language about a language, which they do not yet have. Their own spontaneity . . . is restricted by teachers who do not tolerate answers in "incomplete sentences." The child's flow of communication is constantly stopped by the teacher's instructions "to complete the sentence," which is accompanied by a theoretical discussion of how to do this ("verb missing," "the article is not correct," &ct).

When deaf children write incomplete sentences, it is attributed to their inability to hear, although normal hearing children also write incomplete sentences. Printing is considered a suitable trade for deaf youths because they work well in noisy surroundings. But printing was a trade among the deaf long before presses were very noisy. (Did Ben Franklin or Virginia Woolf run presses because they were deaf?) Printing is attractive to the deaf precisely because the printed word is attractive, and the aesthetics of the craft are considerable. Teachers of the deaf often appear overwhelmed with heartbreak at the thought that their deaf pupils will never experience Mozart or understand fully the wonders of Keats and Shelley. They romanticize the extremes of hearing sophistication to their students, who learn at an early age not to take any of it seriously. Deaf adults pretend, with straight faces, to believe that hearing people spend all their time going to concerts, playing musical instruments, and reading the classics of English literature—aloud—every night.

"If you could only produce a literature in ASL," I heard a college professor harangue a group of young deaf people, "and write it down, then everyone would want to learn your language. If you could produce a Shakespeare," the professor went on, warmly, "or a Goethe. G-o-e-t-h-e," he spelled for the interpreter, who was unfamiliar with the name.

Before oralism defined deafness as failure to speak, failure to hear, failure to create literature and music, the educated deaf person was associated with positive talents and heightened visual sensitivity. Deaf people are, in fact, very visual. It may be less a matter of compensatory talent (a popular theory) than a practiced skill. They certainly seem to prefer chess to Shakespeare. (*The Deaf American* has a chess column, and there is a world organization of silent chess players.) The deaf are interested in many things, including poetry, but seem especially involved with almost every activity that can be described as visual and/or spatial. They love to travel: are tireless sightseers. They enjoy most games and sports: are enthusiastic, disciplined, passionate athletes. They are also interesting and original actors. Modern educators dismiss these pursuits as compromise activities chosen by the deaf "because of their low verbal demands." There may be more to it than that. (Who would say that Pavarotti sings because he can't dance?) Before oralism, artistic talent was strongly encouraged. In the 1890s, the California School for the Deaf sent two students to study and exhibit in Paris.

Today, deaf talent continues to unfold. Though few are encouraged on the larger scale, many deaf artists succeed in the commercial art world, and many find places in excellent graphics and design studios. The deaf community also supports countless amateur painters, sculptors, and craftsmen within their own sphere. Art exhibitions are not uncommon. Many works are created around themes of deaf life and incorporate signs and the handshapes of the manual alphabet, and many are conceived around athletic events.

I watched a captioned baseball game recently, and it was a revelation. The captions were concise, infrequent, carrying only the most essential information. It was pure baseball.

A great deal of physical and cognitive energy is expended in the deaf community on sports. They follow athletic contests in the hearing world keenly and have an intimate network of events in their own. Individual and team sports are played at all residential schools. There are deaf leagues in which the schools compete, and they also compete in leagues with public and private schools throughout the country. *The Deaf American* publishes the results of school games and league standings in virtually every issue during the school athletic season. There are ancient rivalries, and big games are scheduled for homecoming weekends to which old alums flock for occasions of happy reunions. There are standard ASL signs for all sporting teams. There is a wonderfully complex and graceful sign that means *elimination tournament.* Unlike the hearing schools, where only the best athletes make the teams, at schools for the deaf, everyone plays and everyone is allowed to compete; even the youngest work out in the gym. One of the most painful prospects associated with mainstream education is that deaf children will no longer be able to participate in sports.

Involvement in sporting events is many-leveled, complex, and satisfying. Deaf players understand the exact purpose and goals of the game, and all possible variations. Games are free of the kind of ambiguity that accrues to so many other areas of contact with the hearing world, where the deaf are constantly told that they have misunderstood, lack the language competence necessary, or have failed to grasp the implications of a spoken explanation. In sports the rules don't change arbitrarily. When deaf schools win against hearing teams, which they do regularly, the hearing athletes complain that the deaf have the advantage: they can signal unfairly, have better concentration, and cannot be distracted by shouts, taunts, and abuse. Considering that deaf athletes are drawn from a population that is small and unrepresentative, that no auditory cues are available to them, and that many deaf individuals have a sense of balance that is not quite intact, their records are excellent.

Gallaudet College has had a football team since the 1880s—the huddle was invented at Gallaudet. Willy Hoy, deaf outfielder for the Cincinnati Reds, was responsible for the unambiguous hand signals used by major-league baseball umpires. When sports were sports, and not corporate manipulations, there were deaf professional players, and there were all-deaf teams in the semi-pros. Today deaf clubs continue to play a great variety of sports. There is an Amateur Athletic Association for the Deaf, organized in the 1940s, that makes participation and scheduling efficient for deaf teams. Some residental schools open their facilities to adult athletes for practice, and for the all-important tournaments.

The International Committee of the Silent Sports was formed in 1924, in Paris, for the purpose of developing physical education in general and the practice of sports in particular among the deaf of the world. The organization conducts World Games every four years and is recognized by the International Olympic Committee. The United States has been sending athletes to the World Games for the Deaf since 1935.

Jerold Jordan, an administrator at Gallaudet, is a U.S. member of the International Committee of the Silent Sports. I stopped in to see him at his office a few days before he left for the 1979 Winter Games in Europe. Jordan, who is deaf, is middle-aged, dignified, was wearing an elegant blue pinstriped suit, and has the bearing of a world traveler. He has complete fluency in spoken English, and told me he is comfortable communicating with anyone, anywhere in the world. "In Europe, I have no particular trouble. When I'm in the North, I use English. There's always somebody who knows English. My wife is hearing, and if she's with me, she does the talking and listening. If I'm alone, I use pencil and paper." He smiled. "In the South, where people don't have heart attacks when you use your hands, I sign, and have even less trouble.

"A few years ago, I arranged for a group of Gallaudet students to go to France with a tour that included several hearing colleges. The people from the other schools were terribly worried about the Gallaudet kids. When they got to Paris, the deaf students took off. Everybody was amazed. In fact, our kids were much more independent and mobile than the hearing students. Never got lost, and saw everything in the city. Of course, they're *used* to being in situations where they can't talk to people, don't know the language, and can't ask questions. They're used to figuring things out, reading maps, and doing things without help or detailed verbal instruction.

"I was worried about being on the committee for the World Games," said Jordan. "All the members were deaf, and all used different sign languages; but it worked out fine. I'm usually relaxed about communicating across languages, but I thought this would be different. There would be exact rules and regulations, specific schedules to establish, things like that. But it worked out fine. We used natural signs, took our time learning to read each other's sign languages. We kept it simple, of course, avoided 'whereases,' and when we had all agreed on what we would do and the program arrived with all of our decisions written up, it was amazingly accurate.

"People from the Iron Curtain countries came, with signs that many of us hadn't seen for quite a while—or ever. There was one Russian athlete we had some trouble with. I couldn't read his signs and he couldn't read mine, and he couldn't seem to understand anybody else's. We tried every sign language. Nothing worked. We tried everything. Why couldn't we communicate with this guy? He was one of the outstanding athletes on the Soviet team, and, well . . ." Jordan's story suddenly seemed full of embarrassed circumlocutions. The point, when he got to it, was that the Russian athlete wasn't deaf!

"We hated to do it," said Jordan. "After all these years, but we had to. We established a hearing test. Athletes must now produce an audiogram showing fifty-five dBs down in the better ear, or they can't compete."

II

François Truffaut's film *Day for Night* opens with a dedication to Dorothy and Lillian Gish as photographs of the two silent stars appear upon the screen in nostalgic, faded sepia. *Day for Night* is about movie-making; in the film within the film, Truffaut himself plays the director conspicuously wearing a hearing aid—symbolizing again that this is a silent medium.

"A blind man in an ordinary theater," said another French film director, René Clair, "and a deaf [person] in a movie theater should still get the essentials from the performance." Many deaf people were employed by the early motion picture industry as actors, coaches, consultants on how a silent film might be constructed. With the development of the soundtrack and as films got talky, relying on dialogue rather than action to move the plot along, the deaf personnel lost their jobs, and the rest of the deaf population were once more left to their own devices for entertainment. Deaf theater comes out of a long tradition, much older than silent films. It developed not only from necessity, because other theatrical forms were centered on spoken language, but also from a natural urge for culture, a familiarity with the expressive uses of space, and a practiced eye for detail and meaning. The remarkable National Theatre of the Deaf came directly out of that tradition.

There is always a certain amount of conflict in the theater between the text and the performance: word and action. From a literary point of view, the most highly acclaimed dramatists are poets, and the highest expressions of dramatic art are written in verse. Some medieval scholars questioned whether the tragic plays of the ancient Greeks were meant to be performed at all. Since modern theater emerged in the seventeenth century, those who write plays are called "wrights"—builders. Playwrights make drama, not only by addressing the ear with words but also by fabricating a many-dimensional construction of theatrical space, peopled with characters, action, dramatic situations. In the twentieth century, what those characters say to each other has gradually become the central focus of drama, and wrighting has consistently given way to writing. Plays have become discussions, vehicles for the transmission of ideas, sometimes controversial, often didactic; plotted like seminars, they are as likely to be written by professors as by poets.

In the United States the possibilities of a multidimensional theatrical experience have been sacrificed to commercial considerations that limit the number of actors and types of sets, and reduce many plays to a mere exchange of dialogue. Solo performances with few props, scant scenery, and no change of locale are fairly common; two-character plays are also numerous and successful. Many of these plays would fare just as well on radio.

Obviously, the deaf do not have the wherewithal to divide up the senses, assigning language to one and action to the other. Both language and action are in the same mode. However, for the deaf, language is distinct from other body movements, as words are distinct from other kinds of vocal sounds. Each sign carries specific linguistic meaning in the same way that each word carries specific linguistic meaning. The theatrical goal of deaf theater is to translate into sign the original linguistic material of a play, and at the same time to integrate that material into a larger framework of dramatic action. The deaf combine and reconcile the two aspects of theater rather than separating them.

William Gibson began his play *The Miracle Worker* in the mid-1950s. Helen Keller was still living; she consulted with the playwright about the portrait of her famous teacher, and about the depiction of her own moment of revelation. The New York premiere was directed by Arthur Penn, and the role of Anne Sullivan was played by the intelligent young actress Anne Bancroft. In order to broaden their own understanding of the play, Penn and Bancroft read books about deafness and blindness, talked with teachers, and visited institutions. In Washington, they saw a sign language production of the Gallaudet Drama Club. For several years afterward there were discussions between Penn, Bancroft, and officials of HEW about the possibility of bringing a deaf company to Broadway. David Hays, a well-known New York scenic designer, was called in on the project, and also saw the work of the deaf actors. Hays, a visual artist, never forgot it. Long after the original venture had been dropped, Hays was still thinking about the possibilities of a theater using sign language.

Nobody at Gallaudet knows when the drama club began. It may be as old as the college and has always been a center for the extracurricular life of the campus. Theater played no part in the official college program until 1957. In that year, a new dean with an interest in drama and a charge to upgrade the institution arranged for courses to be offered through the English Department (the same dean, George Detmold, and the same reorganization that brought William Stokoe to Gallaudet). A recent graduate of the college, Gilbert Eastman, an art major and former president of the drama club, was hired.

Eastman began teaching courses and producing plays as part of the liberal arts curriculum, and in 1963 he became chairman of a separate Drama Department. David Hays, meanwhile, had been working out a serious plan for a permanent company of deaf and hearing actors. Over the next few years he was spectacularly successful in accumulating artistic and financial capital for the proposed company. In 1967 he brought the Gallaudet Drama Department's spring play, *Iphigenia in Aulis*, to the Eugene O'Neill Theatre Center in Waterford, Connecticut, as the first production of the National Theatre of the Deaf.

The year 1980–81 marked the thirteenth season for the National Theatre of the Deaf (NTD). Some critics consider NTD the best company of actors in the country. They have performed in all fifty states; in legitimate houses on Broadway, on the mezzanines of shopping malls in the Middle West, in regional theaters and college auditoriums. They regularly tour Europe, have been to Asia and Australia, appear on television, and have generated two spin-offs: the Little Theatre of the Deaf, a smaller one-truck group that gives performances mostly for children; and the Theatre in Sign, an ASL company that performs without voice interpretation for deaf communities.

The National Theatre of the Deaf is not a mime theater. The charm of mime lies in the audience's ability and willingness to decipher the actor's gestures in the absence of language. NTD is a linguistic theater. The audience is presented with language twice, in two modes: speech and sign. In some productions, it comes very close to being a bilingual theater.

In a typical season, NTD employs thirteen or fourteen actors; two or three are hearing, the rest deaf. Because the hearing actors are also called readers, I had expected that they would stand at the side of the stage like classroom interpreters and merely relate to the audience the meaning of the signs. Nothing so crude occurs. The hearing actors are onstage, in costume, playing particular characters.

The first time I saw an NTD production and a deaf actor began signing, I was surprised to hear a voice. (A man sitting beside me whispered, "Hey, I thought these guys didn't talk!") A quick search of the stage located the speaker leaning against a prop, accompanying the signer with his voice. It worked very smoothly. The hearing actors also have roles of their own, which they speak and sign. Sometimes they speak their own lines in one register, and the lines accompanying the deaf actor's signs in one or more different registers. They seem to take a deep breath at the opening of the play, then just talk their heads off. The signing of the hearing actors is good (some have been children of deaf parents), but the real virtuoso signing is left to the virtuosi: the deaf actors.

Sign language onstage is engrossing, almost hypnotic, and it's the signing that the audience watches while listening to the spoken words. In some plays, signs and speech are so closely synchronized that a hearing audience has the illusion of reading the signs, understanding both languages. The company reinforces this illusion with a lot of first-rate acting, displaying their craft with unique combinations of signs and gestures, words and gestures, pantomime from the hearing tradition and the visual vernacular of deaf theater. The troupe performs well-known classics, as well as experimental works, with a modern technique that is completely original.

They seem wonderfully distanced, achieving the kind of objectivity that Bertolt Brecht called for in his own theater when he exhorted his players to discard the subjective and abandon the pretense of identification with the characters. Brecht urged actors to get outside their roles and perform them as comments on the written text. I have seen performances of the National Theatre of the Deaf that were masterpieces of objectivity: the signs elegant observations indeed upon the text, and the words, in counterpoint, comments on the signs.

The National Theatre of the Deaf's permanent home is the Eugene O'Neill Theatre Center in Waterford, Connecticut, far up Long Island Sound, close by New London and the Rhode Island line. I visited during a fine dry heat wave at the end of June 1980. The company had just begun a summer session on the spacious grounds of their home, a former seaside estate. The beautifully maintained acres contain a large red barn that is both theater and rehearsal hall, several buildings used for dormitories, an open-air theater under two inspiring beech trees, and a stately frame mansion with awninged porches overlooking Fisher Island. If the Salk Institute with its somber concrete on the Pacific is the fitting center for the deaf's linguistic science, this elegant Eastern retreat is the perfect setting for their linguistic art.

I got there at eight in the morning. The administrators had not yet arrived, and the actors were all at calisthenics. They looked young, beautiful, healthy, energetic, and all lit up. Many were wearing T-shirts with a cartoon character holding an umbrella labeled "Eugene O'Neill Theatre Center and National Theatre of the Deaf."

A number of things go on under the umbrella, but the Theatre of the Deaf is the most substantial. During the summer, NTD runs a Professional School for Deaf Theatre Personnel and an Annual Deaf Playwrights Conference, which was in progress while I was there. Independent of any venture involving deaf talent, the O'Neill also conducts activities tied to the traditional theater: annual conferences for playwrights, choreographers, composer/librettists, critics; and also a school, the National Theatre Institute, which trains hearing college students in the theatre arts. Several readers in the National Theatre of the Deaf were recruited from this program.

I drank coffee, read some of the Center's literature, and watched the actors. Soon David Hays arrived. The impresario. News of his presence created a small flurry, and several people ran to meet him as he walked along a path beside a high stone wall. He has very white hair, a seaman's squint, and a remote, serious face. Most photographs of Hays released by NTD show him in a captain's hat standing against a background of ship's rigging. There is one photograph, however, uncaptioned, of Hays with bent head, sitting on the porch of the mansion in the evening light, playing a long silver flute. He prefers to present himself as a sailor rather than an artist—the captain of a ship, overseer of a large crew. Hays and his family live in a house on an island off New London that is accessible only by boat; he commutes to work every day over water.

David Hays must surely be a theatrical genius. From the most unfashionable corner of American society he has created an impressive institution. He has a permanent company of actors; a permanent, beautiful home for them; schools for training deaf actors, designers, and technicians; and even a school from which he can recruit hearing actors. He has ties with the professional theater, funds for sustaining a staff of professionals and hiring high-caliber directors. The Theatre of the Deaf is well funded —another happy circumstance almost unknown in the American theater. Basic funding (several hundred thousand dollars a year) comes from the Bureau for the Education of the Handicapped; there are also grants from other federal agencies, and occasionally from state and private sources. In return for this support, which is microscopic when compared to the sums spent on the handicapped, the theater has done an extraordinary job of fulfilling its responsibilities. The company has performed throughout the country, bringing professional theater where almost none ever appears, and at very low prices. It rarely turns down an invitation from a community. Often the actors are accommodated in dormitories or in private homes, sometimes as the guests of deaf families.

NTD has trained a generation of outstanding deaf actors. One member, Linda Bove, is a regular on *Sesame Street*. Several former members are employed in excellent regional theaters, have played continuing roles on daytime TV serials, and have had parts written into plays especially for them. *Children of a Lesser God*, which swept the Tony Awards in 1980, was written for Phyllis Frelich, an original member of NTD, by Mark Medoff after he had seen her perform. In the Broadway company of *Children*, and in two national touring companies, the three deaf characters in the play (and their understudies) are played by deaf actors, almost all of whom were trained by the National Theatre of the Deaf.

Not all NTD productions have been equally successful or well received. Sometimes the choice of plays seems eccentric. In 1976, the company did the Virgil Thomson/Gertrude Stein opera *Four Saints in Three Acts.* Considered one of the wordiest and most obscure works for the modern stage, it was arguably not a good choice for a company whose members were reputed to have only a limited interest in words.

"They were *very* interested in the words," Hays protested. "They read the play and said, 'Let's find out what all these words mean.' And they did," he added with pride, as well he might. *Four Saints* in the NTD production simply never looked so good. It looked beautiful; witty and stylish, the signs added a measure of clarity. The plucky young company studied the text, tracked down the references, rehearsed vigorously, gave it an enthusiastic interpretation, and got everything out of it that could possibly be gotten—and it was still rather obscure. It bombed with deaf audiences.

An experimental company, NTD expects to have a wide range of reactions to a wide range of offerings. Some critics have hinted that the company is more successful with comedy than with serious drama, but critical response has been consistently positive. In 1977, during its tenth season, the National Theatre of the Deaf received a special Tony Award for theatrical excellence.

Most of the criticism of NTD has come from the deaf community; and, not surprisingly, most of it is about language. Deaf audiences complain that they can't understand the signs. The theater uses ASL sparingly and prefers to use signs as transliterations of spoken English, creating some of the same problems that exist in platform interpreting. The English signs, however, may be the least of the problems; almost all deaf people are familiar with English signs. Hays has also "theatricalized" the signs, broadening and enlarging them for artistic, visual effect.

The signs become embellishments for the words, like illumina-
tions on a page of manuscript.

Rather than creating poetic forms, which was his intention,
Hays created a style of signing that had begun to lose specific
linguistic meaning. Because the signing usually follows spoken
English, a large number of signs must be used, and the pace can
be lightning fast. (If the actors were using ASL, they would
need fewer signs, delivered at a slower pace.) Productions vary
with the style of the individual director and the verbal density of
the particular script. Some directors insist on high synchroniza-
tion between sign and word. These plays are probably most interesting for hearing audiences, sign and word presented together giving the illusion of a bilingual experience that is quite
breathtaking. It is hardest for the deaf because of the speed
needed to keep up with the English.

There are other problems, equally serious. Fingerspelling is
never used; it's considered theatrically uninteresting and is difficult to read at a distance. When a word is encountered for which
there is no sign, a word that would ordinarily be fingerspelled,
NTD invents a new sign. Inventing new signs is routine for deaf
signers—they do it all the time—but there are special ways to do
it, and certain sequences to be followed that ensure understanding. These sequences are usually bypassed in the theater. New
signs flash by the audience embedded in a stream of signed dialogue. In order to make the signs more interesting visually, and
to make them refer to particular images in the play, handshapes
are made more complex, and more information is packed into individual signs, sometimes extending over entire English phrases.
The result resembles the scrolls and curlicues of sixteenth-
century calligraphy, which became so complicated and ornate
the texts were rendered illegible.

With all the color and action onstage, it is sometimes difficult
for the deaf to know where the signer is. Lacking the auditory lo-
calization of the hearing, the deaf get no information except
through visual cues. Often, before a signing actor can be located

at the back of the stage, for example, the speech is finished. According to all deaf informants, however, this is a minor irritation compared with the general state of the signing.

Though ASL is not the official language of NTD, in all the productions the actors ad-lib a lot in ASL. Hearing members of the audience notice that the deaf people are howling at signs not even seen by the hearing, and not interpreted (some being unprintable). There is also a lot of dynamic acting, sight gags, and many strictly deaf jokes. In NTD's *The Three Musketeers*, for example, they called each other "dummy," and each time it got a bigger and bigger laugh. No hearing person ever got a laugh by calling a deaf person "dummy." It's not unlike the use of the term "nigger" among black people. The Three Musketeers in the play were in fact black, and played their parts culturally black— cool and hip, with an urban swagger—making dummy a three-leveled, cross-cultural joke that got more complex and more meaningful. Everybody certainly understood it.

Management at NTD responded to the various complaints from deaf people by asserting that they were running a theater *of* the deaf, not a theater *for* the deaf. With remarkable lack of apology, they declared that their repertoire was "above the heads of many deaf Americans." An article written by Hays asserts: "This is not the language you see deaf people use in the cafeterias. This is an elevated form of it." The deaf replied that all the spoken English in the plays can be understood by hearing people in the cafeterias. Hearing audiences wouldn't stand for peculiar distortions that had to be sifted through, analyzed, and only ambiguously grasped.

Hays takes the attitude that his theater is educating deaf audiences—as Shakespeare educates—and sometimes says that they will eventually get used to his theatricalized signs. Deaf people who are perfectly fluent in English dispute this contention: It is not their knowledge of English that is inadequate, they insist, but his knowledge of sign. Joseph Papp took Shakespeare into the parks and playgrounds of New York and played to audiences in the least literary neighborhoods of the city, to people who had never read the plays and didn't know how they came out. But he didn't attempt to improve on the English, mispronounce words, or add syllables.

Hays does not view deaf criticism as linguistically or politically serious. Rather, he evaluates it in terms of his own ideals of literary merit; and, as such, he is the sole arbiter. He is not insensitive to the deaf, however, and has given the deaf members of the troupe considerable room in which to maneuver. Several plays were initiated by the company and dealt with the theme of deafness. One of these was *My Third Eye*, their first original script, created in a joint effort by the entire company. It opens with a turnabout sequence in which two hearing people are exhibited in cages. In the one-hour television version that I saw, the ringmaster explains these interesting caged beings. Their body shape is the same, she says, but their behavior is entirely different. You and I use our eyes, but their eyes are blank. Faces frozen. Mouths open and close. They see with their ears and sign with their mouths! Their ears are very sensitive and quick. When they don't want to see, they put their hands over their ears. But they can learn many things, she asserts. When instructed in sign, they are even capable of simple language.

Artifacts from the hearing world are displayed and explained: horns, alarm clocks, whistles, earphones, bells, radios. A ventriloquist with a dummy. Strangest of all, says the ringmaster, is the gadget that controls their lives, "the little dumbbell," she says, producing a telephone receiver. "Their livelihood depends on obeying this machine."

The ambivalence (let's say) expressed in the satire is softened by the light, slapstick comedy, though there were moments in it that made me cringe. Hearing people are portrayed as incessant talkers—talking while walking, dancing, eating, making love. As the lovers embrace and kiss, their mouths never stop moving.

. . .

When the National Theatre of the Deaf was organizing in 1967, very little was known about ASL; and through most of the seventies ASL was still considered slang, or the low form of signing, while signed English was seen as the correct, educated, high form. Gil Eastman, who had left his job at Gallaudet to become a working actor with NTD in 1967, returned to the Drama Department several years later preoccupied with ASL. The sign language preferred at Gallaudet was strictly English. Few ASL plays had been put on public display. In 1972, Eastman studied six different English translations of *Antigone* and worked out an ASL version. Voice interpretation followed the signs. He entered it in a competition of college and university drama productions; it won a prize, and was presented by invitation at the Kennedy Center in Washington.

The following year, Eastman dramatized the problem of conflicting sign languages in a new play, *Sign Me Alice*. The play is a satire on Shaw's *Pygmalion* (and the Lerner and Loewe musical *My Fair Lady*). The haughty professor, who signs in rigid, rapid English, declares: "Why can't the deaf teach their children how to sign correctly?" Alice is the poor, uneducated ASL-using deaf girl who is taken in by the professor. In the end, of course, the professor realizes that it is he who is using the bastard language, and Alice who has the true, rich, and natural ASL. It is a delightful play, with many signed songs and ensembles. Linguistically and politically, *Sign Me Alice* is a consciousness-raising play for the deaf in the same way that Sean O'Casey's plays were consciousness-raising for the Irish. Eastman tapped into a trend already under way, a trend that reflected growing loss of diffidence about the real language of the deaf.

The National Theatre of the Deaf's decision to use signed English rather than ASL had hardly been a decision at all. In 1967, sign language simply meant using signs instead of English words, and it is unlikely that anyone at NTD considered the possibility that there was a real and distinct language at stake. When deaf members of the company began raising ASL as an issue, management reacted with surprise and irritation, but not with entirely closed minds. The problem of presenting both English and ASL with equal artistic clarity—thus creating a *true* bilingual theater—was not attacked directly. Working professionals like to deal with things on a pragmatic level, without theory or prescription. A change in direction would probably come from the company's own momentum, from within, and using its own resources. For a dozen years NTD had been training deaf actors, directors, and production personnel, many of whom had developed into experienced theater people. The deaf playwrights' program was nurturing new talent. Also, since the creation of their newest spin-off, the Theatre in Sign, plays are now being performed in ASL to deaf audiences. Members from the regular company take up residence in deaf communities, conduct workshops, plan programs, give theatrical advice and criticism— all within the ASL tradition.

"We're doing a new play this year," David Hays told me. "For the first time, both the playwright and the director are deaf members of the company."

The new play was entitled *The Iliad, Play by Play;* the author, Shanny Mow; the director, Ed Waterstreet. It was, I had been told, a depiction of the Trojan War as a football game. Shanny Mow was on the premises. I found him in a hot, cluttered office on the second floor of the main building that was filled with chattering people. He was sitting in a tight corner, completely oblivious, typing furiously. We moved to the porch downstairs, shaded by awnings, cooled by an on-shore breeze.

Shanny Mow may be one of a new kind of deaf intellectual—they do research at Salk and are actors with NTD; they teach ASL, organize TV shows, write articles. With any luck, the deaf community will produce more of them.

Mow is in his early forties, a Chinese-American born in Stockton, California, "And if you've never been there, you haven't missed much," he said. I told him I had read about it. Maxine Hong Kingston described Stockton in *Woman Warrior*. "A wonderful writer," he said. "I didn't know her, but of course we're related. My mother married inside the Hong family from Canton." ASL is his third language; his first was Cantonese, his second English. He became deaf at age five after meningitis. "Stopped speaking Chinese at eleven—I asked for a napkin and got a brown bag and cream. I learned ASL at the California School for the Deaf in Berkeley."

He graduated from Gallaudet, got a master's degree from California State, Northridge (CSUN), then taught in schools for the deaf in Montana, New Mexico, and Hawaii. He worked on ASL research at the Salk Institute for several years before joining a group in northern California called D.E.A.F. Media, writing scripts. He's also a photographer and has experimented with movie-making. In 1978 he attended the Deaf Playwrights Conference at Waterford, where he offered a comedy entitled *Billy Pole, Milly, Evelyn, Mike, the Superintendent, and the Spanking Machine.* (He wrote the title out on my notepad; the interpreter was relieved.) At the end of the summer he was invited to join the company. "They made me an actor," he said. "I only acted for two seasons. Now I'm a writer again. Officially, I'm a playwright with the company."

He has written scripts for the Little Theatre of the Deaf. Last season, on their Oriental tour, the company performed an adaptation of a poem by Shanny Mow from an old Japanese folk tale, *Kwashin Koji.*

Mow was reticent about the new play. He was still writing it, he said, still working things out. He seemed pleased, however, and comfortable with this largest of all themes. "They think we're always talking about deafness and aren't interested in anything else," he remarked, but only gave me hints about the forthcoming work.

. . .

I saw *The Iliad, Play by Play* in Pittsburgh. A young deaf actor named Howie Seago was cast as Achilles. I had first met Howie in California in 1979, when he was working in the Bay Area on a TV show for deaf children called *Rainbow's End* (Shanny Mow had written several of the scripts). It was a sort of deaf *Sesame Street*. The locale was not a street but an office, reflecting perhaps, the deaf children's early familiarity with bureaucracy. The secretary was an octopus who could type, answer the phone, and sign at the same time. The shows were all done in ASL with captions and a voice narration.

Rainbow's End had grown out of other shows put together by D.E.A.F. Media, the most important of which was one that's been running since 1974 called *Silent Perspectives*. It was originated by a deaf producer, Ed Ingraham, through the San Mateo Community District of Public Broadcasting, and was shown on the San Mateo channel. It was a talk show—interviews and variety—aired once a week for half an hour. The first year it was put on with no budget and with a student camera crew, and some weeks the producer had a hard time raising money for gas to drive guests from the Oakland offices to the South Bay studio. The show was in sign, interpreted for hearing viewers. Deaf hosts alternated, and there were one or two over the following years who were oral and used speech. Not all the guests were deaf. People from the community, especially parents of deaf children, came forward with a variety of special talents and interests to explore. At the end of the first season, *Silent Perspectives* won an Emmy Award.

D.E.A.F. Media realized that large numbers of deaf children in the Bay Area were watching *Silent Perspectives*. "It wasn't a children's show," Howie told me. "There was hardly anything in it that could be considered for kids. Just grown-ups sitting around, signing. But they were so starved for signing, and starved for information of any kind, and starved for the sight of deaf people on television, that they watched. We got letters from hearing parents of deaf children telling us how much their children enjoyed the program. Naturally, we had the idea of doing a show for kids."

Howie, with Ella Mae Lenz and Betsy Ford, all on the staff of D.E.A.F. Media, applied to the NTD summer school for deaf theatrical personnel. Howie had always been an actor, but Ella Lenz was a linguist—she had written a chapter in the Klima and Bellugi book about ASL, and was developing a program for teaching ASL at the secondary level. Betsy Ford, who is hearing, was a dancer for sixteen years before going to work at the California School for the Deaf, where she taught English and social studies and worked with after-school theater. She was also an interpreter and had been the talent coordinator for *Silent Perspectives*.

Returning from Waterford, they put *Rainbow's End* together and applied for a grant, which was awarded. The show, a series of five installments, was done entirely in ASL. The first installments were shown in the winter of 1979 in California, and were picked up by some, but not many, public television stations in other parts of the country. D.E.A.F. Media was unable to obtain continuing support, and no new episodes were added, though reruns appear occasionally.

In Pittsburgh, the National Theatre of the Deaf was performing at Central Catholic High School, a massive red brick Victorian structure. Its front entrance was set high atop a steep flight of steps, and at four p.m., on a Sunday afternoon, was locked. I walked around to the back and saw a rented truck unloading. The company was in the auditorium. Howie was standing in the aisle, leaning on a pair of crutches. The day before, during a performance in Rochester, New York, he had torn a ligament. Refusing to be left behind, he had received emergency treatment and planned to fly back home to California the following morning. Meanwhile, the company, which included no understudies, was being shifted around, parts were being consolidated, and Howie was rehearsing another actor to replace him as Achilles. I sat in the fourth row, and watched the preparations. Several of the actors and actresses I had met in Waterford waved, or came over to say hello, but only stayed a few minutes. They seemed very busy. Later, they generously shared with me the sandwiches, potato chips, and Cokes that had been brought in for them. All actors live on junk food. As the house lights went on and the ushers began arriving, Howie came and sat with me.

Howie Seago came late to ASL. The language was for him, as for so many others, a life-changing, life-enhancing experience. He prefers to sign, wears a hearing aid offstage, and continues trying to use the oral skills he spent so many years acquiring. He told me that concentrating on my conversation took his mind off his leg. Once, he tilted my head so he could see my face better. "The company is very close," he told me. "It's amazing, we're all good friends; very cooperative and harmonious. Hearing and deaf. No hostility, no undercurrents," he said. "I hope you like the play."

"Is it ASL?" I asked.

"Close," he said. "Closer than most NTD plays. The whole company is strongly inclined to ASL."

The play was about a televised football game, and opened with pre-game interviews in the dressing room of the Trojans. Andy Vasnick, a deaf actor, and the hearing actress, Jody Steiner, were sportscasters, dressed in matching maroon blazers with the network logo on the breast pocket, and it was funny right away. Jody Steiner, who looks like a prototypical ingenue, was wearing a headset, and having trouble with it. "I can't seem to *hear* you," she said. "Something must be wrong with my headset." Big laugh from the predominantly deaf audience.

The play was more than the *Iliad*, it covered the whole of the Homeric legend. In a spirited half-time show, the company, dressed in white band uniforms, polished off the principal episodes of the *Odyssey*. The tableau was stunning. It was amazing how a skinny deaf actor, standing on the knees of a hefty deaf actor, and holding a stick over his head, managed to look like Odysseus' ship in full sail.

There were a few slow spots in the play, perhaps because of the loss of Achilles and the reshuffling of parts. The second act was moving and sad. After the show there was a reception for the cast and guests. The entire audience seemed to be there, drinking wine, eating cheese. The actors arrived, one by one, mingled, talked, signed. They were happy and relaxed, as friendly and gregarious after the performance as they had been concentrated and aloof before. They all seemed relieved that the difficult show had gone so well and was behind them. When I left, after midnight, everybody was still going strong, the actors talking and signing and smiling, sustaining their considerable energy by eating up what remained of the crackers and cheese.

III

Children of a Lesser God is the most important artistic event ever experienced by the deaf community. It is their morality play, performed at last in the mainstream of American culture. Deaf characters are portrayed by deaf actors and actresses, not by hearing players coached in sign language. The star of the play, Phyllis Frelich, was born deaf, raised in a deaf family by deaf parents. ASL is her native language. During the play, she does not speak. She does all her acting in sign. On her own terms, she won not only the respect of the hearing but also their awards.

There is no new information revealed in the play; the strength of the work is in its expression of a typical situation, *the* standard hearing/deaf situation. It is a story of two people struggling for communication: on the level of conflicting lan-

guage and culture, and on the deeper level of human understanding. "It's our story!" Phyllis Frelich said the night she won
the Tony Award. Robert Steinberg, her hearing husband, interpreted her signs into English. He is a set designer; they met
while both were with the National Theatre of the Deaf. She met
the playwright Mark Medoff, who wrote *Children* for her, at the
University of Rhode Island when he was playwright in residence and she was performing. When Medoff returned to his
home in New Mexico, Frelich and Steinberg joined him there at
the Playwrights Lab in Santa Fe, and gave him the stories of
many deaf lives. Medoff in return wrote a brilliant play.

It was first shown in Los Angeles at the Mark Taper Forum,
an interesting and vigorous regional theater that has shown
many experimental works and productions in sign. Although the
play was successful in Los Angeles, the next step—bringing it to
New York—required another magnitude of decision-making.
The prospect of mounting a New York production featuring
deaf actors using sign language and a star who did not speak
filled producers and backers with anxiety. The subject matter of
the play was also considered problematic, though it appeared
less shocking than other subjects enjoying dramatic treatment in
recent decades, such as quadriplegia or stroke, or the story of
Helen Keller, which dealt with both deafness and blindness. (In
The Miracle Worker, the character Helen does not speak at all
until the last scene of the last act, and then she says one word.)

Children of a Lesser God has no conventional inspirational
message. It has no miracle. The central character does not overcome insurmountable obstacles, does not "choose" speech, is not
cured. Her deafness is presented as her own existential condition, part of her personal identity, accepted and shared with a
community. The starring role did not call for a famous actress to
portray a deaf super-being, but showed instead an extremely fine
actress portraying a human being who is deaf.

For the premiere, John Rubinstein was given the male, hearing lead. An attractive actor in his early thirties, he is the son of

pianist Artur Rubinstein. The child of an unusual, possibly an eccentric upbringing, he seemed open-minded about the experiences of the deaf characters in the play. He was a musician and composer, had already mastered an abstract system that was completely independent of verbal language; he learned signs with surprising ease, and established good rapport with the deaf members of the cast. Rubinstein was very successful in the demanding role, and won a Tony Award along with Frelich. Both gave outstanding performances.

It is a clear, honest, moving play that succeeds on its literary and dramatic merits and on superior acting from the cast. It gets no help at all from theatrical embellishments like sets and costumes, which are almost nonexistent; the actors make do with four benches and a few movable props. The rest consists of purely imaginary trees, stoves, hi-fi sets, bridge tables, and so on. The couple make love on the boards.

The story is about an idealistic speech therapist, James, newly arrived at a residential school and trying to persuade a young deaf woman, Sarah, that he can teach her how to speak. Sarah is a former student at the school, now working there as a chambermaid. She has been through it all before. They fall in love, and at the end of the first act, Sarah and James get married.

The other deaf characters are two older students named Lydia and Orin, shown having speech training. Both wear hearing aids, have the ability to speak, and show improvement during the play; but neither experiences worldly success because of it. Orin, in fact, initiates a civil rights suit against the school in an effort to compel them to hire some deaf teachers. Lydia takes over Sarah's old job as chambermaid.

Throughout the play, the signing is beautiful, fluent, and authentic. As in real life, code-switching is frequent. The deaf characters sign ASL when they are talking to each other, and switch to English signs when they talk to the hearing characters. Lydia and Orin speak as well as sign.

The second half of the play brings all kinds of conflict: cultural, political, legal, culinary—when Sarah bakes a quiche, Orin calls it "hearing food"—and physical: James is distraught answering telephones and doorbells, turning timers off, and the volume down on the television set when Lydia visits. Orin's court case approaches and Sarah participates in it with him; she will make a public statement in sign. James is torn between wanting to let Sarah and Orin handle their own affairs, to speak for themselves, and wanting to take over for them. He tries, unsuccessfully, to mediate, then cannot defend himself in the angry confrontation that follows. Angry himself, he accuses Sarah of mocking him, of merely *pretending* that she cannot speak. He commands her to speak. She opens her mouth and screams a high-pitched, grating, unearthly scream. They separate in extreme unhappiness. As the play ends, they appear onstage together promising only to try to help each other.

It is a very moving play, ringing with authenticity. It describes the most difficult problem that deaf people have to face, their relationship with the overwhelming, powerful, mysterious hearing world. It is a world they cannot avoid; a world they wish to engage, if the cost is not too high for them in their own human terms. When the curtain falls, many in the audience are in tears.

The play is not entirely accessible to deaf people, who can only understand the scenes in which deaf actors appear. In scenes between the hearing characters, nothing is signed and no interpreter is provided. There were interpreters for certain performances in Los Angeles, but not in New York or for the national touring companies. Considering the moral message of the play, this lapse seems particularly insensitive. Yet, deaf audiences complain very little. They merely sit and wait for the scenes and the actors who sign, so great is their sympathy with the enterprise.

In Philadelphia, I saw the national company of *Children* with Nancy Frishberg, a linguist, interpreter, teacher, and historian of ASL. She had been an interpreter with National Theatre of the Deaf, and knew all the deaf members of the cast. During intermission she commented that Richard Kendall, the actor who played Orin, had much better speech than he was displaying in the play. I met Richard Kendall, and later was able to make arrangements to talk to him about his career.

Richard Kendall is married to Nanci Kendall, the actress who plays Lydia. They met at the first reading of the play in Los Angeles. Like many of the people I've met and described, Richard Kendall hears quite well in face-to-face conversations in a quiet room, and when his hearing aid is working. If he had to turn his back or move a few feet away, he couldn't hear me. Kendall grew up in Ottawa, he told me, the only deaf person in his family. He has two older brothers he never got to know well, and a younger sister who was the best friend of his childhood and to whom he is still close. "I was mainstreamed," he said, "in the local grade school. They didn't even know I was deaf until I was in the second grade. And my father's a doctor."

Kendall has an expressive, mobile face, a daffy smile. His tone was disarmingly witty, and he reminded me of a young Danny Kaye. "I'm thirty-five," he answered my question. "I know I look like a teenager. That's good for my business." He smiled, then added, "I might even be thirty-six."

"When I finished high school in Canada, I wanted to go to college, but there was nothing for me there. I went to Gallaudet, and that's where I learned how to sign. On my first trip home, my mother commented how much I had changed, how much learning signs had loosened me up."

Kendall seems to have a talent for languages. He told me his French had been pretty good in high school, and that at Gallaudet he had studied French and German: "I only learned to read German. Foreign languages weren't too good at Gallaudet. Just from books. Not much writing. We never got to meet any German speakers.

"I had a good time at Gallaudet. My roommate was Tom

Humphries, do you know him? Yes? Well, if you talked to Tom, you know. He had been raised all oral, too. It was a revelation for us to learn signs. I think I didn't resist as much as Tom did. In fact, I didn't resist at all. In Canada, no one ever prevented me from learning sign language. They just didn't seem to know anything about it.

"My senior year at Gallaudet, Jane Norman asked me to try out for a part in *The Man Who Came to Dinner*. I didn't know a thing about theater. Hadn't been in the drama club or anything. Jane just saw me fooling around with some people on the lawn one day and asked one of my friends to bring me to the try-outs. I had never considered doing any acting before that. But, I thought, what the hell, I'd give it a try. I took the script home, and when I showed up for a reading, naturally, I signed everything in English.

"That's when I got my first real insight into ASL. As a newcomer, an outsider, I suppose I thought of it as a kind of 'in' slang, something that only people from deaf families or deaf schools knew. I don't think I ever thought of it as a *language*. And I couldn't quite get a handle on it until I did that play. Jane took the script and rewrote it. She's a wonderful signer, and very uncompromising about ASL. I think she was the only one doing plays in ASL at the time. Anyway, she put the English words down in flat ASL order, just so I'd get that part right. We worked on the inflections afterwards. I loved it. The show was a big success, and I even won a drama prize when I graduated.

"That year I applied to the summer school at NTD in Connecticut. I still wasn't sure I wanted to be an actor. What I wanted to do was go to California. All my life I wanted to go to California. That's where I was when the acceptance from NTD came: an acceptance and a scholarship. I almost didn't go, but I had a peculiar intuition that if I didn't, I'd be sorry.

"It was all a big success. School was terrific, everybody said I was good and encouraged me. I was invited to join the company. I went on tour that year; it was the company's first tour. We did

Gianni Schicchi, The Critic, and *Under Milk Wood.* The next season, *Gilgamesh.* We were on television a lot, and went to Europe. I was with the company for six years.

"After I left, I didn't quite have the nerve to just go to New York and look for an acting job. I was thinking about going to graduate school. What I did"—he laughed—"what I did was take a job at Fanwood, the New York State School for the Deaf in White Plains. It turned out to be quite an experience. I had never been to a residential school except to give performances with Little Theatre of the Deaf."

"What did you do there?" I asked.

"Dorm counselor," he answered.

I found myself staring at him, shocked. Richard Kendall, with near-perfect oral skills, fluency in ASL and English, a bachelor's degree from Gallaudet, and six years as a professional actor touring the country and the world—if anyone could qualify as a member of the deaf élite, it ought to be Kendall. I was embarrassed to think of Fanwood offering him a job as a dorm counselor.

"I did some teaching, too," he said, returning my stare with a calm, even gaze. "Substituting. All the teaching goes on in the dormitories, anyway," he added. "I really loved being with the kids. I learned so much. I stayed four years, and while I was there I finished a master's degree from Goddard College. *Then* I went to New York. Taught ASL, took acting classes, and did a couple of TV soaps. *The Guiding Light, As the World Turns.* It was fun. They wrote in a part for me in *The Suicide* the first time it was done in America, Off-Off Broadway."

He went back to California and continued getting acting jobs. He was cast in the movie *Voices,* which is about a young deaf woman who wants to be a dancer and a young hearing man who is a rock'n'roll musician. Kendall was one of the few deaf actors in the film. He described the experience as somewhat confusing and frustrating compared with stage or television acting. In deaf acting troupes, and in the wider deaf community, rumors spread with breathtaking speed and remarkable efficiency. In mixed groups of deaf and hearing, the transmission of information breaks down rapidly, and the deaf are typically the last to find out what's happening. They try to take a calm attitude, avoid excessive queries, and fight off natural feelings of isolation that can easily escalate toward paranoia.

"I played the role of Scott Gunther in *Voices*," said Kendall. "In the end, I had only one good scene—in the car with Amy Irving, the star who played the dancer. Hearing," he added. "I had studied three scenes, but two of them were never filmed. After I finished the scene in the car, they told me I could go back to Los Angeles, everything else had been cut.

"I was very upset, mostly because nobody had told me and I had no idea what was going on. After that movie, I did a couple of plays around Los Angeles. The most interesting was *The Trojan Women*. Every role had two actors, one deaf and one hearing. We all had a marvelous time with it. Then *Children* came along, and I became Orin.

"It's an instructive play," he said. "The characters are bound to be exaggerations to some extent. Orin is a very interesting part, and I'm not finished with it yet.

"It's too bad that deaf people in the audience can't have the non-signing scenes interpreted. Some of the hearing actors could use an interpreter, too, frankly. Some of them are having a lot of trouble. The worst part is that they don't know they're having trouble. They think their signing is just fine. Hearing people always think their signing is terrific."

"Why aren't interpreters used?"

"I have no idea how these decisions are made. In Los Angeles we had interpreters at two performances a month but they were dropped when the show went to New York. Just not in the plan. All plays at Mark Taper are interpreted at least twice a month.

"I drove up to Mt. Airy last week to see some people at PSD [the Pennsylvania School for the Deaf]. Pretty place. I always enjoy seeing the kids. And this teacher came rushing over to me, talking and signing." He laughed. "You should have seen those signs. Pathetic, illiterate! 'Oh, Richard,' she said, 'isn't it a disgrace that there aren't any interpreters for your wonderful play? I don't understand how you can put up with it, it's a disgrace, it's an insult. You should insist they get interpreters.'

"And while she was spouting off, putting me down, she was signing the most awful signs you ever saw. She'd been working and making her living off deaf kids for years and never learned to sign, and she was telling *me* I'm insulting the deaf and it's a disgrace. I didn't say anything, but I thought, Here's the disgrace. This is the real disgrace."

Before I left, I asked Richard about his plans for the future.

"I'll be on the road with *Children* for another year or so, and there's talk about making it a movie, but who knows?" He smiled. "*Children* came as a complete surprise. Nobody expected there would ever be a Broadway show with deaf actors. I'm optimistic. Maybe something else wonderful will come along. Don't worry about me," he said with a particularly evil grin. "I can always go back to being a dorm counselor."

Deaf people have been vigorously creating a theatrical tradition ever since they started seeking each other out, forming a community. With the National Theatre of the Deaf, the tradition has become more vigorous. There are now numerous professional, semiprofessional, and amateur deaf companies throughout the country. The appearance of deaf actors in hearing companies has added new meaning and great charm to the American stage. The regional theater movement, which seems to have taken root at last, offers increasing opportunities for deaf players. David Hays sometimes mutters that deaf actors are getting scarce; too many outsiders are dipping into the talent pool. Hays has said, repeatedly, that the deaf are natural actors. They are more than that; they are artists, and professionals. They live day-to-day lives as professionals, on backbreaking schedules, taking risks, honoring commitments, expanding their gifts, refining their skills, doing difficult things seriously and with dedication. So unlike us at the surface, they surprise us with the depth of their talent, intelligence, and imagination. The artists among them are exactly like the artists among us.

Reflections

The handicapped are suddenly visible, in the public consciousness and in the news. Their visibility makes able-bodied people
anxious; makes them wonder if it could happen to them, or to
their children. As a general rule, people would rather think
about the handicapped as little as possible, find broad solutions,
and implement them quickly and generously. Mainstreaming
seems to follow this general rule.

"In the first place," said an advocacy worker, "it's impossible
to write a law for *all* handicapped children. Most congressmen
think that deaf people use Braille. As soon as the whole handicapped movement began, you can't imagine how many crackpot
ideas turned up, most of them completely missing the mark.
There was federal legislation to give hearing ear dogs the same
status on airplanes as Seeing Eye dogs. O.K., some deaf people
do have dogs, and some of them are trained, but they don't function in any way like Seeing Eye dogs for the blind, and if I were
to make a list of all the things that could help deaf people, hearing ear dogs would not make the top twenty. The average legisla-
tor, the average citizen, just can't be bothered to concentrate on
particular problems. Let's make life easier for handicapped people is as far as they can go. That each handicapping condition
might pose different problems, that some different kind of *thinking* might be required, or that complexities might exist—that's
too much. Can't see, can't walk, can't hear—same thing. Let's get
them some dogs.

"They're just not *thinking*." He tapped his forehead. "Since

94-142 *says* that all education must be provided in the least re-strictive environment, the residential schools are in for it. Main-streaming is based on the false assumption that, because they are 'institutions,' residential schools are highly restrictive. Restric-tive for who?

"They have the idea that they're going to move everybody up one notch. The autistic are worse off than the retarded. The retarded are worse off than the deaf. Solution: move the autistic into the less restrictive environment of the retarded, and upgrade the retarded by putting them in those nice schools for the deaf. Then, what happens to the deaf? They have the thrill of getting to go to school with hearing kids. The problem is solved. Every-body's been promoted."

Residential schools are expensive. Some were under-enrolled during the seventies, but not to the extent that neighborhood schools were under-enrolled. Public schools have been closing all over the country. In the schools that remained open, some had empty rooms that could easily be converted to resource rooms and turned over to "special education" projects.

Education is a gigantic industry in the United States, and a powerful force. Schools claim a big slice of all municipal budgets (in rural areas, schools and roads get most of the public money available). The trend has been toward more expensive schools. In order to mitigate costs, teachers have been willing to increase class size. Upward of thirty children in a classroom is now con-sidered manageable, providing that all the children are normal and do not make unusual demands on the teacher's time. Over the last decade, schoolchildren have been vigorously screened and tested in order to detect any inadequacies in their intellec-tual, emotional, cognitive, or social abilities. American class-rooms became fragmented as a substantial percentage of their pupils were diagnosed as "learning-disabled"—a classification that included a range of ill-defined conditions like minimum brain dysfunction, dyslexia, perceptual handicap, hyperactivity, and others.

Children were moved out of regular classrooms for all or part of the school day, sometimes to other buildings, sometimes to schools in completely different kinds of special educational systems. The families of these children were upset and became increasingly unwilling to have their children excluded from neighborhood schools. Many parents perceived their children as completely normal; others insisted that if extra services were necessary, those services must be provided locally; and all became strong supporters of mainstreaming. As special services were expanded in local schools, parents whose children had already been placed in institutions questioned the necessity for keeping them there, and they too demanded special services from the home districts.

In the vernacular of the teaching profession, special education means teaching "exceptional" children, the mentally retarded, learning-disabled, emotionally disturbed, deaf, and blind. Most teachers of the deaf are trained in these programs, and some get additional training through departments of speech pathology and audiology. A few programs are also run by the famous oral schools. In the 1970s, with the arrival of total communication, teachers of the deaf were given instruction in basic sign communication—and so were teachers who worked with mentally retarded, autistic, and aphasic children in special schools.

In the public schools, the number of marginally disabled children grew, and many were found to have speech and language difficulties. They were assigned to speech therapists who worked on improving fluency, teaching the children about nouns and verbs, giving them vocabulary items to learn and drilling them to speak in complete sentences. I was amazed by the teachers as well as the school board members who told me—with conviction—that many of their pupils were language-handicapped to such a degree that they must be taught the names of the foods they eat; that they don't know the names of their own brothers and sisters; and that, because they don't understand the meaning of words like "before" and "after," it is useless to try to teach them arithmetic. The American Speech and Hearing Association changed its name to the American Speech-Language-Hearing Association. Its journal is full of letters complaining that teachers are so busy working with language-handicapped children that there's nobody curing lisps and stammers any more.

There were so many handicapped and exceptional children in the schools, and so many specialists, the schools thought deaf children would not pose any particular problems. In some districts, deaf students were required to have a specially trained teacher of the deaf; but in others, completion of basic special education courses was the only training necessary. An article by Joanne Greenberg and Glenn Doolittle in *The New York Times Magazine* in 1977 gave the following samples of mainstreaming possibilities:

> For some, it seems to mean a sign language teacher in a special room with eight or nine deaf children between the ages of 6 and 13, "integrated" only in music and physical education. . . . For some, it means one deaf child in a class with a sign interpreter. For some, it involves integration in a regular class where the teacher "has access" to a resource person who may or may not know anything about deafness. To a school in a rural district, it may mean nothing at all, a teacher grappling with thirty hearing students who does no more than give the simplest standard individualized reading material to her single deaf student.

The aim of PL 94-142, to provide the least restrictive environment for personal and social development, is actually better served in the state schools. Except for mildly and moderately deaf children, mainstreaming imposes additional and severe restrictions on the environment. At the state schools, deaf children find real acceptance among their peers; a rich and varied dormitory life; and a community of signers. When total communication was adopted and sign language permitted in the classrooms, the schools were recognizing the most fundamental reality of deaf life. The weaknesses of the residential schools are rooted in the century of oralism, just ending, and in the psychology of special education: a reluctance to accept deafness, and a tendency to impose standards of normal behavior based on auditory functioning and English speech. The positive features found in the state schools are not primarily those specifically designed by the educators, but have arisen because of the close relationships among the children, friendships between students and teachers, and contacts with deaf culture.

Deaf adults work in the schools. Though not nearly enough are classroom teachers, active recruitment could enlist more. There are usually deaf shop teachers, athletic coaches, and craft supervisors. Many deaf adults work as dormitory parents—some are older, experienced people, and some are young college graduates. Deaf adults often run the physical plant, the grounds, the kitchen, in small numbers; and deaf adults from the community have traditionally volunteered for a variety of after-school activities. Vocational courses, however, are disappearing in favor of preparatory programs. Like the hearing schools, the deaf schools want to pretend that everybody is going to go to college—or post-secondary education. Many school newspapers are no longer composed by deaf alumni and students on school presses, but have become slick public relations outlets for the administration. There also seem to be fewer deaf Scout leaders and organizers of chess clubs than there used to be. Generally, deaf adults are kept in low-visibility, non-academic, and peripheral positions around the schools.

Academically, the schools have been quite passive about achievement, an attitude largely imposed by oralism. There is still a strong belief that speech is the principal goal of deaf education, and a requisite for all learning. An atmosphere of failure pervades many deaf classrooms, and it has been only partly dispelled by total communication. Lessons are still interrupted for pronunciation drills; the children still receive more practice speaking the words during a reading class than finding the meaning of the text, or the outcome of a story. The teaching environment could use an infusion of professionalism and a more competitive spirit toward the threat of mainstreaming.

Speech training should certainly continue to be a part of deaf education, but not the overwhelming, dominant part. No individual or organization that I know of has called for the elimination of oral training. Deaf opinion has consistently held that teaching speech and teaching signs are perfectly compatible. The most accomplished oral deaf persons I know value their speech highly, but consider ASL their birthright; they bitterly resent suggestions that a choice between speech and sign is ever necessary or appropriate. Oral educators have been interested only in the few who speak, and are cruelly indifferent to the many who do not. Speech must be recognized for what it is in the lives of deaf people: a useful, if sometimes relatively minor, survival skill. Only in extremely rare cases do speech and lipreading ever become the primary language mode for the deaf.

The élite oral schools have trained teachers and determined, to a large extent, the philosophy and methods used in all training courses. If the total communication schools could come to terms with sign language on a more serious, intellectual level, they could play a more important and constructive role in training teachers of the deaf. The schools could upgrade their own staffs, and instruct teacher trainees in sign language as it exists in the deaf community—both ASL and signed English. If the schools would really take the responsibility for training teachers, and exploring the problems of making education and information available to deaf pupils, the academic tone of deaf education would improve. Then teaching the deaf could be taken out of the framework of mental and emotional retardation. (I'm sure that Edward Miner Gallaudet did not persuade Abraham Lincoln to establish a college for the deaf by saying that it was like a special education project to train the retarded. No, he probably said:

"They're only deaf. There is nothing the matter with their intellectual and emotional lives. They are as capable of learning and
developing their talents as the hearing.")

Although educators deny that money is an issue in mainstreaming, day programs, no matter how elaborate, cost much
less than boarding programs. The state and federal budget cut-
ters see great advantages in eliminating residential schools. PL
94-142 supposedly offers choice, but most parents have no
choice. If a local district offers any kind of resource room, there
is no reason to send a deaf child anywhere else. In Pennsylvania,
I met a parent who had moved into a district that didn't have any
hearing-impaired programs just so she could legally send her
child to the Pennsylvania School for the Deaf. I'll call her Mrs.
Williams. "When I informed the school committee that I wanted
my son to go to PSD," she told me, "they acted as if I was trying
to get rid of him. They play on the parent's guilt a lot. Actually,
Peter is a day student. Because I refused local placement, the
state won't provide transportation, either. Me, and five other parents on this side of the river, car-pool the kids over to Mt. Airy
every day. They're all preschoolers and first graders."

"Why do you send him there?"

"So he can be around other deaf children and teenagers. So
he'll be around really good signers. So he can play sports, and be
editor of the school paper, and be in the Boy Scouts, and join the
student government if he wants to. So he can meet some deaf
adults. So he can be in an environment that bends a little for
him, instead of having him do all the bending himself. How can
you ask?" she said. "So he'll get an education and not be stuck in
one room all day long. They say they want deaf kids to learn
how to get along in the hearing world, and that's all they teach
them, the hearing world. He's deaf. He has a right to learn about
the deaf world, too."

Mrs. Williams learned sign language when Peter was two.
"No one ever tried to steer me to an oral program, and no one
ever suggested that Peter not learn signs. The biggest trouble I
had was getting him diagnosed. My pediatrician kept treating me

like a hysterical woman and told me I was worrying too much. I knew something was wrong, he was my third child. When Peter was two, I got a new pediatrician who said to me: 'What are we going to do about his hearing loss?' I took him up to Temple University to be tested. He's profoundly deaf. I had been worrying so much that he was deaf, and then I couldn't believe it. I started taking a sign language course. I remember coming home after my first class. I sat on the floor and practiced my signs. And I cried. That's when I really knew he was deaf.

"Peter started learning signs right away. He was two and a half. I think he learned a sign a minute. It was fantastic. We talked to each other. Look at him. He's terrific." Peter was five and a half years old the afternoon I met him, and he was definitely terrific; a bright and beautiful child. "I have a very normal, spontaneous, happy, communicating boy," said his mother.

"I joined a group, the International Association of Parents of the Deaf, and met other parents who were learning sign language and had children Peter's age. We meet every Tuesday night. All those kids go to PSD. They've been together for almost three years. We try to arrange for them to play together after school, too. Peter has lots of friends. I suppose, in fact I'm sure, that when he gets older he'll want to go and live in the dorm with the other kids, and I'll probably let him. If the school is still there, that is. I was on a state committee to examine the role of the residential schools in Pennsylvania. There are three residential schools in the commonwealth, and I believe that the department of education wants to close one and turn the other two into institutions for the multi-handicapped. In a few years, many students in state schools for the deaf won't even be deaf, but will have a lot of other problems. If that happens, I don't know what I'll do. The whole point of sending Peter to PSD will have evaporated."

Mainstreaming has altered deaf education more drastically than the switch to oralism at the turn of the century. Many concerned people believe that mainstreaming is a new, more heartless form of oralism. At the schools for the deaf, everyone is amazed. Mainstreaming caught them completely off-guard. They might have expected pressure from the right, for more oral training; but not from what seems to be the left, for more integration on civil rights grounds. The schools half expected to be told they were too expansive, not that they were too restrictive. They were prepared to worry about cuts in athletic equipment, in music lessons, field trips, or in the teacher/student ratio. They were willing to serve less ice cream. Some showed signs of trying harder on the reading and math scores. They never expected to face losing students to public schools. Taking cues from the hearing schools, many are trying to fill up empty rooms with other populations, and are seeking out the severely handicapped.

An acquaintance of mine served on the board of trustees at the New York State School for the Deaf in Rome. "Enrollment showed a slight decline in the seventies," the trustee said, "and the school was planning, in a low-key way, to take up the slack. Continuing education for deaf adults seemed to be the way the plan was going, and everybody was very positive. Then, suddenly, mainstreaming got serious, and there wasn't much money anyway for continuing education or community projects, and the whole thing turned around. Suddenly, the school began looking for kids in the really closed institutions, like the Rome Developmental Center. They found them. They're bused in every day and are being taught by the teachers of the deaf. Some of the best teachers at the school are assigned to those children. They're day students now, but I'm sure that in a few years they'll be in the dormitories."

At the Pennsylvania School for the Deaf, enrollment is down from 590 in the 1970s to 340 in 1980; 10 percent of the children enrolled in 1980 are severely handicapped. I asked Joseph Finnegan, headmaster at PSD, if there was a protest from parents about the new kind of student. "A little," he answered, "but I explained to them that, after all, a lot of people felt the same way about deaf children. This is only the second year we've admitted kids with severe handicaps. It's working out very well and I'm sure more will be coming in the future.

"The parents had fewer objections than the alumni," he added. "They really put up a howl!"

In the Dark Ages, the deaf were classed with the feeble-minded and the insane. The history of the deaf is the story of escape from that classification. The source of all deaf pride and dignity comes from the conviction that, even though they cannot hear, they are the same as all other human beings. The hearing world is deeply biased toward its own oral language, and always prefers to deal with deaf people who can speak. But speech is always difficult for the deaf, never natural, never automatic, never without stress. It violates their integrity: they have a deep biological bias for the language of signs.

The story of the deaf is about the development of culture and language of a high order. As with all languages, native competence is acquired in childhood, from people who have native competence. ASL was kept alive, refined, and transmitted in the schools for the deaf. The language not only survived, it became standard throughout the Americas, and is related to many of the major sign languages of the world. Gestuno, the international sign language developed through the United Nations, is based on ASL. Margaret Mead once suggested that American Sign Language might be the ideal universal second language the international community had been searching for.

Deaf Americans are admired all over the world for the richness and precision of ASL. They are envied for the size of a deaf population, distributed all across the continent, who can communicate with each other, travel, and form friendships. Without a standard well-developed sign language like ASL, each generation of deaf persons, in each location, invents its own. New sign systems go through many generations of users before reaching full elaboration. Development is often interrupted, remains incomplete; the cycle begins again in a new direction.

Deaf children with ASL are intellectually, emotionally, and linguistically indistinguishable from hearing children with English. Deaf children of deaf parents are leaders among their peers. "Every year," said the headmaster, "they're the top kids. Since I've been here, the valedictorian and the salutatorian are invariably from deaf families. Not only are they high achievers, they're the children who really challenge the teachers. They ask, 'Why do we have to go to bed at nine, anyway? Who made that rule?'" He laughed. "The teachers don't like it. They like kids who do what they're told. Kids from deaf families think for themselves. They teach the other kids—not only ASL, everything. They're the role models."

It is hard to imagine a cultural group in American society more deserving of respect than the deaf, or more willing to earn it. They are independent; they have consistently refused an income tax exemption similar to that given the blind. They maintain their own clubs, have built a tradition of conviviality, self-help, and mutual support. They have created art and theater, and like to play sports. Ruthlessly excluded from active influence on policy in the education of the deaf, the deaf adult community continues to show a strong, sensitive, altruistic commitment to all deaf children—most of whom are other people's children.

Educational policy in the past has done much to discourage deaf culture, and now appears actively trying to destroy it. But deaf people have deep convictions about themselves; they understand deafness completely. They also have a long history of resistance to theories and policies that threaten those convictions. The deaf have dug in their heels, cried out with their hands, and preserved the better part of their humanity: their spirit, their intelligence, and their language.

Notes

PROLOGUE

PAGE 3 *500,000:* Wilbur (1979), p. 1. Also Benderly (1980), p. 169.
   3 *Polynesian signer:* Kuschel (1973).
   4 *invented sign languages of children:* Goldin-Meadow and Feldman (1977); Feldman, Goldin-Meadow, and Gleitman (1978).

IN SEARCH OF SIGN LANGUAGE

   14 Mindel and Vernon (1971).
17–19 *abbé L'Epée, and the early history of deaf education:* See (e.g.) Bender (1970), Stokoe (1960).
   23 On lipreading, see Conrad (1977), Heider and Heider (1940).
   24 *The Deaf Population of the United States:* Schein and Delk (1974).
   26 *Bell's life:* Bruce (1973), Bender (1970).
   27 *Gray's remark:* Bruce (1973), p. 279.
   35 *Memoir:* Bell (1883).
 36–7 *hereditary deafness:* Gallaudet College (1975).
   45 *"Sign Language Structure":* Stokoe (1960).
   47 *historical change in ASL:* Frishberg (1975, 1979).
   48 *nouns and verbs in ASL:* Supalla and Newport (1978).
   49 *Dictionary of American Sign Language:* Stokoe, Casterline, and Croneberg (1965).
   50 Chomsky (1957).
   51 *simultaneous signing and speaking:* Marmor and Petitto (1979).
   57 *Deaf Like Me:* Spradley and Spradley (1978).

SIGNS AND SCIENCE

PAGE 63   Bronowski and Bellugi (1970).

65   Wundt (1973).

66   ". . . American linguists regarded the aim of their discipline as being the classification of the elements of human languages. Linguistics was to be a sort of verbal botany. As Hockett wrote in 1942, 'Linguistics is a classificatory science' "—Searle (1974).

68   See Culler (1975) for discussion of structuralism and literary criticism.

70   *"the lowliest South African Bushman . . ."*: Sapir (1921, p.22).

70   *"essentially perfect"*: Sapir (1960), p. 1.

70   Whorf (1956) is a collection of articles edited by J. B. Carroll. In the Introduction, Carroll describes Whorf's experiences with the Hopi (p. 17).

71   *"In our language . . ."*: Whorf (1956), pp. 139–140.

71   For one major discussion of Whorf's hypothesis, see Hoijer (1954).

72   *color naming by English speakers:* Brown and Lenneberg (1954).

72   Rosch (1977).

78   *The outcry against him:* See Mehta (1971) for a lively account of this conflict.

78   The comparison between Chomsky's theories and modern chemistry was made by Lees (1974).

79   *"informed doubt"*: Hymes (1974), p. 329.

80   Chomsky's definition quoted in Klima and Bellugi (1979), p. 35.

82   The biological implications of ASL research are discussed in a review of Klima and Bellugi's book by Studdert-Kennedy (1980).

83   Data about short-term memory appear in Chapter 4 of Klima and Bellugi (1980). The rate of speaking and signing is in Chapter 8.

85   Watson (1964), p. 118.

88   Gibson (1966) has an especially interesting account of the visual world. See also Gibson (1979).

89   *"reaching, grasping . . ."*: Hewes (1977), pp. 111–112.

90   For a straightforward statement about the gestural origins of language, see Hockett (1978).

90   Burgess (1981).

PAGE 91 Mallery (1972) has an excellent history of gestural languages.
92 West (1960).

NATURE: THE INNATE LANGUAGE ENDOWMENT

94 Epigraph quoted in Langer (1948).
94–5 Rawlinson's translation of Herodotus (1858).
103 *cued speech:* See Cornett (1967), pp. 3–13.
108 Peet, *Fifteenth Annual Report* (1833).
110 Ling, Ling, and Pflaster (1977).
111 *isolated channels:* See Neisser (1967).
113 Ling, Ling and Pflaster (1977), p. 217.

NURTURE: SCHOOLS FOR THE DEAF

122 Silverman (1975).
127 *educational levels of Clarke School students:* Elish (1976).
129 Silverman (1975), p. 5.
135 *cost of MSSD:* According to information from the Gallaudet College Office of Planning, MSSD's operating budget for 1978–79 was $9,217,000. Dividing that figure by the number of students enrolled, 276, gives a cost per pupil of $33,395.
151 "Some scientists hypothesize that natural selective pressure may have relaxed somewhat among whites but not among blacks"—Benderly (1980).
151 Underenumeration is discussed by Schein and Delk (1974).
152 *the Fitzgerald Key:* Fitzgerald (1969).

INFORMATION

173 See Lash (1980).
176–7 Lash, pp. 106 and 431.
176 Keller (1961).
188 *courses:* National Technical Institute for the Deaf, RIT *Official Bulletin,* (October 1976). Course description is that of English of Contemporary Literature (p. 102).
188–9 *paper bags:* Ibid., pp. 78–79.

APEING SIGN LANGUAGE

203 *"the sixteenth month"*: Gardner and Gardner (1969), p. 666.
204 *"Behavior is lawful"*: Gardner and Gardner (1978), p. 38.
205 Chomsky (1980), p. 239.
205 *132 signs*: Gardner and Gardner (1978), p. 38.
205 *eliciting signs*: Cited in Savage-Rumbaugh, Rumbaugh, and Boysen (1980), p. 56.
206 *comprehension*: Gardner and Gardner (1978), p. 65.
207 Hahn (1971).
208 *second language*: Linden (1976), p. 119.
208 *last photograph*: The photo appeared in the *APA Monitor* (American Psychological Association, January 1980), p. 5.
209 Van Lawick-Goodall (1971).
211 Morris and Morris (1966), p. 151.
213 *gorilla on the cover*: The accompanying article, "Gorilla Talk," is by Patterson (October 1978).
217 Seidenberg and Petitto (1979), Petitto and Seidenberg (1979).
217 Terrace (1979).
231-2 *vocabulary size*:
　　　Washoe, 132: Gardner and Gardner (1978), p. 38.
　　　Nim, 125: Terrace (1979), p. 137.
　　　Koko, 100: Patterson (1978), p. 72.
　　　Sarah, 130: Premack and Premack (1972), p. 92.
　　　Lana, 75: Savage-Rumbaugh *et al.* (1980), p. 54.
　　　Roger Fout's colony at Norman (between 40 and 90 signs): Linden (1976), pp. 117 and 128.
232 Napier (1980), pp. 68-73.
233 Napier, pp. 113-116.

A WAY OF LIFE

237-8 Gannon (1981), p. 325.
238 *spelling*: See Templin (1948).
238 *"precocious performances"*: Hoemann, Andrews, Florian, Hoemann and Jensema (1976), p. 491.
239 Lenneberg (1967), pp. 320-323.
242 See Gannon (1981) for a full account of deaf sports.

REFLECTIONS

275 Greenberg and Doolittle (1977).

Bibliography

Bell, A. G., *Memoir upon the Formation of a Deaf Variety of the Human Race.* Washington, D.C.: Alexander Graham Bell Association for the Deaf, 1883 (reprinted in 1969).

Bender, R., *The Conquest of Deafness.* Cleveland: Case Western Reserve Press, 1970.

Benderly, B. L., *Dancing Without Music.* Garden City, N.Y.: Doubleday, 1980.

Bronowski, J., & Bellugi, U., "Language, Name and Concept," *Science 168* (1970), 669–673.

Brown, R., and Lenneberg, E., "A Study in Language and Cognition," *Journal of Abnormal and Social Psychology 49,* (1954) 454–462.

Bruce R. V., *Bell: Alexander Graham Bell and the Conquest of Solitude.* Boston: Little, Brown, 1973.

Burgess, A., "Creating a Language for Primitive Man," *New York Times Magazine,* Nov. 15, 1981.

Chomsky, N., *Rules and Representations.* New York: Columbia University Press, 1980.

———, *Syntactic Structures.* The Hague: Mouton, 1957.

Clarke, B., and Ling, D., "Cued Speech: A Follow-up Study," *The Volta Review* (January 1976), 23–34.

Conrad, R., "Lip-Reading by Deaf and Hearing Children," *British Journal of Educational Psychology, 47,* (1977), 60–65.

Cornett, O., "Cued Speech," *American Annals of the Deaf, 112* (1976).

Culler, J., *Structuralist Poetics: Structuralism, Linguistics and the Study of Literature.* Ithaca, N.Y.: Cornell University Press, 1975.

Feldman, H., Goldin-Meadow, S., and Gleitman, L., "Beyond Herodotus: The Creation of Language by Linguistically Deprived Deaf Children," in A. Locke, ed., *Action, Gesture and Symbol.* New York: Academic Press, 1978.

Fitzgerald, E., *Straight Language for the Deaf: A System of Instruction for Deaf Children.* 14th printing, Washington, D.C.: The Volta Bureau, 1969.

Frishberg, N., "Arbitrariness and Iconicity: Historical Change in American Sign Language," *Language, 51* (1975), 696–719.

———, "Historical Change: From Iconic to Arbitrary," in E. Klima and U. Bellugi, eds., *The Signs of Language*. Cambridge: Harvard University Press, 1979.

[Gallaudet College], *Hereditary Deafness*. Washington, D.C.: Public Service Programs, Gallaudet College, 1975.

Gannon, J., *Deaf Heritage: A Narrative History of Deaf America*. Silver Spring, Md.: National Association of the Deaf, 1981.

Gardner, R. A., and Gardner, B. T., "Comparative Psychology and Language Acquisition," *Annals of the New York Academy of Sciences, 309* (1978), 37–76.

———"Teaching Sign Language to a Chimpanzee," *Science 165* (1969) 664–672.

Gibson, J. J., *The Senses Considered as Perceptual Systems*. Boston: Houghton Mifflin, 1966.

———, *The Ecological Approach to Visual Perception*. Boston: Houghton Mifflin, 1979.

Goldin-Meadow, S., and Feldman, H., "The Development of Language-like Communication Without a Language Model," *Science 197* (1977), 401–403.

Greenberg, J., and Doolittle, G., "Can Schools Speak the Language of the Deaf?" *New York Times Magazine*, Dec. 11, 1977.

Hahn, E., "On the Side of the Apes," *The New Yorker*, April 17, 1971; and "Washoese," *The New Yorker*, Dec. 11, 1971.

Heider, F., and Heider, G., "An Experimental Investigation of Lipreading," *Psychological Monographs 52* (1940), 124–153.

Hewes, G. H., "A Model for Language Evolution," *Sign Language Studies, 15* (1977), 97–168.

Hockett, C. F., "In Search of Jove's Brow," *American Speech, 53* (1978) 243–313.

Hoemann, H., Andrews, C., Florian, V., Hoemann, S., and Jensema, C., "The Spelling Proficiency of Deaf Children," *American Annals of the Deaf* (October 1976), 489–493.

Hoijer, H., ed., *Language in Culture: Conference on the Interrelations of Language and Other Aspects of Culture*. Chicago: University of Chicago Press, 1954.

Hymes, D., Review of "Noam Chomsky," in G. Harman, ed., *On Noam Chomsky: Critical Essays*. Garden City, N.Y.: Doubleday, 1974.

Johnson, G. W., "Residual Vision," *The Deaf Spectrum*, vol. 5, nos. 5 and 6, (May/June 1974).

Keller, H., *The Story of My Life*. New York: Dell, 1961.

Klima, S., and Bellugi, U. *The Signs of Language*. Cambridge: Harvard University Press, 1979.

Kuschel, R., "The Silent Inventor: The Creation of a Sign Language by the Only Deaf-Mute on a Polynesian Island," *Sign Language Studies, 3* (1973), 1–27.

Langer, S. K., *Philosophy in a New Key.* New York: New American Library, 1948, p. 97.

Lash, J. P., *Helen and Teacher.* New York: Delacorte Press/Seymour Lawrence, 1980.

Lees, R., Review of "Syntactic Structures," in G. Harman, ed., *On Noam Chomsky: Critical Essays.* Garden City, N.Y.: Doubleday, 1974.

Lenneberg, E., *Biological Foundations of Language.* New York: John Wiley, 1967.

Linden, E., *Apes, Men and Language.* New York: Penguin, 1976.

Ling, D., and Clarke, B. R., "Cued Speech: An Evaluation Study," *American Annals of the Deaf,* vol. 120, no. 1 (1975), 480–488.

Ling, D., Ling, A., and Pflaster, G., "Individualized Educational Programming for Hearing-Impaired Children," *The Volta Review,* vol. 79, no. 4 (May 1977), pp. 204–230.

Lyons, J., *Noam Chomsky.* New York: The Viking Press, 1970.

Mallery G., *Sign Languages Among North American Indians, Compared with That Among Other Peoples and Deaf-Mutes.* The Hague: Mouton, 1972.

Marmor, G. and Petitto, L., "Simultaneous Communication in the Classroom: How Well Is English Grammar Represented?" *Sign Language Studies,* 23 (1979), 99–136.

Mehta, V., *John Is Easy to Please.* New York: Farrar, Straus, and Giroux, 1971.

Mindel, E., and Vernon, McC., *They Grow in Silence.* Silver Spring, Md.: National Association for the Deaf, 1971.

Morris, R. and Morris, D., *Men and Apes.* London: Hutchinson, 1966.

Napier, J., *Hands.* New York: Pantheon, 1980.

Neisser, U., *Cognitive Psychology.* New York: Appleton-Century-Crofts, 1967.

Patterson, F., "Conversations with a Gorilla," *National Geographic Magazine,* vol. 154, no. 4, (1978), 438.

———, "The Gestures of a Gorilla: Language Acquisition in Another Pongid," *Brain and Language, 5,* (1978), 56–71.

Peet, H., *Fifteenth Annual Report of the Directors of the New York Institution for the Instruction of the Deaf and Dumb.* New York: Mahlon Day, 1833, pp. 25–26.

Petitto, L., and Seidenberg, M., "On the Evidence for Linguistic Abilities in Signing Apes," *Brain and Language, 8,* (1979), 162–183.

Premack, A. J., *Why Chimps Can Read.* New York: Harper & Row, 1976.

———, and Premack, D., "Teaching Language to an Ape," *Scientific American* (October), 1972, 92–99.

Rawlinson, G., *The History of Herodotus*, vol. 11. London: John Murray, 1858, pp. 2–3.

Rosch, E., "Linguistic Relativity," in P. N. Johnson-Laird and P. C. Wason, eds., *Thinking*. London: Cambridge University Press, 1977.

Sapir, E., *Culture, Language, and Personality*. Berkeley: University of California Press, 1960.

———, *Language*. New York: Harcourt, Brace & World, 1921.

Savage-Rumbaugh, E. S., Rumbaugh, D. M., and Boysen, S., "Do Apes Use Language?", *American Scientist, 68* (Jan.–Feb. 1980), 49–61.

Schaff, A., *Language and Cognition*. New York: McGraw-Hill, 1973.

Schein, J., and Delk, M. Y., *The Deaf Population of the United States*. Silver Springs, Md.: National Association of the Deaf, 1974.

Searle, J., "Chomsky's Revolution in Linguistics," in G. Harman, ed., *On Noam Chomsky: Critical Essays*. Garden City, N.Y.: Doubleday, 1974.

Seidenberg, M., and Petitto, L., "Signing Behavior in Apes: A Critical Review," *Cognition, 7,* (1979), 177–215.

Silverman, S. R., *Apostrophe to Dr. Bell*. Northampton, Mass.: The Clarke School for the Deaf, 1975.

Spradley, T., and Spradley, J., *Deaf Like Me*. New York: Random House, 1978.

Stokoe, W. C., *Sign Language Structure*. Studies in Linguistics: Occasional Papers 8, University of Buffalo Press, Buffalo, 1960.

———, Casterline, D., and Croneberg, C., *A Dictionary of American Sign Language on Linguistic Principles*. Washington, D.C.: Gallaudet College Press, 1965.

Studdert-Kennedy, M., "Language by Hand and by Eye: A Review of Klima and Bellugi's *The Signs of Language,*" *Cognition, 8* (1980), 93–108.

Supalla, T., and Newport, E., "How Many Seats in a Chair? The Derivation of Nouns and Verbs in American Sign Language," in P. Siple, ed., *Understanding Language Through Sign Language Research*. New York: Academic Press, 1978.

Templin, M., "A Comparison of the Spelling Achievement of Normal and Defective Hearing Subjects," *Journal of Educational Psychology, 39* (1948), 337–346.

Terrace, H. S., *Nim*. New York: Alfred A. Knopf, 1979.

Van Lawick-Goodall, J., *In the Shadow of Man*. New York: Dell, 1971.

Watson, D. O., *Talk with Your Hands*. Published privately by David O. Watson, Jr., Winneconne, Wis., 54986, 1964.

West, La Mont. *The Sign Language, An Analysis*. Unpublished doctoral dissertation in two vols. University Microfilms International, Indiana University, 1960.

Whorf, B., *Language, Thought, and Reality*, ed. J. B. Carroll. Cambridge: MIT Press, 1956.

Wilbur, R. B., *American Sign Language and Sign Systems*. Baltimore: University Park Press, 1979.

Wundt, W., *The Language of Gestures*. The Hague: Mouton, 1973.

Index

A NOTE ON THE TYPE

This book was filmset in Janson, a recutting made direct from type cast from matrices long thought to have been made by the Dutchman Anton Janson, who was a practicing type founder in Leipzig during the years 1668-1687. However, it has been conclusively demonstrated that these types are actually the work of Nicholas Kis (1650-1702), a Hungarian, who most probably learned his trade from the master Dutch type founder Dirk Voskens. The type is an excellent example of the influential and sturdy Dutch types that prevailed in England up to the time William Caslon (1692-1766) developed his own incomparable designs from them.

Composed by American-Stratford Graphic Services, Inc., Brattleboro, Vermont. Printed and bound by Fairfield Graphics, Fairfield, Pennsylvania.

Designed by Virginia Tan.